CHARACTER PATHOLOGY:
Theory and Treatment

AMERICAN COLLEGE OF PSYCHIATRISTS

Officers (at time of 1983 Annual Meeting)
ROBERT L. WILLIAMS, M.D., *President*

HAROLD M. VISOTSKY, M.D.
President-Elect
ROBERT O. PASNAU, M.D.
First Vice-President
JERRY M. LEWIS, M.D.
Second Vice-President

HENRY H. WORK, M.D.
Secretary-General
CHARLES E. SMITH, M.D.
Treasurer
SIDNEY MALITZ, M.D.
Archivist-Historian

Program Committee for 1983 Annual Meeting
ALLAN BEIGEL, M.D., *Chairperson*

KENNETH Z. ALTSHULER, M.D.
JOHN M. DAVIS, M.D.
JAMES S. EATON, M.D.
GEORGE L. ADAMS, M.D.

RICHARD T. RADA, M.D.
PAUL L. ADAMS, M.D.
GAIL M. BARTON, M.D.
DAVID J. KUPFER, M.D.

Publications Committee
MICHAEL R. ZALES, M.D., *Chairperson*

CARL EISDORFER, M.D.
BENJAMIN BRAUZER, M.D.
ROBERT E. JONES, M.D.
GEORGE SASLOW, M.D.
JOHN S. TAMERIN, M.D.

JOE P. TUPIN, M.D.
CHARLES E. WELLS, M.D.
MILTON KRAMER, M.D.
RICHARD C. PROCTOR, M.D.
JOE YAMAMOTO, M.D.

HENRY H. WORK, M.D.

Character
Pathology:
Theory and Treatment

Edited by

Michael R. Zales, M.D.

Associate Clinical Professor of Psychiatry
Yale University

BRUNNER/MAZEL, *Publishers* ● New York

Library of Congress Cataloging in Publication Data
Main entry under title:

Character pathology.

   Papers presented at the annual meeting of the American College of Psychiatrists held in New
Orleans, La., 1983.
   Includes index.
   1. Personality, Disorders of—Congresses. I. Zales, Michael R., 1927-   . II. American College
of Psychiatrists. [DNLM: 1. Personality disorders—
Congresses. WM 190 C469 1983]
RC554.C47 1983   616.85′82   83-18996
ISBN 0-87630-347-5

Copyright © 1984 by The American College of Psychiatrists

Published by
BRUNNER/MAZEL, INC.
19 Union Square West
New York, New York 10003

All rights reserved. No part of this book may be reproduced by any process whatsoever without the
written permission of the copyright owner.

MANUFACTURED IN THE UNITED STATES OF AMERICA

Contributors

GERALD ADLER, M.D.

Director of Medical Student Education in Psychiatry, Massachusetts General Hospital; Lecturer in Psychiatry, Harvard Medical School, Boston, Massachusetts

ARNOLD M. COOPER, M.D.

Professor of Psychiatry and Director of Education, New York Hospital-Cornell Medical Center; Training and Supervising Analyst, Columbia University Psychoanalytic Center for Training and Research, New York City, New York

SHERVERT H. FRAZIER, M.D.

Professor of Psychiatry, Harvard Medical School; Psychiatrist-in-Chief, McLean Hospital, Belmont, Massachusetts

THOMAS G. GUTHEIL, M.D.

Associate Professor of Psychiatry and Director, Medical Student Training, Massachusetts Mental Health Center, Harvard Medical School, Boston, Massachusetts

PHILLIP L. ISENBERG, M.D.

Assistant Professor of Psychiatry, Harvard Medical School; Director of Residency Training, McLean Hospital, Belmont, Massachusetts

WILLIAM S. JAMES, M.D.

Instructor in Psychiatry, Harvard Medical School; Associate Psychiatrist, McLean Hospital, Belmont, Massachusetts

DOROTHY OTNOW LEWIS, M.D.

Professor of Psychiatry, New York University School of Medicine, New York City, New York

W. WALTER MENNINGER, M.D.

Director, Division of Law and Psychiatry, The Menninger Foundation, Topeka, Kansas

JOHN C. NEMIAH, M.D.

Professor of Psychiatry, Harvard Medical School; Psychiatrist-in-Chief, Beth Israel Hospital, Boston, Massachusetts

E. MANSELL PATTISON, M.D.

Professor and Chairman, Department of Psychiatry, Medical College of Georgia, Augusta, Georgia

DOUGLAS A. SARGENT, M.D., J.D.

Associate Professor of Psychiatry and Adjunct Professor of Law, Wayne State University, Detroit, Michigan

GERALD J. SARWER-FONER, M.D.

Professor and Chairman, Department of Psychiatry, University of Ottawa School of Medicine; Director, Department of Psychiatry, Ottawa General Hospital, Ottawa, Ontario, Canada

STEVEN S. SHARFSTEIN, M.D.

Deputy Medical Director, American Psychiatric Association, Washington, District of Columbia

PETER E. SIFNEOS, M.D.

Professor of Psychiatry, Beth Israel Hospital and Harvard Medical School, Boston, Massachusetts

FREDERICK J. STODDARD, M.D.

Assistant Clinical Professor of Psychiatry and Clinical Associate, Department of Psychiatry, Massachusetts General Hospital, Harvard Medical School, Boston, Massachusetts

ERNEST S. WOLF. M.D.

Assistant Professor of Psychiatry, Northwestern University Medical School; Training and Supervising Analyst, Chicago Institute for Psychoanalysis, Chicago, Illinois

Contents

Preface

Perhaps it is not entirely fortuitous that the topic selected for the Twentieth Anniversary Meeting of the American College of Psychiatrists was "Character Disorders," for reaching one's twentieth year represents one's "coming of age" and signals the end of adolescence and the beginning of adulthood. Possibly an organization matures at a different rate, but the analogy does not seem too farfetched.

Just as character structure helps shape or misshape the adult, so can philosophies, goals, and modus operandi shape the image and structure of an organization. This year's program illustrates ways in which the developmental process can be misshapen, so as to produce the psychopathology described in the various disorders. The format of the meeting reminds us of the history of our organization and illustrates the *successful* results of years of fine-tuning of the educational process. The College was organized by a group of psychiatrists who were recognized as outstanding in the field. Over the years the membership has grown as additional outstanding colleagues have been invited to membership and younger colleagues who showed promise for achievement of excellence were recruited.

In the early years, when the objectives of the College were being formulated, it was decided that provision of education of the highest quality would be the principal goal of the organization. Planners of the early programs felt that it would be most productive to concentrate on a single theme, or at best two or three closely related themes, as topics, and to view these in depth. It was decided to utilize the leading experts in the field as teachers, whether or not they were members of the College. The arrangement of one or two lectures in a plenary session followed by discussion in small groups proved to be very successful when begun in the early 1970s. The speaker-experts rotate from group to group during the course of the meeting and thus are much more available for discussion and enhancement of the educational process than they are in the more typical discussion periods during plenary sessions. The expertise of the College members who make up the small groups further enhances the educational process.

Thus, the joining together of a group of outstanding psychiatrists, dedicated to the very highest quality of continuing education, which has been organized in the fashion described and which utilizes the very top experts as teachers, are all factors that have shaped the College to produce a strong "character," so that its image in the field and the reputation of its programs are truly outstanding. I am gratified that the program this year has continued at this high level.

ROBERT L. WILLIAMS, M.D.
President, 1982-1983
American College of
Psychiatrists

Introduction

It has always been the hope of the American College of Psychiatrists that the annual volume, through the topical contributions contained therein, would provide the reader with material useful in clinical practice. This is the fifteenth such volume and is the product of the 1983 scientific meeting held in New Orleans, Louisiana. The theme was "Character Disorders." Credit for developing the program and assembling the outstanding experts whose essays follow is due the Program Committee, whose very able Chairperson was Allan Beigel.

"Character disorder," also known as personality disorder, has been defined as a pattern of personality distinguished by maladaptive, inflexible behavior (1). Descriptions of pathological characters can be complex and confusing, since personality types are rarely found in pure forms. It was primarily psychoanalysis which conveniently divided these various disorders into higher and lower orders. In the former are included the hysterical, phobic, compulsive, depressive, cyclical, passive-aggressive, and impulse-ridden. Their pathology generally reflects a reasonably well-organized ego and superego. The group of lower-order pathologies includes the narcissistic and schizoid characters, as well as the borderline personality. One also finds here the alcoholic and addictive personalities, as well as the delinquent and criminal. These individuals generally demonstrate significant defects in ego and superego development with resultant difficulties in object relationships.

As one would expect, some of the diagnostic terminology has changed over the years; however, an examination of DSM-III (2) reveals basically the same or remarkably similar concepts as had previously prevailed.

This volume is an attempt to present new and synthesized material, leading to the best application of psychiatric knowledge, principles, and treatment. The emphasis is placed, with few exceptions, on the lower-order pathologies, since they reflect the vast bulk of contemporary interest and literature.

The reader will quickly appreciate how far research and clinical experience have brought us in the area of character pathology. Yet we have only, as this year's contributors repeatedly remind us, scratched the surface in our knowledge. It is thus the timely significance of the essays that comprises the substance of this work.

The chapters in this book fall rather naturally into an order of presentation. Part I is devoted to Theories of Character Development. Sarwer-Foner's chapter leads the way, and he completes with grace the Herculean assignment of delineating the basic concepts of character in character neurosis and disorder. He begins by defining "character" as "the usual way one is as an adult," then turns to the linking concepts of heredity and constitution, and proceeds to examine the psychopathology involved. His concept of character pathology and of character neurosis follows along with his own, original contribution in terms of the continuum of ego defenses. After a thorough review of orality and anality and the defenses of sublimation and displacement, he focuses on some specific forms of character pathology, the concept of normality, and, as one has come to expect and appreciate from Sarwer-Foner, therapeutic training and manpower implications.

Wolf's chapter is an extraordinarily straightforward presentation of his and Kohut's work. Moving into psychoanalytic self-psychology per se, he defines the self, empathy, the self as structure, and selfobjects, the latter with a fascinating, illustrative example. The major part of his essay concerns selfobject relations disorders, wherein he covers all the essentials, i.e., etiology, classification, psychopathology, behavioral patterns (characterology), and treatment. This chapter provides an invaluable presentation of Kohut, making understandable and enlightening what might otherwise be difficult and mysterious.

Completing the theory section is Cooper's chapter. He reviews the contributions of Freud, Erikson, and Vaillant to his thinking. Following Wolf, Cooper's analysis of the work of Kohut and Kernberg, from his own perspective, proves not to be repetitive, but, rather, thoughtful and complete. Despite the many apparent and real differences in the conceptualizations of narcissism which he discusses, Cooper's attempt at synthesis is rich and rewarding. He deals first with normal narcissism; then with grandiosity; the integrated self-image; narcissism, object relations, and the superego; self-esteem; narcissism and the "normal" Oedipus complex; narcissism and the body; he then concludes with idealization in normal development.

Part II is devoted to Prominent Symptomatic Derivatives. Frazier, James, and Isenberg provide an interesting overview of the subject of violence. They state from the outset that violent acts are committed by people with or without mental impairment, and then they review the categories of illness in which violence might occur. After presenting an historical survey of the causal theories of violence, from Pinel through psychoanalysis to the present, they follow with their experiences at the Bridgewater State Hospital for the Criminally Insane.

Their description of the violent individuals who suffer from either a character neurosis or a paranoid, schizoid, schizotypal, narcissistic, or borderline personality disorder are informative and clinically useful. In delineating the developmental failures in the child and adolescent which create the violent individual, they come to an interesting conclusion: We remain unsure today regarding the causes of violence secondary to our fear of becoming its victim (as well as our helplessness in the face of the magnitude and horror of the problem). The plea implied here is for further research in this relatively neglected area.

Lewis, in discussing the biopsychosocial correlates of conduct disorders in children and adolescents, begins with two, age-old assumptions: 1) that an unjust society is the basic cause of children's antisocial acts; and 2) that delinquent children are essentially characterologically impaired. After reviewing the sociological theories of Hewitt and Jenkins, she then turns to her own extensive research in this area. The major thesis is that the aforementioned assumptions (misconceptions) have created an unscientific atmosphere in which little effort has been made to search for underlying medical, psychological, or psychoeducational factors. She presents recent studies that focus on those often overlooked factors, neurological and psychiatric, that now appear so closely associated with severe behavior problems. Finally, she makes a very strong case for calling into question the very diagnosis of "conduct disorder" as an entity and asks that it be eliminated from the nomenclature of child psychiatry.

Pattison's chapter on alcoholism concludes this section. It is erudite, thorough, comprehensive, and impressive in utilizing multiple sources of data for diverse theoretical perspectives. It represents a grand attempt to integrate a developmental and psychodynamic model of character typologies in the grouping, "the alcoholisms." One major contribution is his delineation of various subgroups of alcoholics who may respond preferentially to different therapeutic approaches. Pattison makes a strong statement that alcoholism is not a unitary disease and provides the reader with a fascinating attempt at reclassification, representing an important addition to this field.

Although each chapter in this volume makes reference to the therapy of character disorders, Part III focuses primarily upon Treatment Approaches. It consists of two essays, the first by Sifneos and Nemiah. They begin by reminding the reader of the wide spectrum of characterological disturbances, ranging from the psychotic to the neurotic. Following this, they describe the nature of insight psychotherapy and the four major criteria for this type of treatment. Then they elaborate on their specialty, short-term anxiety-provoking psychotherapy (STAPP). Here they discuss the special criteria for the selection of patients—a circumscribed chief complaint, documentation of a meaningful childhood relationship, and motivation. Of great significance is their experience that even severe narcissistic character problems may improve with STAPP, if only the patient dem-

onstrates keen motivation for change and is functioning well in one area of his*
life, especially in work performance.

Using lengthy excerpts from a videotaped evaluation interview, Sifneos and
Nemiah make their point convincingly. The reader begins to appreciate the timing
and precision of appropriate confrontations, the delicate nuances of transference
reactions, the ability of a superb therapist to focus on a particular conflict, to
engage the patient, and then to summarize accurately. The chapter evokes a
desire to see the entire videotape and is reflective of the magnificent quality of
the authors' work.

Adler's essay deals with both borderline and narcissistic disorders. He asks
whether these diagnoses are useful, whether there exists some type of relationship
between them, and how they both might be related to schizotypal, antisocial,
paranoid, and schizoid personality disorders.

Beginning with the DSM-III (2) descriptions of both, he makes his most
important and beguiling observation, that borderline patients in successful treatment *over time* will look increasingly like narcissistic personality disorders. He
describes both types in treatment, again carefully looking at the contributions
of Kohut and Kernberg in a synthetic rather than adversarial manner in order to
create his own theoretical framework. Calling on the works of Winnicott, Piaget,
and Fraiberg, among others, he approaches major treatment issues, i.e., aloneness, self-worth and incompleteness, validation, and countertransference. Here
he makes a unique contribution to the understanding and treatment of these
extraordinarily difficult patients.

Part IV is concerned with Related Management Issues. Leading off is Sargent's
chapter on how the reciprocal interaction between the imposing demands of
practice and flaws in the physician's character may harm his practice and even
shorten his life. Spicing the essay with quotes from Heraclitus, Samuel Butler,
Shakespeare, and others, he defines the "ideal" physician and the "medical
character" in the context of practice. Through a series of absorbing and fascinating vignettes, he presents physician caricatures, all of which demonstrate
elements generally believed to be virtuous, but which occasionally prove lethal.
Sargent makes a plea for the treatment and rehabilitation of the impaired physician, but he leaves it to the reader to consider for himself the possibilities of
prevention.

Menninger's essay on the interface of law and psychiatry follows. All of us
have become accustomed to his unusual ability to use source material to substantiate his findings, and, once again, he does not disappoint. He begins by
employing three clinical cases to demonstrate how mental health practitioners
may be called upon to work with individuals with character problems who have
violated the law. He then asks the three critical questions raised about the capacity

* Throughout this volume the generic "he" shall be used unless otherwise indicated.

of psychiatry: 1) to diagnose or understand those with behavior disorders; 2) to make predictions about their future behavior, both with and without clinical intervention; and 3) to make recommendations and/or provide treatment for them with particular concern for what might prompt them to change and no longer engage in antisocial behavior.

Menninger deals with each of these areas in depth and presents the special treatment problems involved, particularly those falling under the aegis of transference/countertransference issues between therapist and offender/patient. His final recommendation (even demand) is that law and psychiatry find a mutuality of purpose and respect, an effective method of communication, a recognition of individual or shared shortcomings, and the open acknowledgment that certain goals may only be accomplished through genuine collaboration.

The final chapter is most timely. Sharfstein, Gutheil, and Stoddard present one of psychiatry's major reimbursement concerns. Initially, they deal with the history of third-party payers for character disorder patients—how outpatient treatment might violate insurance rules for coverage, the concept of "moral hazard" in which the use of a service or treatment is encouraged by insurance (and not by illness) status, consumer demand, peer and claims review, and, finally, problems with provider credentials. The authors make the topic stimulating and informative.

Sharfstein et al. then look at money as a clinical issue in the psychotherapy of these patients. Through a series of 15 interesting (often amusing) case studies, they cover such topics as the interactions of reimbursement and the dynamics of psychotherapy, ethical and countertransference considerations, and when the therapist should either turn to insisting on cash payment or enlisting the services of a collection agency. Finally, the authors give cogent recommendations for a hopeful outcome.

As one can see, the material contained in this volume is reflective of one of the major problems in psychiatry today. The authors have remained ever-vigilant in their essays to the needs of the practitioner, and for this I must extend my deep appreciation. In addition, I would like to express my personal gratitude to Robert L. Williams, President of the College, for his support and encouragement, and to the entire Publications Committee for their diligent efforts.

Michael R. Zales, M.D.
Greenwich, Connecticut

REFERENCES

1. KAPLAN, H.I., FREEDMAN, A.M., and SADOCK, B.J. (Eds.): *Comprehensive Textbook of Psychiatry/III*. Baltimore: Williams & Wilkins, 1980.
2. *Diagnostic and Statistical Manual of Mental Disorders*, Third Edition. Washington, D.C.: American Psychiatric Association, 1980.

Part I

THEORIES OF
CHARACTER DEVELOPMENT

1

The Basic Concepts of Character in Character Neurosis and Character Disorders

Gerald J. Sarwer-Foner, M.D.

"Character" in adults can be defined as "the usual way we are"—the normal "sets" of adult ego defenses forming the habitual overall patterns of the way we adapt to things. In this definition there are several features. First is the fact that it is an *adult* adaptation. We are delineating the forming of one's "character" or "personality" in adult life. Here we are considering the form and the structure of the way we are, as seen throughout life. Second, we refer to "something" that is acceptable to the conscious visualization of one's self, to how the person is, i.e., features that are not conflicted in the ego—or at least are not in great conflict with the person's ego. There are exceptions to this, for we do see patients with "a character" that troubles them.

LINKING CONCEPTS

Heredity and Constitution

At birth there are constitutional capacities and inherited tendencies present forming a genetic pool for such factors as the speed of sensory reaction and the metabolism of the individual. At one level, this can be seen as the way (the speed and intensity of) cellular energy becomes available to various parts of the body, including the brain (1-5). Constitutional and hereditary aspects of how this energy becomes available and develops, as broad concepts, would include the individual variation, manifesting the instictive (present in every member of the same species) influence in the evolution of the brain, central nervous system,

5

and the autonomic nervous system as a series of biologic "sets," gestalt-receiving structures. Thus, by their innate structure (genetically inherited structure), they are "ready" for certain stimuli and functions which "fit" them. Their variable readiness for function, that is to say, the speed with which they are ready to receive a stimulus or respond to it—the rapid, or slow, capacity for switching from one to the other, for synaptic fusion of many neurons to become a "system" or "systems," or for integration of series of motor responses—may be inherited. Those "innate" (genetically inherited) features are developed better when fed by a "proper metabolism" (an optimum flow of nutrients and essential conditioning of the internal milieu).

Meeting the needs of such developing systems from outside of the body in properly timed sequences nurtures all the attachment, or bonding, interactions with the gratifying environmental elements. If these inner, sequentially timed biological needs are not met in proper sequence, then frustration occurs, increasing the biologic need. This is expressed as a physiological heightening (increase) in the need for relief of tension in that system (3, 6). The way the increased tension builds up and the manner of its discharge in relationship to the externally frustrating (non-gratifying) parenting figures condition these as object (bonding) relationships. These determine the *affective* responses that accompany these processes. Love or hate, their strength and intensity, are thus conditioned. The initial strength and speed of the buildup of rage and aggression as conditioning responses to such frustration are consequences of such factors. The registration of these reactions in the association areas of the brain forms symbols (sensory and memory traces). These include the affective associations linked to them. These symbolic-affective representations help develop our ego and ego defenses. Many terms and concepts are encompassed here.

First there is the concept of heredity and what is inherited. In terms of this discussion, we are talking about a series of instinctual drives—energetic forces in the cells and brain, action tendencies (which do not have to be learned through experience), which on being registered in association areas of the brain become symbols-linked-to-affect, used by that person to relate to the world. Instinctive tendencies (innate tendencies) are present in all members of the same animal species. They are not present in all *to the same degree* of "manifestation," "drive," "presence," "sensory modality," and "action tendency." All instinctive drives evolve in their manifestation over time, with the increased maturation of the brain and other organ systems (for example, maturation of the locomotor system, striated muscles and their supporting bones; systems coming under voluntary control, etc.) (2).

Thus, heredity, at one level of logic, includes the resultant of biological, developmental forces received from the genes and the regulatory forces of organic development. These interact with environmental nurturing, molding, and melding forces.

Most psychiatric illnesses in which one may suspect hereditary factors are not "inherited," i.e., the disease is not directly produced. Rather, a series of biological tendencies (for example, greater and more easily triggered startle responses; more capacity for rage, aggressive responses, and motor activity; less tolerance for inner pain or for intense proprioceptive sensation with intolerance for the resulting increased psychologic tension) makes some persons vulnerable to bad environmental interaction, producing, over time, the vulnerability to a decompensation of function, resulting in the disease. Such greater than average biological sensitivities make the interaction with the environment crucial for "this person" and are the general genetic "set" of the vulnerability for the later development of a disease entity. Here we have the concept of a more diffuse, less specific inheritance of a series of vulnerabilities, rather than the direct inheritance of a disease or tendency to later develop a disease.

Constitution

This leads us to the looser concept of "constitution." Constitution means the inherited tendencies forming a describable series of factors, which orient the organism in certain directions, but are not themselves determinate of a particular characteristic or disease. They may be conditioned, i.e., modified, by the environment, or released in full or in part by particular environmental conditions. There have been many attempts to delineate constitutional factors and to describe bodily structure, build, and biological reactivity. The works of Kretschmer (7) on body build, the "asthenic," "pycnic," and "athletic," are a classic example. Kretschmer and his students at Tubigen spent many years trying to match psychopathology (the pathology seen in the psyche) with bodily build. Later Sheldon (8) and his associates in the U.S. did anatomic studies based on similar ideas, using a somewhat different typology and scientific methods. Sheldon, using "somatotyping," measured the relationships of skin, connective tissue and bone to establish a typology of body build, which he attempted to link with biological reactivity. His "endomorphic," "mesomorphic," and "ectomorphic" body typologies corresponded roughly to Kretschmer's earlier typology. There was more interest in these phenomena 30 years ago than there is today.

There have also been attempts by such authors as Szondi (9) to fuse constitutional and psychodynamic concepts in identifying constitutional typologies represented by facial appearance of late 19th and 20th century "types" with particular character structures and "characterologic" action tendencies, particularly in terms of criminality, hysterical tendencies, depressive tendencies, etc.

There is still some interest today in the use of various versions of the Szondi test to correlate psychopathology and constitutional body build.

In terms of personal reactivity to external object relationships, Jung spoke of "extroverted and introverted personalities" as two normal variants, while Bleuler termed essentially the same *normal* range of personal reactivity "syntonic and schizoid." The syntonic or extroverted was the outgoing, oral (but normal) type of personality, while the schizoid or introverted was the withdrawn, quiet, not outgoing, reserved, but *normal* type of individual. There was the implication that if either of these normative personality types were to become mentally ill, the schizoid-introverted would develop the autistic and withdrawn types of illnesses tending to autistic or severe schizophrenia with negative symptoms, while the syntonic-extroverted would tend to have a manic-depressive or schizo-affective type of illness with "productive" or "positive" symptomatology.

The overall emotional coloring or affective tonality of the *affective responses*, including their bodily reactivity, has been called "temperament" and is seen as a constitutionally determined characteristic. Studies of temperament (1-5, 10-12) and its "unrolling" as a child grows up have been important in child psychiatry and developmental pediatrics.

The "quality" of the emotional responses, with their "coloring," represents the interactions between constitution and environment producing temperamental qualities: the introverted and placid or the extroverted (outgoing), often with development of a particular body build, and the *speed* and type (intensity) of reactivity. Features such as joyful calmness or placidity, without great need to reach out, seize, and explore, or great joy, enthusiasm, and outgoing energy, with intense curiosity about the outside world, are seen as "temperamental." Other examples are: the need to move and vigorously initiate movement versus a more placid ability to wait and to accept waiting, with tolerance to being moved etc.; the speed of response, such as the capacity to react with startle and great fear, versus a more placid, nonfearful, accepting, or not overwhelmingly fearful, slower reply; the speed with which rage develops; the speed with which whatever responses being observed in newborns and developing children are seen; the speed with which screams of rage and hunger are emitted and the pace at which they die down as children are comforted; and the rapidity, or step-like "slowness" of falling asleep at the breast contented when feeding. These factors can be seen as fused-to-constitutional, genetic-constitutional, and environmentally adapted and conditioned. In their turn they influence the development of temperamentally-linked expressive, energetic, relational, and adaptive qualities. Temperament, however, is the emotional reactive coloring of these qualities. This reactivity does not exist in a vacuum. Obviously, it develops in relationship to the conditioning of life experience and to the nature of the outside object relationships which are formed by the way basic biological needs are met, gratified, or frustrated in a timed schedule that either consistently fits or frustrates the needs of the individual.

Psychopathology

Psychopathology is seen as the form that disease resultants take in the psyche (mind). In the classic German view of psychopathology (13, 14), this included study of the signs and symptoms, the forms and manifestations of their presence in the mind (psyche). There was always an assumption of an organic basis, but also acceptance of their psychological expression in the symbols of the mind, in thought, affect, cognition, language, and feeling. From this the German psychopathologists attempted to assume—and these tendencies spread to England, Switzerland, and the United States, etc. (while France tended to deveop its own view of such phenomena)—that there may be correlations between physiological process (even when the nature of the physiological process was not known) and the development of the "*psycho*pathology" being studied.

Psychoanalysts and the general psychopathologists both evolved concepts of what psychopathology was. The Freudians came up with their concepts of psychopathology and metapsychology, particularly the ideas that there were only certain ways in which intrapsychic conflicts could express themselves—in sustained successful resolution, i.e., normality (15), or in psychopathologic resolutions, i.e., neuroses, psychoses, or sexual deviations ("perversions"). Conflict can have a symptomatic expression in *neuroses* with symptoms of anxiety, persistent depressive affect, conversion, obsessions, compulsions, phobias, dissociative phenomena, partial depersonalization, fugue states, etc., symptoms which represent and include a partial breach of reality-testing around the issues which produce these symptoms. These patients nevertheless remain with reasonably intact reality-testing and judgment in other areas of their lives.

In psychoses, there are major breaks in reality-testing with symptoms demonstrating feelings of unreality, delusions, hallucinations, ideas of reference, in some cases thought and affective disorders, and exaggerated outbursts of aggression. Poor judgment, psychomotor retardation, projection, great impulsivity, and poor control are also seen. There are deviations in the individual's investment of biological energy and drives in contacting external reality, with resulting distortions of the use of the senses and therefore of reality-testing.

Psychopathology can be represented as "symptom equivalents" in *sexual deviations* ("perversions" in the older literature). Here the sexual instinctual drives are diverted from the usual course of development to become arrested at some form other than normal heterosexuality. These sexual attachments are largely (but rarely entirely) ego-syntonic. Here is a link with the "characterological," since this "symptom equivalent" becomes the usual way that a person is, as to his sexual object attachment. Here it is a "symptom equivalent" but the intrapsychic conflicts in the sense of personal identity are not expressed as a neurotic or psychotic symptom, but as a "masked symptom equivalent," in the ego-syntonic sexual expression. In some, aggressive drives become linked in a largely ego-syntonic, specifically sexual way. A person can have such a sexual deviation and be "normal" in the ordinary sense, the sexual expression being ego-syntonic. Some with a sexual deviation develop a psychopathological decompensation, with symptomatic expression in neurosis or psychosis, on top of the sexual deviation.

THE CONCEPTS OF CHARACTER PATHOLOGY (16-28) AND OF "CHARACTER NEUROSIS" (23, 29-39)

This concept means that the major pathology is largely expressed in defense mechanisms, using behavioral action tendencies which become part of the normal character structure of that individual and are thus largely ego-syntonic. They disturb his entourage and get him into trouble with the law (40-42). He may, after the event, feel sorry or regretful or realize that something is wrong, but at the time the adaptive tendencies are expressed, the individual has no awareness of the problem or ability to behave differently.

Instead of ordinary neurotic symptoms, which are ego-"dystonic" (i.e., the symptoms cause distress, pain, discomfort to the patient), or psychotic symptoms, which are also "dystonic" in the reduction produced in the person's overall functioning, there is something else. *Here there is an adaptive way of dealing with intrapsychic conflict by expressing it in daily behavior.* The tensions produced by the conflicts are expressed in the behavior of the patient and in ways of discharging the accumulation of biological drives from intrapsychic conflicts. These patterns of discharging inner biological tension in the direction of its overall baseline or "resting level of excitation" have other interesting facets:

1) They *are* (i.e., have become) *usual* and *automatic* (i.e., without thought or conscious struggle about whether or how to accomplish the biologically required discharge of tension to a more comfortable level). Many people so affected are not even partially aware that anything of any consequence is going on.

2) The ways of accomplishing this are part of the usual way this person is and in that sense "don't bother" him.

3) In some circumstances these behaviors bring overt conflict with external authority (e.g., antisocial, psychopathic, or intolerable-to-others behavior). Though aware of the disastrous *consequences* of their behavior in these terms, their inner sense of personal identity as oppositional to the group with whom their behavior produces the conflict is still relatively unconflicted and ego-syn-

tonic (16, 43, 44), i.e., "this is the way I am," "I'm against the establishment, the adults, my father, the school system, the stuffed shirts, etc." (29).

4) The majority of these "characterological" (19), i.e., ego-syntonic expressions are not as dramatic as delinquency (34, 39-42, 45) or antisocial behavior. Rather, they represent a very large group of commonly seen adaptive defenses classed as "personality disorders." Some examples include aspects of obsessive-compulsive personality (22, 44, 46-48), in which all relationships are approached around the issues of "control" (who controls whom) (44, 48), or passive-aggressive phenomena, such as exaggerated surface politeness or apparently friendly compliance, with an underlying, stubborn inability to conform to very reasonable requirements if set at someone else's initiative, standards, or timing. Other examples are: addictive, all-encompassing personalities who overeat, are addicted to drugs, and over-drink; self-centered persons "totally" preoccupied in an ego-syntonic way with their own desires or needs, to the exclusion of consideration or concern for others; and grandiose narcissistic personalities, etc.

5) If one has understood some of the implications of the above, then another facet emerges—that even in symptomatic neuroses and psychoses or in the "unsymptomatic" sexual deviations, it is often possible to see pathologic ego defenses (including symptoms) which become "a chronically painful way of life." Those chronic depressive patients who feel that depression is permanent (49) and residual schizophrenic patients who automatically use their symptoms to keep you off and to maintain their "Schizophrenia as a Way of Life," in Lewis Hills' phrase (50), show this.

Here *a part of* a symptomatically expressed and ego-dystonic illness, with its pain and sorrow for the sufferer, encompasses areas of adaptive expression and reponse, used to *keep* the condition going. These adaptive responses are automatic ego defenses that are *ego-syntonic* at a particular time. If they become part of a clinical condition, they are "characterological," i.e., "the way I usually am and react." Defenses such as these are exemplified in residual schizophrenia, used as a "way of life" (50).

Hill (50) has theorized that the purpose of such action is to minimize the patient's personal pain. The present author agrees. This is the patient's "usual psychotic personality way" of keeping you out of their defended, painful areas. These are the characteristic tendencies which residual schizophrenic patients present in their psychotic ego defenses, their psychotic way of testing reality and of forcing you off the areas where they feel frightened because they do not know how to cope. Often, these characteristics are not that difficult for the doctor to see or understand and result from the forces impinging on the patient, so that this becomes the "way the patient is." The "way the patient is" can become extremely difficult to manage if one is attempting to change the patient's ego defensive style and functioning. Thus, we have examples of schizophrenic patients and some depressive patients who oscillate up and down a range or spectrum of their particular ego defenses. These patients have a characteristic set of ways and a range of modalities for getting better or worse, all of which operate within a certain framework. The patient progresses and regresses, moves up or down, on a scale of patterns of ego defenses, but about an individual mean point. The patient keeps the therapist out of a defended area and automatically falls back with great skill on these "fortified positions" (if you want to look at ego defenses as "fortified positions") as his usual way of being and dealing with such intrusions.

The Continuum of Ego Defenses

I have worked with the concept of the continuum of ego defenses. This theoretical view is "a straight-line continuum" model of ego defenses linking diagnostic entities, with a non-existent theoretical "normality" at the top, and a non-existent theoretical "rock-bottom" psychosis (as a model of the most severe psychosis) at the bottom.

A listing of diagnostic entities that can be made would demonstrate one aspect. The main point for our purposes is that all individuals have a range or spread of their own ego defenses. When ill they slip further down and when recovering move further up their own scale. When someone becomes ill, our task is to help move him upward with "an ego-patching job" towards a greater integration of reality-testing in ego defenses and thus to a higher position on his own scale.

This theoretical concept allows one to look at character neurosis and character defenses, as well as at typical ego-syntonic patterns of expressing a sense of personal identity, in relationship (often oppositional) to father, mother, family (i.e., an inner establishment), or to the outer establishment—one's sense of community, of belonging to, or being isolated and alienated from, the outside world. There are often aggressive visualizations of this world. One often sees the symbolic "reliving" in transference-triggering settings (10, 12, 23, 51) of patterns of family relationships in expressive, largely ego-syntonic, personalized habit patterns. This is seen in the personalized expression of both aggressive (46, 47) and libidinal drives (52) and in "characteristic sets" for dealing with social situations, e.g., exaggerated politeness to all, but an impulsive and accidental spilling of coffee on someone when he has enhanced aggressive tension.

The continuum of ego defenses has particular relevance to the adolescent and young adult phases of life (53). With adolescence, an unconscious and conscious reworking of the earlier identificational processes occurs, as well as a tendency for a social break with the parents. There is thus a move towards personal independence, with a turning to a peer group for the reworking and revalidation of personal sets of values—particularly superego (moral and cultural) and re-lationship values—towards a definitive adult sense. This reworking of sexual and aggressive goals is now aim-related toward definitive adult objects with sexual intercourse and reproductive capacities. The form of an adult ego ideal is also reworked—for some definitively, for others as something which will still evolve. This includes the capacity to be ashamed if he violates some aspects of his ego ideal (that ideal of what one should be). This reworking takes place in the context of an enormously increased thrust of the sexual instincts and drives, with, therefore, relatively diminished reality-testing and introspective capacity. There is a concomitant turning away from introspection to replacement of this by age-related peer group consensus. Adolescents turn from their parents to their friends, producing the peer group pressures common for each generation in each society. This enhances any capacity for greater behavioral expression of sexual and aggressive conflicts, rather than for introspective thought and feeling. This tendency of not looking internally, but expressing conflicts in activity, leads to the prominence of such patterns in this age group. As the adolescent emerges from this cauldron of experimentation and turmoil, if these patterns are retained, they remain as definitive adult characterological traits (60).

In other words, in those who develop character neuroses, the roots, originating in early childhood, are clearly seen in the patient's adolescent turmoil. They are reworked partially here in terms of the values and behavior of the peer group. Acting-out of aggressive conflicts, anti-authoritarian and anti-adult morality be-havior, violations of "good conduct," little or no respect for current authority, stealing, violent fighting, sometimes killing, and attacking property and the rights of individuals are commonly seen. Those who have already been delinquent as latency-aged or younger children rework this in adolescence. Here the issues of a final identification with have-nots and the criminal classes or with other antinomian models of adult life are established. There are many who, after an initial period of adolescent turmoil, redevelop former solid identifications with the values of their parents and their culture and settle down with culturally conforming, ego-syntonic, characterological patterns.

In short, some adult sociopathic and other character neuroses emerge as de-velopmental defects of the period of adolescence and youth, even though they are also reworkings of earlier stages of development in childhood and infancy.

Orality (43, 52, 54, 55), Anality (22, 31, 32, 44, 48), Sublimation and Displacement

When consistent, "I care for you and your needs" nurturing takes place in the first year of life, and gratification occurs, encouraging further exploration of what becomes the outer world. Here we have the emergence of clear-cut oral patterns which create and reinforce object relationships and "the taking in" of outside things. Many authorities (43), Grunberger (44, 52), for example, have characterized the oral phase as an "open-ended funnel, taking all in," as a phase in which one wraps oneself around the environment, and as a phase in which everything flows into the individual (52). The persistence of these traits as the way one approaches the world and the outside, thus as oral character traits (17, 43, 52), is often seen. For example, one sees the development of out-reaching curiosity, of outgoingness, of human warmth, of optimism, of readiness to have new experiences, of an enthusiasm and zestfulness for life, for new contacts and for new things while still savouring the old and valued, and for the tasting and savouring of the world, of love of food and good experience, including good sexual object relationships. Thus, orality can be kept as an unchanged character trait in those who have it, with no great intrapsychic difficulty. It does not have to be transformed into other things. It is seen in its oral aggressive manifestations in encompassing avidity, greed, or actual overeating, which are ego-syntonic and can cause problems. Verbal domination of others can also be a partially oral, aggressive trait, and can cause problems as well. In other words, characterological traits derived from the oral erogenous zones or orality in terms of liking food, bonbons, cigarettes, pipe smoking, chewing on the end of a pencil, sucking a thumb, etc., do not have to be transformed into other things to be able to persist in adult life as "reasonably socially acceptable" characteristics.

Manifestations of anality (22, 32, 44, 46-48), on the other hand, must be transformed into something else, less anal, in adult life. It cannot continue as an unmodified character trait, but has to be changed into something else. Anality can have a symptomatic persistence (e.g., miserliness), but cannot win social acceptance in its pure, unchanged form.

Interest in and pleasure from the anal mucosa seen in the second year of life during toilet training, magical thinking and feeling seen in both the oral and anal phases, the issue of confusing a thought, a wish, and the causing of an act, particularly an aggressive or destructive one—all are important aspects of this stage of psychosexual development. An interest in feces—the desire to see what is in it, what is homogenized in it, is part of this phase. The pleasure derived from the sensations of the anal mucosa at this age—the touching and experimenting with anal objects and products, or literal "playing with your bum"—are not acceptable as a regular, "the way I am" trait in adult life, and must be transformed into other things. This is also true of behavior around urinary tract control. The inability to control urine has been linked in some patients to a later inability to control other impulses, and the "badness of bed-wetting," if it persists, becomes the "badness of delinquency" in the minds of older children (33, 41). One can suck a pencil as an adult when talking to a group, or even put one's finger in one's mouth, as an uncouth gesture, and still find relative acceptance. One cannot, however, stick one's finger up one's bum, defecate on the floor, pass flatus, etc.; the anal traits must be transformed into something else.

Sublimation and Displacement

The normal mental mechanism for this is *sublimation*. Although this applies to some degree also to the oral, it comes into its own mainly as a solid basis for the healthy transformation of anal traits and for the development of healthy characterological traits in their place. In sublimation, the instinctual cathexis (investment) of the zonal drives is stripped of anal qualities and attachment to the anal mucosa, and free, non-zonally linked energy is thus available for investment in other things. This is a normal process. For example, the development of self-discipline, the putting off of immediate gratification of a desire to a more appropriate time, politeness and consideration for others, interest in intellectual pursuits, appreciation of art, literature, mathematics and music, etc., can all be seen as developments and sublimations of anal cathexes. Indeed, some of our finest, most civilized traits are sublimations of anal erotism. Control and discipline needed for these purposes—the capacity for self-sacrifice, the ability to control aggression—create the so necessary "thin veneer" of civilization.

The less normal mechanism than sublimation is *displacement,* which on the surface resembles sublimation. In displacement, however, zonal, biologically linked energy remains attached to its original anal erotism or aggression. It thus remains "shitty energy" linked to direct contact with the anal mucosa, and it leads to the approach to object relationships so characteristic of the anal phase.

What are some of the characteristics of this phase? In contrast to the oral phase, which is an "open-ended funnel with everything taken in" (44, 52) and with the individual embracing the world through his senses, tasting and putting everything into himself, the anal phase is rather preoccupied with distinctions, with the separateness and the discreteness of things. The issues include separation, being superior or inferior, and the value or worthlessness of an object. Is it totally owned and possessed; is it a slave or a master? The *control* of objects and the distinctions between objects that are "defecated out" are important. The separateness, the completeness of the discreteness, the superiority or inferiority of the object, of belonging or not belonging, of having ownership are important. Above all, the mechanisms and the affects of owning, the energetics of control, of possessing and of being able to crush, attack, or keep, preserve and own are the issues. Concerns with creating, disturbing, smashing, separating from, expelling, keeping in, keeping out, having one's way, being superior or inferior, submitting or conquering—all are central. These qualities are retained as character traits by those heavily marked or fixated here.

Transforming this phase of life by sublimation or displacement creates qualities that can become *the central theme* in one's personality or can color everyone's personality to some degree, becoming central themes only in some. When these themes persist in adult life, they represent the persistence of these anally-linked elements as character traits. One extreme form is the miser who must hoard everything and keep it in. Some such people are often chronically constipated. They are chronically sour in temperament and often sadistically controlling. The masochistic victim who always submits to some injustice; the chronically messy, with inability to submit to anyone's control, and who must create a mess, be late, be incompetent; those who throw away money, are spendthrift—all are examples of characterological traits representing transformation of unresolved anal cathexes.

In displacement, as compared to sublimation, the original anal cathexis, with its unchanged biological "tension" of either aggressive or possessive anal qualities and its magical causality factor, is kept invested in at least some object relationships. Thus a proctologist, who has a sublimated interest in his work, does not primarily like looking up an anus because it is an anus. Rather, he uses the instrument because it is important and necessary for the appropriately realistic purpose of discovering lesions. By contrast, someone who has an anally displaced interest in proctology would *really enjoy* sticking the tube up an anus, and the looking for the lesions would be incidental to this other major interest. Similarly, a surgeon who cuts to get at lesions and remove them shows sublimation of his controlling and aggressive interest in getting at things and definitively solving problems. By contrast, a surgeon who is really interested in cutting, tearing, ripping, and bleeding, rather than removing the lesions, would be someone who demonstrates a displacement of anal aggressive urges. The way these issues are dealt with and transformed into the beginnings of character traits colors the following developmental phases, acting as a template for them.

Some Specific Forms of Character Pathology

The characteristics, tonalities, ways of being, including the characteristic patterns of our parents' ego defenses, fuse with our hereditary-constitutionally determined central nervous system "sets," forming our own distinct fusion of temperament and character, as part of our identificational process with our parents. So, the "styles" of being—the styles of tasting, of feeling, of hearing, of coping, of having object choice and object relations—become fashioned in our own way and emerge as our character structure and sometimes as our character problems. These problems can take the form of a definitive character neurosis

(28, 34, 35, 37) or other character pathology (2, 4, 10, 16-18, 21, 25, 29, 33, 38, 41, 57).

Some important examples of character pathology include Grinker el al.'s (57) study of borderline personality patients. Kernberg's (58, 59) definition of the Borderline Personality Organization patient as a psychoanalytic or psychodynamic diagnosis of specific character pathology must be mentioned. Masterson's (60) and Sarwer-Foner's (61, 62) elaboration of this clinical concept are examples of other papers dealing with this entity. It is important to use the term for this particular character disorder in its strict sense, thus separating it from a looser current usage (63), in which a broader category of patients with prepsychotic and postpsychotic ego defenses is included. Many anal defenses are seen in such patients, including important aspects of sadomasochism and the struggle for control.

One sees many anal aspects in character types, among them the particularly controlling, the domineering, the obsessive and compulsive, the emotionally and morally rigid, the steely aggressive, the most conformist "stuffed shirt" (29), and the totally messy, alienated, and dirty oppositionist.

The clearest example is, perhaps, the obsessive-compulsive personality, with its features of control and accent on distinctions between objects, on being above or superior, or submitting and being inferior, and on being a sadist or a masochist, or on approaching all relationships to control them (29, 31, 32, 44, 46, 47).

It is not my intention to enumerate an entire list (almost without limit) of variations in character pathology, but merely to mention some of importance that are frequently seen: the psychopathic or antisocial, the aggressive, the impulse-ridden (34, 40), the accident-prone, those fated to failure, those who must be first, those orally addictive or orally incorporative individuals. One must include those showing the various aspects of anal pathology, from miserliness to the much more commonly seen need to control everything (44). In passive-dependent (10, 12) and passive-aggressive personalities, clinical issues of the ease of dependency and compliance are important.

Normality

A word should be said about "normality," which has been described by Sabshin and Offer (15). It can be seen as a state in which there is good integration of heredity and constitution with the development of one's own temperament; good reality-testing for the norms of society, a particular culture, and a particular family; and ego-syntonic defenses with a considerable capacity for constant object relationships. Consideration for others and the capacity to work successfully, to have ongoing, successful object relationships, to play successfully, and to have good sexual outlets within the norms of a particular society, including the capacity to reproduce, are essential components of this state of being. The integration of all or most of these, in a reasonably ego-syntonic way of functioning, is defined as "normal."

This concept of the normal leaves room for the existence of some psychopathology within it. This is often congruently linked with overall apparent "normality," i.e., the psychopathology sometimes indirectly supports, or is masked by, some of these "normal" aims. One sees supportive congruent relationships with interrelation of normal and psychopathological elements in major, lifelong object relationships with spouse, friends, etc., in an ego-syntonic way. Pathology, on the other hand, breaks the limits of congruent support, causes difficulties in work, in social relationships, and in the maintenance of ongoing, constant object relationships (including love and sexual relationships). It will produce inability to play and relax successfully. This means that the person becomes "ill." We have already discussed many aspects of illness manifesting as character neurosis, character pathology, or personality disorders.

THERAPEUTIC TRAINING AND MANPOWER IMPLICATIONS

There are important implications from these concepts, for none of our current (modern) organic therapeutic treatments, from psychosurgery and electroconvulsive therapy to psychotropic drugs, has any major influence over time on the development of character pathology. Character pathology and residual psychiatric character defenses are what remain in patients with unremitting pathology. These patients show acute and residual symptoms, but also suffer from characterologically defensive aspects of their residual psychoses. Others show persistent psychopathic disorders or other important character disorders, and some suffer from personally troublesome sexual deviations. By "personally troublesome" I mean troublesome to them, troublesome to society, or both.

We must not only teach these clinical, diagnostic, and therapeutic concepts in a general way, but also develop in-depth teaching and training in these areas as well. In that way we would produce sufficient medical manpower trained in the techniques available to us, such as psychoanalysis or the long-term intensive psychotherapies that are aimed at changing character structure. This is crucial for at least those selected individuals who will have to deal with these problems, if one hopes to help such patients in a definitive way.

There is a large body of literature and knowledge which shows that many can be dealt with in a definitively helpful way, at least by some skilled people. It is important to know this and teach this. It is important to keep this in the foreground of our minds as a therapeutic focus and issue.

Understanding character pathology enables one to use the other treatments more knowledgeably. It enables one to distinguish between the acute symptomatic expression of pathology and its more chronic and often characterological expression. Sometimes one is able to intervene effectively, over the short haul, even in a patient with character pathology, by concentrating on specific items. For example, in psychomotor retardation, one can increase the person's outgoingness with psychotropic drugs. Having done this, one can then raise some of the character problems as issues for the patient's consideration, so that the patient can, if motivated to do so, look at them and seek help over the long haul. A good concept of "normality" and what it involves is crucial here. One must not have an exaggerated or distorted sense of what is normal. Either of these would skew therapeutic expectations and adversely affect therapy.

SUMMARY

Concepts of character and character pathology have been presented. These included "heredity-constitutional" factors leading to the development of "temperament," and the molding of these factors by the environment, leading to the development of ongoing object relationships and personal identifications forming one's own character. Character has been defined as the usual way one is as an adult. This includes the normative, ego-syntonic way one feels about it. Pathology of these processes, producing character neuroses and personality disorders, has been discussed.

The linking concepts, involving many aspects of the ego and ego defenses, have been presented. The concept of the need to change and transform into character structures certain zonal cathexes of the anal phase, particularly those seen in the second (toilet training) year of life, has been stressed (64). The concepts of sublimation and displacement, as well as the continuum of ego defenses, have been demonstrated.

Early childhood identifications and identificational processes crystallized at the resolution of the Oedipus complex are reworked definitively during adolescence. The emergence of adolescent, characterological psychopathology and its possible persistence in adult life, when adolescent and young adult resolution is unsuccessful, have been discussed.

Some specific types of character disorders have been mentioned and compared with a concept of normality. The "complementarity" of some psychopathology in normal people and the normative aspects of complementary object relationships (mutually supporting) with spouses or friends have also been mentioned. The importance of using the concept of character disorder and character pathology in understanding and treating all pathology, relating to a concept of normality, has been outlined.

The need to teach these concepts, to train medical manpower in the techniques needed for long-term characterological treatment with the aim of changing char-

20   *Character Pathology: Theory and Treatment*

acter pathology, has also been stressed. This remains one of the major concerns. The fact that certain character pathology of a narcissistic kind (16, 26, 27) is prevalent in our current society makes these issues of great relevance to the current North American scene, as well as having a broader clinical and theoretical interest.

REFERENCES

 1. ALPERT, A., NEUBAUER, P.B., and WEXL, A.: Unusual variations in drive endowment. *Psychoanal. Study Child*, 11: 1956.
 2. FRIES, M.E.: Some hypotheses on the role of the congenital activity type in personality development. *Inter. J. Psychoanal.*, 35: 206, 1954.
 3. LOURIE, R.S.: The role of rhythmic patterns in childhood. *Am. J. Psychiat.*, 105: 653, 1949.
 4. LOURIE, R.S.: The role of individual constitutional differences in early personality development. *Clin. Proc. Child. Hosp., D.C.*, 22: 282-284, 1966.
 5. THOMAS, A., and CHESS, S.: *Temperament and Development*. New York: Brunner/Mazel, 1977.
 6. LOURIE, R.S.: Studies of head banging, bed rocking and related rhythmic patterns. *Clin. Proc. Child. Hosp. D.C.*, 5 (11): 295, 1949.
 7. KRETSCHMER. E.: (1921) *Physique and Character*. London: Kegan, Paul, Trench, Tralner, 1925.
 8. SHELDON, W.H.: *Varieties of Human Physique*. New York: Harper, 1940.
 9. SZONDI, L.: Analisis del yo y analisis del caracter. *Rev. Psical, Gen. Apl. Madrid*, 8: 595-639, 1953.
10. BRODY, S.: *Passivity*. New York: International Universities Press, 1964.
11. HARTMANN, H., KRIS, E., and LOEWENSTEIN, R.M.: Comments on the formation of psychic structure. *Psychoanal. Study Child*, 2: 11-38, 1946.
12. PARENS, H., and SAUL, L.J.: *Dependence in Man*. New York: International Universities Press, 1971.
13. FISH, F.: *Fish's Clinical Psychopathology*. M. Hamilton (Ed.), Revised Ed. Bristol, England: John Wright, 1974.
14. JASPERS, K.: *General Psychopathology*. Translated by J. Hoenig and T.W. Hamilton. Chicago: Univeristy of Chicago Press, 1964.
15. SABSHIN, M., and OFFER, D.: *Normality: Theoretical and Clinical Concepts of Mental Health*. New York: Basic Books, 1981.
16. ADORNO, T.W., FRENKEL-BRUNSWICK, F., LEVINSON, D.J., SANFORD, R.N., et al. (Eds.): *The Authoritarian Personality*. New York: Harper, 1950.
17. ALEXANDER, F.: The neurotic character. *Inter. J. Psychoanal.*, 11: 292, 1930.
18. BLANE, H.T.: Characterological patterns of defense. *Int. Psychiat. Clinics*, 3: 139-162, 1966.
19. CHRISTENSEN, R.L.: Character disorder: The twentieth century "neurosis." *U.S. Armed Forces Med. J.*, 6: 1597-1604, 1955.
20. FREUD, S. (1914) On narcissism: An introduction. *Standard Edition*, 14: 69-102. London: Hogarth Press, 1957.
21. FREUD, S. (1926) Inhibitions, symptoms and anxiety. *Standard Edition*, 20: 77-174. London: Hogarth Press, 1959.

22. GABE, S.: The genetic determinants of obsessive-compulsive phenomena in character formation. *J. Am. Psychoanal. Assoc.*, 13: 591-604, 1965.
23. GIOVACCHINI, P.L.: Transference, incorporation and synthesis. *Int. J. Psychoanal.*, 46: 287-296, 1965.
24. GLOVER, E.: The neurotic character. *Int. J. Psychoanal.*, 7: 11, 1926.
25. GREENACRE, P.: *Trauma, Growth and Personality*. New York: Newton, 1952.
26. KOHUT, H.: *The Analysis of the Self*. New York: International Universities Press, 1971.
27. KOHUT, H.: *The Restoration of the Self*. New York: International Universities Press, 1977.
28. NUNBERG, H.: Character and neurosis. *Int. J. Psychoanal.*, 37: 36, 1956.
29. BERGLER, E.: The type "Mr. stuffed shirt." *Am. Imago*, 17: 407-412, 1960.
30. BOYER, L.B., and GIOVACCHINI, P.L.: *Psychoanalytic Treatment of Characterological and Schizophrenic Disorders*. New York: Science House, 1967.
31. FREUD, S. Character and anal erotism (1908). *Standard Edition*, 9: 167-176. London: Hogarth Press, 1959.
32. JONES, E. Anal-erotic character traits. In: *Papers on Psychoanalysis*. New York: Wood, 1913.
33. MICHAELS, J.J.: Character structure and character disorder. In: S. Areti (Ed.), *American Handbook of Psychiatry*. New York: Basic Books, 1959.
34. MICHAELS, J.J.: Character disorder and acting upon impulse. In: H. Levitt (Ed.), *Readings in Psychoanalytic Psychology*. New York: Appleton-Century-Crofts, 1959.
35. REICH, W.: *Character Analysis, 3rd Ed*. New York, Orgone Institute Press, 1949.
36. REICH, W.: On the technique of character analysis, In: C. Thompson, M. Mazen, and M. Wittenberg (Eds.), *The Outline of Psychoanalysis*. New York: Random House, 1955.
37. STERBA, R.: On character neurosis. *Bull. Menninger Clinic*, 17: 81-89, 1953.
38. STERBA, R.: Clinical and therapeutic aspects of character resistance. *Int. J. Psychoanal.*, 35: 438-439, 1954.
39. VALENSTEIN, A.F., MICHAELS, J.J., and EVJE, M.: Aspects of character in the neurotic veteran. *J. Nerv. Ment. Dis.*, 117: 445-457, 1953.
40. KAUFMAN, I.: Delineation of two diagnostic groups among juvenile delinquents: The schizophrenic and the impulse-ridden character disorder. *J. Amer. Acad. Child. Psychiat.*, 2: 292-318, 1963.
41. MICHAELS, J.J.: *Disorders of Character: Persistent Enuresis, Juvenile Delinquency and Psychopathic Personality*. Springfield, IL: Charles C. Thomas, 1955.
42. STIERLIN, H.: Treatment dilemmas with psychotic and psychopathic patients. *Brit. J. Med. Psychol.*, 36: 75-84, 1963.
43. GLOVER, E.: Notes on oral character function. *Int. J. Psychoanal.*, 6: 131, 1925.
44. GRUNBERGER, B.: Étude sur la relation objectale anale. *Rev. Française Psychanal.*, 24: 138-160, 166-168, 1960.
45. MUSTA, W.: A technical problem of acting out. *Ann. Surv. Psychoanal.*, 7: 327, 1956.
46. HARTMANN, H., KRIS, E., and LOWENSTEIN, R.M.: Notes on the theory of aggression. *Psychoanal. Study Child*, 3/4: 9-36, 1949.
47. HARTMANN, H., KRIS, E., and LOWENSTEIN, R.M.: Notes on the superego. *Psychoanal. Study Child*, 17: 42-81, 1962.
48. SARWER-FONER, G.J.: Some aspects of anal object relationship. Seminars Presented

to Students at Canadian Institute of Psychoanalysis, 1972-73.

49. SARWER-FONER, G.J.: A psychoanalytic note on a specific delusion of time in psychotic depression. *Canad. Psychiat. A.J. Supple.*, 11: S221-S228, 1966.

50. HILL, L.B.: The nature of extramural schizophrenia. In: D.H. Rifkin (Ed.), *Schizophrenia in Psychoanalytic Office Practice*. New York: Grune & Stratton, 1957.

51. THOMPSON, C.M.: The role of the analyst's personality in therapy. *Amer. J. Psychother.*, 10: 347-367, 1956.

52. GRUNBERGER, B.: *Narcissism: Psychoanalytic Essays*. New York: International Universities Press, 1979.

53. SARWER-FONER, G.J.: Denial of death and unconscious longing for indestructibility and immortality in the terminal phase of adolescence. *Canad. Psychiat. A. J.*, 17: Sp. Suppl. II, 51-57, (July) 1972.

54. PETERFREUND, E.: Some critical comments on psychoanalytic conceptualizations of infancy. *Int. J. Psychoanal.*, 59: 427-441, 1978.

55. WINNICOTT, D.W.: Transitional objects and transitional phenomena. *Int. J. Psychoanal.*, 34: 89-97, 1953.

56. SARWER-FONER, G.J.: Patterns of marital relationship. *Amer. J. Psychother.*, 17: 31-44, 1963.

57. GRINKER, R.R., SR., WERBLE, B., and DRYE, R.C.: *The Borderline Syndrome*. New York: Basic Books, 1968.

58. KERNBERG, O.: Borderline personality organization. *J. Am. Psychoanal. Assn.*, 15: 641-685, 1967.

59. KERNBERG, O.: *Borderline Conditions and Pathological Narcissism*. New York: Jason Aronson, 1975.

60. MASTERSON, J.: The splitting mechanism of the borderline adolescent: Development and clinical aspects. In: J.E. Mack (Ed.), *Borderline States in Psychiatry*. New York: Grune & Stratton, 1975.

61. SARWER-FONER, G.J.: An approach to the global treatment of the borderline patient: Psychoanalytic, psychotherapeutic and psychopharmacologic considerations. In: P. Hartocollis (Ed.), *Borderline Personality Disorders*. New York: International Universities Press, 1977.

62. SARWER-FONER, G.J.: The intractable borderline patient: Treatment considerations. In: A. Gralnick (Ed.), *Treatment of the Seriously Ill Patient*. Port Chester/Rye Brook, New York: Gralnick Foundation, 1983.

63. KOLB, J.E., and GUNDERSON, J.G.: Diagnosing borderline patients with a semistructural interview. *Arch. Gen. Psychiat.*, 37: 34-41, 1980.

64. MENNINGER, W.C.: Characterologic and symptomatic expressions related to the anal phase of psychosexual development. *Psychoanal. Quart.*, 12: 2, 1943.

2

Selfobject Relations Disorders

Ernest S. Wolf, M.D.

INTRODUCTION

Thirty years ago, when I was a young psychiatric resident, it seemed to us that most of the problems of psychiatric nosology had been resolved. We had learned about Kraepelin and about Freud, who had given us descriptive and dynamic diagnoses. To be sure, it was not easy to fit the protean variety of human kind that crowded our wards and clinics into the proper categories that would allow us to understand them and to help them. But, in fact, our conceptualizations were powerful tools, and, I flatter myself to say, we did quite well and helped a great many people. Maurice Levine, a superb teacher, introduced us to the principles of psychiatric diagnosis and treatment that still guide my approach to patients today. I shall recall those basic principles very briefly because, in essence, they are as valid today as they were 30 years ago (1).

Levine's principles were really those of all good medical practice. It seems obvious but it bears repeating that treatment based on adequate diagnosis is superior to treatment which is focused simply on the relief of symptoms. It follows that "the prescription for treatment is written by the understanding of the problem rather than by a set of therapeutic rules." Adequate understanding implies thinking about the patient within a framework of five simultaneous considerations:

1) Clinical diagnosis
2) Dynamic diagnosis
3) Genetic diagnosis

23

4) Transference
5) Countertransference.

Clinical diagnosis was subdivided into five major categories:

1) Normal
2) Psychosis
3) Mental deficiency
4) Neurosis and neurotic character disorder
5) Psychosomatic illness.

It is evident that there is much overlapping in these relatively simple diagnostic categories, even before the simultaneous consideration of dynamic and genetic factors. Dynamics and genetics, of course, were the important contribution which psychoanalysis had made to the diagnostic-therapeutic process in psychiatry.

CHARACTER

The first writing by Freud specifically devoted to a discussion of character was "Character and Anal Erotism" (2). Though there have been many additions and modifications to this original conceptualization of the anal character, it is necessary to point out that the central and essential idea of character as the more or less stable outcome of the interaction of drive-conflict and defenses with the impinging environment has remained a pillar of most psychoanalytic formulations. However, these pioneering advances made by psychoanalysis had some major shortcomings. There are internal contradictions arising from the difficulty in assigning an appropriate share of the character-forming process to either internal, i.e., drive derived, or to external, i.e., social factors. Furthermore, and this is of the greatest practical importance to the psychiatrist who treats patients and teaches students, the therapeutic effectiveness of the psychoanalytic conceptualizations are not on a level with their theoretical elegance. It is not unequivocally clear whether therapeutic results are related more closely to the therapist's theories or the therapist's personality. Or, perhaps, the therapist's theories and the way he makes use of them depend to a significant extent on his personality. We struggle still with this problem today, though we are impressed that our advances in theory have freed us of many of the distorting effects of our personalities, e.g., we are more aware and more accepting of our countertransference attitudes which, thus, become less of an interference in the therapeutic process (3-5).

PSYCHOANALYTIC SELF PSYCHOLOGY

I wish to focus now on one particular set of accomplishments in the further development of psychoanalytic theory and treatment during the last two decades, namely the work of Heinz Kohut and his colleagues. Heinz Kohut's opus, the Psychoanalytic Psychology of the Self, or, more informally, Self Psychology, consists of a number of essays and books that are of enormous significance for any serious consideration of character (6-12).

Kohut was nurtured and worked within the mainstream of psychoanalysis. He was relatively uninfluenced by the other main psychoanalytic contributors to the post-Freudian era, whether relatively traditionalist-classical or neo-Freudian. He developed a systematic psychoanalytic approach that was original, comprehensive, and innovative without deviating from the basic principles of the psychoanalytic body of knowledge. But in order to grasp the self psychological approach without the distortions imposed by prior commitments to alternate points of view, it is necessary, temporarily, to set aside prior notions and to listen to Kohut openly without wondering about id, ego, and superego, or about drives, defenses, conflicts, and resistances. All these concepts are, of course, of the greatest usefulness at the proper time, but temporarily they should be displaced to the periphery of attention. Instead, the self and its selfobjects should be placed in the center of concern. And, here, we run into the first major difficulty.

THE SELF

What is the self? How can it be defined? And what are selfobjects? What kind of a neologism has been coined here? Indeed, I will have a hard time satisfying epistemological urges. I am also afraid that if I really attempted to give a philosophically and philologically sound definition, provided that were possible, it would lead us off into airy realms of theoretical speculation—but without arriving at a good understanding of what Kohut meant to convey to his colleagues. Therefore, we have to accept that theories in self psychology are incomplete, ill-defined, imprecise, and constantly changing to reach a better internal consistency and a better articulation with other sciences. But that is the process by which scientific advances come about, ever so slowly. So instead of the clear scientific definitions that one may rightfully expect, I will present clinical descriptions selected to highlight and evoke the inner experiences that correspond to the ideas and the concepts that we have been using in self psychology. The distinguishing feature of this approach is a stance, a point of view, that does not attempt to assess the other person from the outside, so to speak, as an object in the world, not even as an object on the couch, but, rather, attempts to assess what this person is *experiencing* both consciously and unconsciously. I might add that we are just as fastidious in the objective assessment of our patient's subjectivity as the natural scientist is in the objective assessment of his object of study.

EMPATHY

We call the process of objectively assessing our patient's subjectivity empathy. Empathy is a method for gathering data by imaginatively placing oneself into another self to gauge what the other's experience is likely to be. Cognitive processes, such as reason and logic, are used to combine the empathic data with other data, such as memories, fantasies, knowledge, and ideas about events of the past, present, and future, into scientific explanations, which in psychoanalysis are called interpretations. Empathically obtained data are just as reliable as other observational data and are subject to the same limitations of personal bias and of being influenced by psychological necessities such as resistances. Their use needs to be carefully monitored by trained observers. But that is true for the use of any kind of data in scientific inquiry. The untrained medical student is hardly a more reliable reporter of microscopic pathology than the untrained fledgling analyst is of empathic data from his patients. But the trained microscopist discerns three-dimensional structures where the student could see only confusing chaos. Similarly, the trained psychotherapist can grasp the most complex mental states empathically where the student is overwhelmed in a turmoil of thoughts and feelings.

THE SELF AS STRUCTURE

But let us get back to the self that I have asked you to put into the center of your attention. I am going to postpone a precise definition of the self, except to indicate that the self is that psychological structure that makes its presence evident by providing us with a healthy sense of self and well-being. It seems that the essence of the self is elusive, as the essence of an electron is elusive. All we can really know about these structures are their manifestations, the phenomena they give rise to. Even the quality of being a psychological structure means no more than that the self can be shown to have a history—a past, a present, a future—and that over this history there are certain aspects that change only very slowly, if at all, Structure merely means stability over time. Of course, this stability can be lost; there may be sudden or rapid changes in function and manifestation, such as an altered sense of self, or a lost feeling of well-being, and then we conceptualize that structure has been lost or altered. Thus, we talk about cohesive selves and fragmented selves. But, clearly, these are metaphors. The importance of the self is not a new discovery and precedes psychoanalysis. Psychoanalytic psychology, until recently, however, did not pay much attention to the self. There are a number of reasons for this neglect:

1) I think the most important reason for bypassing the self was the urgent need to investigate those psychological constellations that had been newly discovered, especially the conflict-laden sexual drives and their vicissitudes. The study of the latter had to proceed in the face of stubborn resistance both from within and from without. Therefore, any deviation from the program to investigate instinctual drives, conflicts, and defenses was suspect as a probable manifestation of a hidden or well disguised resistance.

2) Morally speaking, furthermore, any focus on the self coupled with a concern for the self's well-being looks selfish. To be called narcissistic is, in our Judeo-Christian culture, not a compliment. Yet, scientists readily recognize that such moralistic biases have no legitimate place in investigative endeavors. If Freud could make it legitimate to talk about and study sexuality, then one could hope that Kohut might make it legitimate to talk about and study narcissism without any pejorative connotations.

3) One further aspect of the study of the self makes it unpalatable for many people. Here I am referring to the inevitable discovery when studying the self that the self cannot exist for very long in a psychological vacuum, in fact, that the very emergence and maintenance of the self as a psychological structure depend on the continuing presence of an evoking, sustaining, responding matrix of selfobject relationships. This discovery heralds the end of another cherished illusion of Western man, namely, the illusory goal of independence, self-sufficiency, and free autonomy. Thus, self psychology strikes deeply at a politico-religious value system in which the self-made man is hero. Man and his environment are inseparable. They cannot be studied in isolation. The psychoanalytic study of the individual inevitably, via self psychology, becomes not the study of the person-in-vacuo but the study of man in his surroundings, i.e., the study of the self and its selfobjects.

SELFOBJECTS

What are selfobjects? While it is difficult to define the self, it is fairly easy to define selfobjects. Selfobjects are those objects in the surroundings, who—in addition to whatever other psychological functions they may perform—function to evoke and sustain the self as a cohesive structure. Strictly speaking, therefore, selfobjects are neither selves nor objects but functions performed by objects for selves. However, the self experiences the selfobjects as part of its own structure, since the cohesiveness of the structure depends on them. Analogously, the mortar that binds the bricks into a building becomes part of the building.

Perhaps the easiest way for me to explain what is meant by the selfobject concept is by an illustrative example. Imagine a speaker in front of an audience. As he stands in front of his audience of respected colleagues, he feels pretty good but slightly apprehensive. How will they receive what he has to say? He tells them what he has on his mind, and they listen, more or less attentively. That makes him feel he is being listened to and he feels responded to. As a result, he feels good, more sure of himself; in other words, his self-esteem is enhanced. And, perhaps, the audience will think that this fellow has it "all together." To put this a little more theoretically, apparently he needs such responsiveness because his self, a psychological structure as we see it, needs certain sustaining psychological responses from its surroundings in order to maintain its cohesion, vigor, and harmony. Because usually they are performed by objects, we call these needed responses selfobject responses, or, more precisely, selfobject functions of the object.

But suppose the audience had been getting a little bored with what it had been hearing. Perhaps the speaker would notice a lot of yawning or stretching and restlessness in the room; maybe people were beginning to walk out. What would happen to him? I think he would begin to feel rather uncomfortable, a little distracted, and then he would probably begin to be unsure of himself, perhaps begin to stumble over his words or lose his place. His voice might give out; he might blush, break out in a sweat. Well, I am sure I need not give a detailed description of what it is like when one suddenly feels unresponded to, disconnected from one's surroundings, because I assume everyone has experienced it at times and knows that the unconnected state is a most unpleasant experience. If you noticed someone in that state you might comment to yourself that the poor chap seems to be "falling apart." To conceptualize this we would say that his self had fragmented because of insufficient selfobject responses. Of course, there are many other ways of conceptualizing these phenomena. But final judgment should be withheld until a more comprehensive picture of what self psychology is attempting to conceptualize has emerged.

SELFOBJECT RELATIONS DISORDERS

You may well wonder why I have spent so much time just talking about definitions of self and of selfobjects and why I have gone to such lengths in demonstrating some fundamentals of self-selfobject relations. But it seems to me that having a clear grasp of these fundamentals will greatly facilitate my task of elaborating on the disorders of the self, or, as I have called them here more precisely, the disorders of selfobject relations.

Etiology

Faulty interaction between the child and his caretakers, especially during the early years when the self first emerges, is experienced by the nascent self as inappropriate or even injurious selfobject responsiveness. The result is a diffusely damaged self or a self that is seriously damaged in one or the other of its constituents.

On a previous occasion Kohut and Wolf outlined as follows:

> In view of the fact that the disorders of the self are, by and large, the result of miscarriages in the normal development of the self, we shall first present an outline of the normal development of the self. It is difficult to pinpoint the age at which the baby or small child may be said to have acquired a self. To begin with, it seems safe to assume that, strictly speaking, the neonate is still without a self. The newborn infant arrives physiologically pre-adapted for a specific physical environment—the presence of oxygen, of food, of a certain range of temperature—outside of which he cannot survive. Similarly, psychological survival requires a specific psychological environment—the presence of responsive-empathic selfobjects (12).

To give firmness and cohesion to his fragile self, the child needs two kinds of responses from his selfobject environment. Mirroring selfobjects provides confirmation for the child's innate sense of vigor, greatness, and perfection. Idealized selfobjects are available to the child as images of calmness, infallibility, and omnipotence with whom the child can merge. Faulty interactions between the child and his selfobjects result in a damaged self, which predisposes the child to the later outbreak of a disorder of the self. Depending on the nature of the damage, therefore, adult selves exist in varying degrees of cohesion, have various levels of vigor, and are balanced in varying degrees of harmony.

Classification

Significant failure to achieve cohesion, vigor or harmony of the self may be said to constitute a state of self disorder, i.e., etiologically speaking that means selfobject relations disorder. The disorders of the self can be subdivided into a number of groups, depending on the nature of the damage to the self. If the damage to the self is relatively permanent and the defect is not covered over by defenses, then the resulting syndrome is like those that are traditionally referred to as the *psychoses*. Constitutional factors combine with the effects of deficient mirroring to produce the noncohesive psychopathology of *schizophrenia*. In another category, inherent organic factors combine with the psychological depletion resulting from lack of joyful selfobject responses to leave a predisposition toward *empty depression*. Absense of structure-building experiences attending the merger with calm, idealized selfobjects is likely to result in insufficient self-soothing or self-supportive structures and, therefore, predispose to *mania* or *guilt depression*.

Borderline states are characterized by similar relatively permanent injuries to the self, except the damage is covered by complex defenses. A borderline self may protect its fragile structure against further serious damage from the rough and tumble, as well as the intimacy, of social intercourse by using schizoid mechanisms to keep involvement shallow or by using paranoid mechanisms to surround itself with an aura of hostility and suspicion that will keep noxious selfobjects at bay.

Less severe and more temporary damage to the self is found in the *narcissistic behavior disorders*. Characteristically, these persons attempt to shore up their crumbling self-esteem through perverse, delinquent, or addictive behavior. In the *narcissistic personality disorders* we find even less severely damaged selves. Here the injured state of the self is experienced directly in the form of subjective symptomatology, such as hypochondria, depression, hypersensitivity to slights, lack of zest, inability to concentrate on tasks, irritability, insomnia, etc.

Psychopathology

A chronically faulty selfobject environment, rather than single traumatic events, causes the developmental failures which leave the child vulnerable to specific constellations of damage to the self. Certain characteristic types of self pathology stand out, though they are usually found in mixtures rather than in pure culture.

Prolonged lack of stimulating responsiveness from the selfobjects of childhood results in *understimulated* selves. Such people lack vitality and experience themselves as boring. In order to ward off painful feelings of deadness, they need to create a pseudo-excitement by the use of any available stimulus. Depending on the developmental phase, one may see head-banging among toddlers, compulsive masturbation in childhood, dare-devil activities in adolescents and adults. Adults, of course, can be quite inventive in producing innumerable kinds of self-stimulating behavior. Such diverse activities as deviant sexuality, drug and alcohol abuse, and frenzied lifestyles in business or social spheres serve as examples. Even such splendid exercises as jogging or running can be transformed into pathological excesses by a self's need for stimulation to maintain its cohesion. The "highs" that can be experienced during these self-stimulating exertions are familiar to all of us and are a reminder of the extraordinary sense of well-being enjoyed by a really cohesive self. On the other hand, in a damaged self, the ubiquitous empty depression is kept at bay by creating pleasurably stimulating sensations in parts of the body or mind, since the joy provided by healthy functioning of the total self is unavailable.

A 53-year-old accountant came into treatment because of moderate chronic depression and anxiety which made his daily life a miserable experience, though he was able to perform his work well. He was constantly concerned that he was not really fully accepted by his partners; in fact, he felt that he did not really belong anywhere. He exuded a general aura of pessimism and negativism. There was no trace of enthusiasm for anything, either people or objects.

Occasionally he would engage his wife in bitter discussions, in which he expounded his black view of the world. The arguments that developed might evoke a kind of pseudo-excitement in him.

He had been born in Western Europe to moderately well-off parents. Father was a grocer; mother helped in the store; and their two children were cared for by a series of maids. The vicissitudes of war caused a separation from the parents at age seven, and subsequently he grew up in a series of foster homes in America. It is not clear why he was unable to make any lasting human relationships in any of these homes, but a chronic bed-wetting problem may have been an important factor.

During treatment it became apparent from both the reconstruction of his history and manifestations in the transference that he had no expectation of any real interest in him from anybody. Yet, equally apparent was his need for recognition and confirmation of his worth by his co-workers, and, especially, from me. His understimulated self manifested as a chronic depression.

Lack of integrating responses to the emerging infantile self predisposes to states of *partial fragmentation*. These people react to narcissistic injuries with a disturbed sense of the continuity of their self or the smoothness of its functioning. Characteristically, they are anxious, hypochondriacal, awkward, and clumsy in posture, gait, or speech.

A 35-year-old research chemist was unhappy with his professional career because of lack of advancement, though he was well trained by an Ivy League university. His first marriage had ended in divorce when his wife tired of his obsessive-compulsive nagging and ran off with a college boyfriend. The patient suffered greatly from a number of minor illnesses that assumed life-threatening proportions in his mind. His awkward posture and clumsy movements, as well as his chronically morose anxiety, had caused him to be ridiculed by his college classmates, resulting in a general feeling of mortified alienation.

He was the only child of two chronically sick elderly parents who, though well-meaning, were quite unable to adequately respond to their youngster. They were at once overprotective, impatient, and authoritarian. From this confusing milieu he withdrew into a rich fantasy life and compensated himself with the deserved recognition he received for his outstanding intellectual achievements in school. But underneath this compensating structure he remained in a partially fragmented state. In treatment he responded well to the integrating effect provided by a stable and accepting therapeutic ambience.

Excessive or inappropriate selfobject responses may lead to an *overstimulated* state of the self. These people are fearful of the tension induced by being flooded with fantasies of their own greatness or the excited fantasies about the greatness of others. As a consequence these persons will be shy or lack the normal capacity for enthusiastically pursuing a goal.

Overburdened selves lacked the opportunity to merge with the calmness of an omnipotent selfobject. Therefore, they lack the self-soothing structures that protect the normal individual from being traumatized by the spreading of his emotions. Even gentle stimuli cause painful excitement, and the world is experienced as hostile and dangerous. Somatic hyperirritability and migraines have been observed.

A woman in her early thirties had married a widower with three teenage children after the children's mother died following a sudden, overwhelming illness. The patient's father had been a somewhat sociopathic man whose acting-out behavior had led to his premature sudden death when his daughter was a preadolescent. The patient's mother had been an overly anxious woman more concerned with the neighbor's good opinion of her than with the traumatic shock to her daughter caused by father's untimely and disreputable demise. In fact, the little girl was accused of being very much like her father, and, by a kind of loose association, she was burdened with some responsibility for her father's sins. Or so at least it seemed to her. During treatment she often experienced even gentle questions as assaultive, and at times she would think the whole psychoanalytic situation as inimical. At such times or when extra-analytical demands on her were especially heavy, she might suffer attacks of migraine headache.

The intense suffering associated with pathology of the self impellingly motivates towards amelioration by either alloplastic or autoplastic modifications. Intensity of need combined with expectation of rebuff causes deep shame. Stridently expressed demands may alternate with total suppression. Demands, whether expressed in fantasy or in behavior, whether they are related to grandiosity or to being accepted by idealized figures, are not derived from the normal, healthy, self-assertive narcissism of childhood, but from the fragments of archaic selfobject needs or from the defenses against them.

Here is an example of a narcissistic behavior disorder:

> A young artist felt compelled to go "cruising" until he had made a homosexual pick-up every time that he experienced a faulty selfobject response from his co-workers. The momentary sexual encounter usually would suffice to provide sufficient responsiveness to avoid fragmentation of the self, even though no ongoing relationship ever developed.
> *Selfobject dynamic:* Faulty selfobject response threatens self with fragmentation, which is avoided by "emergency" homosexual relation.

Behavioral Patterns (Characterology)

So far we have discussed psychopathology, i.e., the different types of *pathological states* of the self that we have learned to distinguish. We come now to different types of *behavioral patterns* that are characteristic of all disorders of the self, including also the narcissistic personality disorders and the narcissistic behavior disorders. The latter refer specifically to prominent acting-out behavior, such as delinquency, addiction, and perversion. The former, however, also express in their behavior aspects of their psychopathology and also give rise to characteristic behavioral patterns.

Thus, we see *mirror hungry personalities* who are impelled to display themselves in order to evoke the attention of others, who through their admiring responses will perhaps counteract the experience of worthlessness.

> This young woman had come into analysis because of severe depression following a social rebuff by a community organization she had attempted to join. During treatment it was very important to her to tell me about all her social successes, her children's achievements, her husband's professional honors, and her own many accomplishments. On one occasion she proudly told me about how she had persuaded a friend to do something very difficult but beneficial and expected me to acknowledge her skill as well as the generosity of her effort. At the time I was preoccupied with some other important issues in her analysis and, instead of interpreting her intense need for acknowledgment by me, I erroneously interpreted her denial of separation fears regarding her friend. Her response was icy, and when she returned for the next session, she reported having been extremely upset after the last session to the point that on the way home she "inadvertently" ran a red light.
> *Selfobject dynamic:* Fragmentation following insufficient mirroring response.

We also see *ideal hungry personalities* who can only experience themselves as worthwhile by finding selfobjects to whom they can look up and by whom they can feel accepted.

This man, during treatment, suddenly became enraged with me when he found out that I was going abroad via a charter-airline flight. His need for an idealized selfobject was so intense that he needed to see me as superior to the type of people who take cheap charter flights. The sudden disappointment in the idealized selfobject temporarily fragmented his vulnerable self with the transformation of his healthy self-assertiveness into pathological rage.

Alter-ego hungry personalities need confirmation by being associated with another self whose appearance, opinions, and values they share.

This analysand, during a major part of his analysis, could not bear and would become very upset when he detected that I had a different opinion from that held by him on almost any topic.
Selfobject dynamic: The need for confirmation of this fragile self required the selfobject to enact in front of patient's eyes and ears the image of the self's alter-ego.

Merger hungry personalities need to control their selfobjects because they use them in lieu of self-structure. Their need to control often is experienced by their selfobjects with a feeling of being oppressed, since the merger hungry person cannot bear the other's independence or separation from him.

In *contact shunning personalities* the intensity of their need for others is exceeded only by their sensitivity to the expected rejection. Therefore, isolating defenses come prominently into the foreground, not as symptoms of disinterest but, to the contrary, as symptoms of the widely excessive need. The two major defensive constellations here are schizoid or paranoid in appearance. *Schizoid* defenses withdraw and hide the vulnerable self from the feared vicissitudes of social intercourse. Alternatively, *paranoid* defenses may surround the vulnerable self with such an aura of suspicion and hostility that potentially dangerous intruding selfobjects are held off at a safe distance.

SOME GENERAL COMMENTS

After having proceeded so blithely to present a nosological scheme to facilitate an orientation to the disorders of selfobject relations, it is necessary to point out and to warn that such systematic classifications are not to be taken as more than an orienting and guiding framework. To be sure, the classic psychoanalytic typology of character into oral, anal, urethral, phallic, genital, and phallic-narcissistic characters suffers from similar shortcomings and should similarly not be used as a defining classification.

There exists a number of difficulties that give rise to serious objections to almost any of the usual character nosologies. First of all, as has been already pointed out, "the simplified correlation of specific patterns of manifest behavior with universally present psychological conditions which of necessity forms part of any such typology will, in the long run, impede scientific progress" (12, p.420).

Second, the impression is created, inevitably, when presenting such a classification within a schema for ordering disorders, that the conditions so classified are, in fact, of a pathological nature. But that is plainly not true. Indeed, the constellations of structures that are designated as character-types vary in significance all the way from normal to severely pathological. The boundary between illness and health is vague and undetermined. The confusion originates from the fact that the sources of our conceptualizations are psychopathological phenomena.

Third, there is no stable correlation between etiological factors and the descriptive-phenomenological patterns. The behavior described as "mirror-hungry," for example, does not necessarily imply a deprivation of mirroring as the etiological agent. Only in the most general sense is it true that faulty selfobject relations during the formative stages of infancy and childhood will eventuate in adult behavior patterns that are characterized by faulty selfobject relations.

The complexity of human psychological experience, no less than the complexity of human behavior, is of such a degree that the precise representation in the exact formulations of scientific theories remains at present an elusive goal. This inescapable fact, however, does not significantly detract from the usefulness and epistemological soundness of the scientific theories that we create to order the chaos of observations in and around us. Similarly, the typologies to which we feel so attracted need not be shunned because of the limitations discussed above. But we should avoid going beyond their usefulness as direction-setting guides, and we should make sure that our misguided zeal for theorizing does not lead us into building fancy systems of thought, unless the latter clearly articulate harmoniously with contemporary contiguous scientific fields.

TREATMENT

General Comments

Even a cursory discussion of the multiple issues of treatment would go far beyond the confines of this chapter. Nevertheless, certain principles can and should be stated. A weakened self stands at the center of all selfobject relations disorders. A weakened self is weak for two reasons: first, because of the injury sustained as a result of faulty selfobject relations during the developmental phases, mostly in childhood, but also during certain developmental crises such as adolescence, midlife, and aging; second, the vulnerable self is kept weak by its own fragility, which forces it into defensive postures that interfere with current selfobject relationships and thus effectively hinder the establishment of self-sustaining and self-healing selfobject relations in the here-and-now. Rational treatment, therefore, should address itself to strengthening the weak self, if possible.

There are two paths to strengthening the self psychotherapeutically, but especially through psychoanalysis. For a small number of patients, the accepting ambience of being in the presence of a respected person who is seriously, nonjudgmentally, and empathically interested in the patient's experience may be a "first" in their life, and the first occasion to be in a milieu that facilitates the healing of the self. Thus, the self may finally recover somewhat from the early trauma. Still, there will remain scars and at least part of the pathologically heightened needs for distorted selfobject relationships. To totally cure and restore the injured self remains an elusive goal for most.

Fortunately, there is a second and psychotherapeutically extremely important avenue for strengthening the weakened self. This restoration of a strengthened self comes about via the psychoanalytic process, which in a stepwise fashion replaces the archaic (and thus pathological) needs for selfobject responses with age-appropriate ones, i.e., specifically with a selfobject response that we might label *reciprocal empathic resonance*. Without going into the technical details for activating the psychoanalytic process, let me outline the steps:

1) Allowing and facilitating the emergence of the archaic selfobject needs in the treatment situation by providing a proper ambience of non-interference (13);
2) The emerging selfobject needs will spontaneously focus on the therapist, i.e., a selfobject transference develops;
3) This transference will be disrupted, often very painfully, when inevitably the therapist somehow fails to respond in precisely the manner required by the patient;
4) This disruption is explained and interpreted in all its dimensions but particularly with reference to analogous early and presumably etiological situations with the significant persons of the past;
5) Explanation and interpretation restore the previous harmonious selfobject transference, but the mutual understanding achieved and *experienced* has served to replace the previously frustrated archaic selfobject need with a reciprocal empathic resonance which strengthens the self.

Specific Comments

The therapeutic process outlined above is predicated, among other factors, on the self being sufficiently strong to withstand the process, and, especially, the painful disruptions of the transference, without undue regression or total and perhaps irreversible fragmentation of the self. Patients who never achieved a cohesive self, therefore, are not suitable for psychoanalytic treatment. This eliminates most of the functional psychoses, in particular schizophrenia and the severe dysthymic disorders, from psychoanalysis as a treatment method. Though the lack of a cohesive self is covered over by defenses in the borderline states, these patients also are disposed to regress severely with loss of structure. As a rule they are not analyzable, though this is difficult to predict; the final diagnosis should be based not on any kind of theoretical definition or on any brief clinical assessment but only on a trial and failure of psychoanalytic treatment.

Injured selves which nevertheless achieved a measure of cohesion such as we find in the narcissistic personality disorders and in the narcissistic behavior disorders are the prime candidates for psychoanalysis. What about the psychoneuroses? In my experience, the pure symptom neurosis has become a rarity, and the patients that I have had the privilege of seeing during the last years all suffered from primary selfobject relations pathology. Many also suffered from a variety of neurotic sexual pathology derived from pathological Oedipal complexes, but, in each case, the Oedipal pathology was the result of faulty responses by the oedipal selfobjects of childhood. Psychoneurosis, thus, seems to be a particular variety of selfobject pathology and is treated as such.

REFERENCES

1. LEVINE, M. Principles of psychiatric treatment. In: F. Alexander and H. Ross (Eds.), *Dynamic Psychiatry*. Chicago: University of Chicago Press, 1952.
2. FREUD, S. (1908) Character and anal erotism. *Standard Edition*, 9: 169-175. London: Hogarth Press, 1959.
3. WOLF, E. Transference and countertransference in the analysis of disorders of the self. *Contemp. Psychoanal.*, 15: 577-594, 1979.
4. WOLF, E. Empathy and countertransference. In: A. Goldberg (Ed.), *The Future of Psychoanalysis*. New York: International Universities Press, in press.
5. WOLF, E. (1983) Disruptions in the treatment of disorders of the self. To be published in the Proceedings of the 4th and 5th Annual Conferences on the Psychology of the Self. In preparation.
6. KOHUT, H. (1959) Introspection, empathy and psychoanalysis. In: P. Ornstein (Ed.), *The Search for the Self*. New York: International Universities Press, 1978.
7. KOHUT, H. (1966) Forms and transformations of narcissism. In: P. Ornstein (Ed.), *The Search for the Self*. New York: International Universities Press, 1978.
8. KOHUT, H. (1968) The psychoanalytic treatment of narcissistic personality disorders.

In: P. Ornstein (Ed.), *The Search for the Self*. New York: International Universities Press, 1978.
9. KOHUT, H. *The Analysis of the Self*. New York: International Universities Press, 1971.
10. KOHUT, H. *The Restoration of the Self*. New York: International Universities Press, 1977.
11. KOHUT, H. Reflections on advances in self psychology. In: A. Goldberg (Ed.), *Advances in Self Psychology*. New York: International Universities Press, 1980.
12. KOHUT, H., and WOLF, E. The disorders of the self and their treatment. *Int. J. Psychoanal.*, 59: 414-425, 1978.
13. WOLF, E. Ambience and abstinence. *Annual of Psychoanal.*, 4: 101-115, 1976.

3

Narcissism in Normal Development

Arnold M. Cooper, M.D.

INTRODUCTION

Any discussion of narcissism in normal development must confront two significant and self-evident handicaps at the outset. The first of these is that the concept of normality in psychiatry remains poorly defined, and there is no uniform agreement on modes for separating health and illness. The second difficulty is that the term narcissism has accumulated a large number of meanings referring to different psychological functions or concepts, and despite the intensity of recent discussions, there is still no agreed-upon definition. The fuzziness of the term reflects the complexity of the concepts, while the persistence of the term reflects their central importance. I shall briefly review some of the pertinent considerations concerning normal development and narcissism before discussing the relationship between the two.

NORMAL DEVELOPMENT

Normality in medicine, and surely in psychiatry, is always an approximation of some theoretical goal which is approached by balancing a number of qualities. First, the concept of normality must include consideration of externally given, culturally prescribed norms, as well as the psychological mode by which individuals internalize those norms as part of their own prescriptions for value and behavior. Most psychiatrists today would regard it as dangerous to accept social norms as an indicator of psychological health, but would simultaneously regard it as pathological if an individual did not have a fully internalized awareness of the social values of his culture. One aspect of normal reality-testing is the full

39

recognition of cultural imperatives, leaving open the option to accept or reject those directives, that is, to conform or rebel.

Second, normality and normal development imply that within some range of variation all individuals share the full array of human psychological capacities. Within a large range of quantitative difference, we expect that all basic psychological functions are operative.

Third, our ideas of normal development include a balance between stability of the psychological organization, enabling integrated functioning at any point in time, and flexibility of functions, enabling growth and adaptation to changing circumstances. Since all behavior may be regarded as attempted adaptation, the concept of normality requires a fourth dimension, namely, a value system as a yardstick. Psychiatry shares the core values of medicine in assuming that normal (healthy) development facilitates the achievement of the capacities for happiness, joy or contentment, and the fulfillment of innate potentials and self-realization. The distinction between normal and pathological is, of course, relatively easy in the case of those deviations of behavior which fit our criteria for illness, and difficult or impossible in the case of milder forms of deviation and discontent. Freud's contrast of neurotic misery and normal human unhappiness is pertinent, but still beyond easy definition.

Assuming an average expectable, that is, normal, endowment of bodily and mental capacity, various attempts have been made to describe normal development in terms of expected sequences through which all individuals, at least in Western society, must pass. Probably the two best known developmental sequences are those of Sigmund Freud (1) and Erik Erikson (2). They are well-known and have done yeoman duty in our field. Freud's description of the course of libidinal development from a state of primary autoerotism to mature genitality which includes another person has provided a set of categories for understanding many aspects of behavior. Erikson's sequence in terms of the interaction of innate task and social setting, proceeding from basic trust, through the establishment of identity, on to generativity and integrity, attempts to describe normal development in terms of the psychosocial achievements which are considered developmentally normal through the life cycle. Erikson's sequence has provided useful guideposts and has focused attention on the issue of identity, a core aspect of narcissism.

I would like to bring up two other ways in which the developmental sequence has been conceptualized, since these modes provide data and opportunities for data-gathering. Anna Freud's concept of "developmental lines" (3) is an attempt to dissect behavior into discrete components, each of which may be followed sequentially from the time of its earliest precursors through its vicissitudes during the life cycle. Such sequences include, for example, development from primitive forms of play to mature forms of work, development from earliest manifestations of shame to mature operations of conscience, development from earliest body awareness to mature body control, development from infantile dependence to mature emotional relationships, etc. The concept of developmental lines provides opportunities for understanding normal development in much more detail than is provided by either Freud's or Erikson's holistic schemata. First, one can examine whether any given capacity is developing at the expected rate and in the expected mode, and, second, one can examine whether all capacities are developing in some appropriate balance. Anna Freud (3) said, "the disequilibrium between developmental lines . . . is not pathological as such but it becomes a pathogenic agent when the imbalance is excessive. Moderate disharmony does no more than produce the many *variations of normality* with which we have to count." Assuming that two forces are always at work—the biological unfolding of inherent potential and the effects of the actions of the environment, especially the actions of the family, upon the developing organism—one can then establish considerable precision in attempting to identify developmental abnormalities.

George Vaillant's work (4) is a second mode of study of aspects of normal development. Vaillant has described the 40-year follow-up of a group of 99 men who were first studied as college students. He demonstrated that in the course of normal development there are significant changes in the nature of the prevailing defense mechanisms. During adolescence and earlier there tends to be a predominance of immature or even psychotic defenses: examples would include denial, fantasy, and acting-out. If development proceeds successfully, these defenses tend to fade and are replaced by defenses that Vaillant considers either neurotic (i.e., ordinary), such as displacement, repression, and intellectualization, or healthy mechanisms, such as humor, sublimation, altruism, and anticipation.

Vaillant also found that clear indicators of later success or failure in life could be detected in adolescence and extrapolated to earlier phases. Failure of identification with the father, domination by the mother, poor childhood environments, and poor interpersonal adjustment all indicated high probabilities of later failure in life, as measured by unhappy marriage, financial failure, inability to achieve one's goals, poor relations with children, etc.

I believe that Anna Freud's concept of developmental lines and Vaillant's empirical study are complementary and indicate that the concept of normal development is robust and subject to study through experimental design. Their work also makes it clear that, while there are some outcome predictors for normality, no single variable is determining for adult functioning, which is always the sum of many interacting factors.

THE CONCEPT OF NARCISSISM

There have been a number of recent reviews of the historical development of the term narcissism (5, 6), and I will briefly present only some of the major issues here. It is surely the case, as Pulver (7) pointed out, that Freud used the term narcissism in at least four different ways:

1) Clinically, to denote a sexual perversion characterized by the treatment of one's own body as a sexual object.
2) Genetically, to denote a stage of development considered to be characterized by the libidinal narcissistic state.
3) In terms of object relationship, to denote two different phenomena:
   a) A type of object choice in which the self in some ways plays a more important part than the real aspects of the object.
   b) A mode of relating to the environment characterized by a relative lack of object relations.
4) To denote various aspects of the complex ego state of self-esteem (p. 323).

It is unfortunate that Freud chose to follow Havelock Ellis' lead in using the term narcissism which, following the theme of the myth, clearly connoted a pathological syndrome. Freud was interested in describing a line of development which he believed to be universal and normal in its origins. He was also interested in describing the vicissitudes of this line of development and its pathological outcome. This confusion between narcissism as pathology and narcissism as an aspect of normal development has significantly handicapped our understanding. Wilhelm Reich, following Freud's lead, used the concept of narcissism as the basis of his description of character. He said (8), "Character is essentially a narcissistic protection mechanism . . . against dangers . . . of the threatening outer world and the instinctual impulse." Reich made it clear that aspects of narcissism are central and normal in considering development. In fact, he placed the maintenance of narcissistic well-being in the center of personality development and regarded character formation as a set of defensive structures designed to protect the individual against narcissistic injury.

A further difficulty plaguing our discussions of narcissism has been our confusion in coping with such words as ego, self, and person. American psychiatry, certainly American dynamic psychiatry, has tended to follow Hartmann's lead in defining the self as a function of the ego and in considering narcissism as the libidinal investment of the internalized self representation. Recently, Bruno Bettelheim (9) has suggested that there is a systematic mistranslation of Freud's *"das ich"* in the English *Standard Edition*. Bettelheim asserts that Freud used *"das ich"* to refer to the self, the person, and even to the "soul," and that these meanings took precedence over his use of the term to refer to a structure of the mental apparatus. Laplanche and Pontalis (10) have also suggested that Freud deliberately avoided clarity in his use of *"das ich,"* intending to convey ambiguity and the broadest frame of reference. The ambiguity which Bettelheim and Laplanche and Pontalis state that Freud intended to convey is surely with us today. Despite many attempts to clarify the definitions of the terms, to organize the interrelationships of the ideas in a dynamic theory, and/or to facilitate the usage of the concepts clinically, we remain with more ambiguity than is desirable or useful.

THE WORK OF KOHUT AND KERNBERG

Heinz Kohut's Views

During the past decade, the works of Kohut and Kernberg have been central in discussions of narcissism, and a brief review of their influences is pertinent.

Kohut (11), in his attempt to understand the treatment behavior of patients with narcissistic personality disorders, made a crucial suggestion which greatly broadened the field of inquiry. It was Kohut's idea that the narcissistic patients' seeming inability to establish an ordinary transference relationship—the distance, demandingness, grandiosity, impersonality, merging, rage, lack of empathic contact, and overall lack of the sense of an intimate relationship one experiences with narcissistic patients—that these characteristics were not the result of an inability to establish a transference but were, in fact, the particular mode of transference of narcissistic patients. In effect, Kohut stated that narcissistic manifestations, contrary to the traditional view, whether in myth or in psychiatry, indicated not the absence of a tie to an object but a specific primitive form of object tie which appeared in patients who had suffered significant damage to the nuclear self during early psychological development, with a consequent arrest in the development of a cohesive self.

After initially attempting to place his findings concerning narcissism into a framework which would be compatible with traditional psychoanalytic theory, Kohut abandoned that effort and developed his own theory of the bipolar self. Kohut asserted that the establishment of the nuclear self is the primary program of the developing organism, with all other structures and drives being derivatives of and shaped by vicissitudes of the self. In this view, the self represents an independent center of initiative with two major characteristics. On the one hand, tendencies for idealization and grandiosity lead the developing individual toward goals, while, on the other hand, the inherent tendencies toward exhibitionism, striving, and ambition drive the organism forward toward its goals.

For the self to develop normally, the infant requires empathic mothering, i.e., a caretaking person with the emotional capacity for phase-appropriate responsiveness to the infant's needs to idealize and to receive acknowledgment and encouragement for its striving and exhibitionistic displays. In this framework of empathic mothering, the foundation for the development of a unified nuclear self takes place, as the infant gradually acquires the skills and capacities for linking ambitions and ideals. Adequate and empathic mothering provides the framework of reality-testing within which the primary grandiosity and untrammeled strivings of infancy are tamed to meet the limitations of the physical world and the infant's capacities.

In Kohut's view, the linkage of infant with empathic mother is central for normal development, and he coined the term "selfobject" to refer to the relationship to another person in which the other is psychologically perceived to be either wholly or in part an aspect of one's own self. The selfobject is a source of strength and structure, providing the necessary feelings of completeness and vigor while the infant's nuclear self is still weak and incomplete. The relationship of the self to one's selfobject in earlier infancy is heavily weighted towards the sense of the selfobject as entirely an aspect of one's own self with little outer reality or autonomy attributed to the other. With maturation the selfobject is increasingly perceived as having autonomous qualities rather than being entirely an aspect of inner needs.

In Kohut's later work he came to the conclusion that all individuals throughout the life cycle require for their sense of vigor and well-being the nurturance which comes from relationships to selfobjects. Mature relationships to selfobjects include the capacity for recognition of the autonomy of the object and empathy with the other's needs, while, simultaneously, using the object as an aspect of oneself.

Empathy—the capacity to perceive and feel another's inner psychological state and needs—plays a central role in Kohut's schema of normal development. Without empathic responsiveness, the infant cannot develop a vigorous nuclear self. The ability, in turn, to be empathically responsive to another is a measure of health.

It is of interest that Kohut's value systems for health or normality are significantly different from those of Freud. Where Freud defined psychological health in terms of the capacities for love and work, Kohut used as his criteria the capacities for joy and creativity. Love and work would be avenues towards these higher achievements. This fits Kohut's claim that he is describing Tragic Man, in contrast to Freud's Guilty Man; Tragic Man struggles for self-fulfillment in the universe and is only secondarily concerned with resolution of his inner conflicts.

Otto Kernberg's Views

Kerberg (12), in working with narcissistic and borderline patients, has had the theoretically less radical aim of achieving an ingenious combination of traditional ego psychology and object relations theory, utilizing concepts of Mahler and Jacobson with regard to individuation and the self. Kernberg maintains the tripartite schema of ego, superego, and id, and sees the self as a structure of the ego. The self derives from the internalized representations of the interactions of the infant's drive states with the objects in the environment and of the affective dispositions which arise in these interactions and are attached to these representations.

Where Kohut saw pathology as a consequence of the developmental arrest of the natural tendency towards a firm cohesive nuclear self, Kernberg sees pathology as a progressive development of distorted abnormal forms of the internalized self-image and internalized objects; prototypically, these pathological forms consist of denigrated, rageful, grandiosely compensatory, greedy self-images. For Kernberg, adult narcissistic pathology is not a consequence of the absence or enfeeblement of self-development, but, rather, a consolidation of the pathological self-representations and pathological self-idealizations, characterized by failures of reality-testing of the real self, the fusion of idealized self and real self, and distortions by hatred and rage.

Both Kernberg and Kohut agree on the importance of maternal responsiveness and warmth for the development of healthy self-representations. Kernberg, however, places far greater emphasis on the pathological role of rage in the genesis of narcissistic pathology. Kohut sees the genesis of narcissistic pathology in the failure of vigorous self-development resulting from empathic failure of the mother, and rage as a secondary indicator of that failure rather than a pathogenic element.

SYNTHESIS

Despite many apparent and real differences in the differing conceptualizations of narcissism, I shall suggest the following integrations of current views of a few of the topics at issue.

Normal Narcissism

While it might be desirable for the term narcissism to be dropped, it seems unlikely to happen, and so I shall use the term in the broadest sense to refer to aspects of the psychological interest in the self. The development of a sense of unified selfhood is essential in normal development and, therefore, narcissism—that is, aspects of the self—is a part of all psychological activity, whether normal or pathological. The continuing pejorative implications of the term narcissism do not fit our modern models for self-development, and both our patients and ourselves tend to confuse our discourse because of the older "bad" implications of the term.

Grandiosity

There is general agreement that infantile stages of the adult self are characterized by fantasies of grandiosity, perfection, and unlimited idealization. There is an infantile sense of the self as all-controlling, all-powerful, all-encompassing. This infantile version of the self-representation is present whether one sees the infant as an autistic creature unrelated to its object or as in complex interaction, "using" the object as a source for the maintenance of its primitive self-system. Infantile grandiosity is, of course, not an abnormality of which the adult has rid himself; it is a normal developmental stage appropriate to early infancy, which will forever show residues in psychic life in the form of the potential for the appearance of derivatives of these states in normal functioning and during regression under special circumstances. Grandiose fantasy during phases of creative work, or during aspects of sexual experience, is a source of enrichment and vitality and is clearly not pathological. The ability to revive modified versions of primitive experience to serve higher adaptive functions in later development is a measure of healthy psychological flexibility.

The Integrated Self-image

A vital aspect of normal self-development is the achievement of an internalized, integrated self-image. Each individual must integrate into a single and coherent whole a huge number of discrete, and often disparate, self-representations, which derive from the many different roles one plays under differing life circumstances. One important measure of normality is the ability to maintain an overall sense of unity while keeping the flexibility for diverse roles.

The integrated stable sense of self also requires the establishment of adequately firm boundaries between self and others. The borderline personality syndrome has been labeled a disorder of identity diffusion, characterized by psychic merging of self and other; in severe forms this loss of boundaries is a characteristic of certain forms of psychosis. The capacity to maintain an acceptable and unified self-image—which includes residues of infantile, idealized, and grandiose selves; realistic, actual self-images; and bad and denigrated self-images in varying balance, dependent on inner and outer vicissitudes—is significant for every aspect of behavior.

Different workers have referred to these integrative capacities and failures in a variety of ways. Kohut spoke of enfeebled selves lacking cohesion. Kernberg speaks of splits in self-representations. Erikson referred to identity diffusion, and Winnicott spoke of the False Self. Under many different headings, every investigator in this area has emphasized the core importance of the creation of a unified, coherent, integrated inner sense of self.

Narcissism, Object Relations, and the Superego

The assessment of functioning of the self requires consideration of at least two other psychological capacities: the nature of object relations and the structure of the superego.

1) Contrary to Freud's early formulation of narcissism as an excess of self-love, capturing so much of the available quantity of libido that love of others was impoverished, most psychiatrists would today accept Horney's (13) correction and agree that the capacities for object-love and self-love are parallel and mutually enhancing rather than competitive. The ability for a sustained attitude of generosity and love, tempered but not damaged by realistic, critical faculties, is likely to be displayed both toward one's self and toward one's objects—or toward neither. The self-representations and object-representations develop in the interaction of infant and caretaker, and the internalized representations of each will be linked as more or less satisfactory or unsatisfactory. While it is abundantly clear that early in development the support of a loving, empathic object is essential for the development of a normal self, there is greater dispute about whether, in later pathological states, a good selfobject can in itself be a healing element, as Kohut suggested.

2) The self-representations are always a reflection of the state of ego-superego integration. Defects of self-development and the development of pathological self-systems are always accompanied by superego pathology. The reasons for this are not entirely clear, but at least one element can be understood as the consequences of narcissistic rage on superego formation. Under conditions of excessive frustration of infantile, omnipotent, grandiose strivings, the mastery or disposition of the rage of narcissistic frustration is a major psychological task. Under healthier circumstances, with the aid of an empathic mother, both the narcissistic failures and the grandiose strivings are tempered over time, and the rage of frustration is likely to be met by soothing ministrations and will not reach disorganizing levels with consequent terror of some form of annihilation. If these integrative processes fail, then accusatory, paranoid tendencies remain powerful, and the target of that paranoid rage will include the self and the external object. The general tendency for the demands and the punishments of the superego to

be far harsher than reality has been noted by many, and it seems that the more serious the failure of narcissistic integration, or the less gratifying is the internalized self-image, than the harsher the superego will be. These individuals perceive every discrepancy between idealized and actual selves as a circumstance of utmost failure and danger, with denigrating and punitive consequences.

Self-esteem: Real and Spurious

The failure of the self to provide pleasure or to meet ego ideal standards is reflected not only in the sense of guilt from superego accusations, but also in the lowering of self-esteem. The inability to maintain some level of satisfying self-representations with consequent adequate self-esteem, even in the face of internal accusations related to realistic or fantasied failure, is an indication of a weakened self-system. Self-esteem may crudely be considered a reflection of the continuing inner measurement of the success of the self as a pleasure giver. However, self-esteem as seen from the outside cannot be taken at face value. For example, individuals sometimes described by their friends as smug and self-satisfied, with an overweening, all-encompassing self-esteem which prevents closeness to others and interferes with empathic recognition of others' needs, are likely on closer psychological scrutiny to reveal that what appears as self-esteem is an unstable façade. What we see in these individuals is a highly exaggerated, aggressively tinged, aggrandizing caricature of self-esteem which is inwardly designed to do hopeless battle against an overly harsh superego and to bolster a weakened inner self. These persons are often incapable of integrating positive and negative aspects of the self and are likely to show other characteristics of narcissistic pathology, such as sudden descents into empty depression, feelings of secret fraudulence despite their displays of outward, supreme self-confidence, and an inability to maintain a sustained interest in their own activities and achievements.

Self-esteem, like every other psychological quality, requires examination in depth and cannot be gauged by simple self-rating. Individuals with healthy self-esteem can tolerate criticism without collapse or the need for revenge; they can even contemplate changes in their self and do not experience feelings of depletion at the prospect of sharing their sources of well-being with others.

When infantile needs for admiration, mirroring, responsiveness, and idealization are shattered too early or too harshly, the individual is in peril of developing feelings of nothingness, annihilation, hopelessness, and invisibility. To counter these intolerable feelings of dread, children as well as adults seek and find desperately needed forms of exaggerated self-inflation which temporarily enhance the sense of well-being. Horney (13), who chose to confine the term narcissism to pathological situations of unrealistic self-inflation, said the following about narcissistic pathology:

> It means that the person loves and admires himself for values for which there is no adequate foundation. Similarly, it means that he expects love and admiration from others for qualities that he does not possess, or does not possess to as large an extent as he supposes. . . . These two tendencies—appearing unduly significant to one's self and craving undue admiration from others—cannot be separated (p.89).

In her view, the pathologically narcissistic individual is someone whose emotional ties to others are tenuous because they have suffered loss of a "real need." Under conditions of parental coercion, which have impaired the child's self-sufficiency, self-reliance and initiative, pathologic, narcissistic tendencies represent an attempt to cope with the painful feelings of deficiency.

> He escapes the painful feelings of nothingness by molding himself in fantasy into something outstanding—the more he is alienated not only from others but also from himself, the more easily such notions acquire a psychic reality. His notions of himself become a substitute for his undermined self-esteem. . . (13, p.90).

Remarkably similar views were expressed by Winnicott, who spoke of a "True" and "False Self." Winnicott (14) said:

> A True Self begins to have life, through the strength given to the infant's weak ego by the mother's implementation of the infant's omnipotent expressions. The mother who is not good-enough is not able to implement the infant's gestures; instead she substitutes her own gesture which is to be given sense by the compliance of the infant. This compliance on the part of the infant is the earlier stage of the False Self and True Self and belongs to the mother's inability to sense her infant's needs (p.145).

We all know the narcissistic patients with whom we feel that we are speaking to a mask and whose elaborate façade conceals from us an individual with feelings of desperate passivity and helplessness.

The intensive study of issues of narcissism in recent years has lead to a much greater understanding and clinical usefulness of the concept. As these few examples may indicate, we do not yet have an adequate map of the normal developmental stages of narcissism through the life cycle, but we do expect that derivatives of both infantile narcissism and newly created narcissistic constellations will be part of all normal human behavior. Any assessment of adult psychic functioning requires an assessment of the stage and quality of sel development. Self-esteem provides a fine calibration of the summation of acti ities with narcissistic consequences. At one extreme, narcissistic humiliati leads to plummeting self-esteem, a consequence we normally guard agains while, at the other extreme, untamed narcissistic grandiosity threatens a re mergence of infantile undifferentiated merger and omnipotent fantasies, posi another danger. Superego functions are finely tuned to register every discrepan between our internalized ideal self and our actual behaviors, and self-estee fluctuations mirror those measurements.

I would like now to give several examples of ways in which newer thinki concerning the role of narcissism in normal development may significantly al some of our usual clinical ideas.

NARCISSISM AND THE "NORMAL" OEDIPUS COMPLEX

The Oedipus complex has been regarded traditionally as an expectable c velopmental crisis stemming from the biological arousal of socially forbidd sexual and aggressive wishes and the consequent fear of punitive castration mutilation. Out of this crisis, and the need to maintain both the ties to need objects and one's bodily integrity, there results the internalization of structur control systems which we label the superego.

Looked at from the viewpoint of the developing narcissism, one may, perha somewhat narrowly, regard the Oedipus complex as a phase-appropriate atten to gratify infantile grandiosity in the context of emerging sexuality. For purpos of simplicity, I will follow tradition and speak only of the male child. In fa tasizing an Oedipal triumph, the child attempts to escape the narcissistic inju of acknowledging the power of his mother's almost absolute control over h and his dependent need for mother's care and elevates himself to the role of t idealized, all-powerful father, reducing mother to a sex object submissive to will. Simultaneously, in fantasy, he deposes father from a position of power a might and places himself in father's large shoes and aggrandizes father's lar penis as his own.

In this view, while sexual aims are clearly a central portion of the Oedi phase, they assume their importance and their subsequent terrifying quality t cause of the narcissistic intention which the child seeks to gratify throug sexual mode. The child's aim is omnipotence, grandiosity, and power over object, with sexuality and aggression providing the instrumentalities for realization of these narcissistic goals. It has always been the traditional psyc dynamic view of the Oedipus complex to assume that there is, indeed, an avoidable crisis as the child acknowledges a three-person world and that structu building of the superego occurs in the context of the terror of castration.

In recent years, a different view of the Oedipal phase has been put forward, most notably by Searles (15) and Ornstein (16). They suggest that the child's Oedipal strivings are a phase-appropriate narcissistic expression of the child's grandiosity, exhibitionism, and ambitious strivings, which are not in themselves a source of terror or conflict. In this view, they become a source of conflictual crisis only if the parents respond to the child's sexual and assertive strivings unempathically. If the mother humiliates and crushes the child in his—to adult eyes—absurd and ridiculous sexual exhibitionism and grandiosity, and if the father reacts with anger, as if the child were a genuine competitor rather than a child engaged in idealizing imitation of the adult, then indeed the child will become angry and frightened and will increasingly distort the nature of his wishes and the responses of his parents. Under these circumstances, he will construct one or another variety of neurotic defenses designed to protect him from both humiliation and wrathful retaliation.

However, the parents may empathically perceive the child's strivings as a harmless, growth-enhancing form of pleasurable self-aggrandizement, as a phase-appropriate alteration in his relation with his selfobjects, and as practice for living in a more complex multiperson world with externally directed assertiveness. And if they perceive that the child requires not squashing but assistance in deflecting his new needs and capacities toward other creative pathways, then the child will not develop the usual residua of pathological Oedipal conflict. Searles and Ornstein, using different frames of reference, both suggest that appropriate parenting responses will enable the child to obtain confidence in both his sexual abilities and his assertive capacity through the Oedipal experience, and that the child will enter latency with new strengths and new relational and creative capacities.

A recent summary of a discussion of Ornstein's paper on "Self Psychology and the Concept of Health" reported the following:

> The developmental vicissitudes of the Oedipus complex are phase-appropriate opportunities for the further development of a creative-productive-active self that can both fulfill its program of action and meet the demands of its particular sociocultural context. These Oedipal passions are positive, enriching experiences and in and of themselves are not pathological. Only when the nuclear self cannot retain its firmness or cohesiveness and responds to traumatic injury with enfeeblement or even fragmentation, do these stirrings appear in isolated, intensified form as breakdown products of the self and express underlying self-pathology (16, p.16).

In this connection, Ornstein went on to say that it is quite likely that our view of the highly conflict-laden, ubiquitously pathological infantile Oedipus complex is an artifact of our erroneous reconstructions from the transference neurosis.

What is revived in the transference neurosis is the Oedipus complex that in childhood had already developed its pathological form, content, and intensity, rather than its so-called "normal" infantile precursor.

In other words, if earlier stages of self-development were successfully traversed as a result of the selfobject's provision of need satisfaction and the learning of anxiety control, then the Oedipal phase becomes one more opportunity for complex structuring of selfobject relations without the interference of distorted aggressive and sexual "disintegration products." However, more data will have to be accumulated before one can accept this revision of traditional views.

NARCISSISM AND THE BODY

The central role of bodily experience in narcissistic development has been emphasized by most writers on the subject and is, of course, at the heart of the Narcissus myth. In recent years, clinicians have paid increasing attention to the effects of bodily change during the life cycle upon self-image and self-esteem. An important segment of a satisfying self-representation derives from images of the body-self as a pleasure source at least concordant with, if not under the control of, one's conscious self. The role of sexuality, for example, as providing healthy, narcissistic gratifications necessary for the maintenance of self-esteem for most persons is, of course, obvious. We are clinically more likely, however, to concern ourselves with *pathological* aspects of the defensive use of sexuality for pathological narcissistic enhancement and to pay relatively little attention to the *normal* replenishment of narcissistic needs through sexual pleasure.

The effects of changing bodily experience and perception on self-esteem regulation throughout the life cycle is highly significant for most persons. The extraordinarily rapid changes of body habitus during adolescence, the decline of bodily strengths and capacity during middle and old age, the loss of beauty with age in the eyes of most self-beholders, and the vicissitudes of the body during illness will have profound effects upon the internalized self-image.

Much of the turmoil of the adolescent identity crisis relates not only to problems of one's place in the social order but also to the significant disturbances of self-representation occasioned by rapid changes in body size, shape, and function. That period is for some persons never successfully traversed, and they forever retain a lack of ease in their own skin and a hypersensitivity to bodily change. Others, achieving more stable identity, are able to adapt to the large variety of bodily alterations which life brings. Those individuals whose self-structures are relatively fragile will experience these "body blows" to self-esteem as heavy indeed and are liable to react with an array of narcissistic defenses, ranging from the search for the fountain of youth through plastic surgery or exercise to the search for beauty in a partner whom one can hold up as an emblem of one's desired self.

Under not too pathological circumstances, the individual can compensate for failures of the body image by maintaining the self through one's selfobjects and through higher-order intellectual, creative or spiritual ambitions and idealization. Self-esteem through love and work and even joy and creativity is potentially separable, over the course of development, from its original sources in bodily joy. Most of us, however, have relatively little capacity to separate our self-image from its conscious bodily representation and its actual appearance and function. We all know those whose entire well-being collapses with a common cold.

IDEALIZATION IN NORMAL DEVELOPMENT

Idealization has received a great deal of attention in the literature on narcissism. Kohut, particularly, has stressed the normal role of idealization in early self-development, the special features of normal and pathological idealizations in the transference, and the more subtle ongoing idealizations which influence later stages of the life cycle.

Idealization throughout life serves at least two important interrelated functions. First, it is a mode of identification with a grand, powerful, and admired figure who functions as a selfobject, thereby enhancing one's own sense of power and capacity. In this way, idealization provides a template for one's own development, enabling one to imagine and undertake activities which might otherwise seem beyond attainment.

Second, idealizations also serve as a vehicle for revivals of regressive grandiose fantasies when these are needed for self-inflation in times of stress or in a certain group setting. By modeling one's self on an internalized ideal, one can, with relative freedom from superego reproaches, pursue otherwise unacceptable grandiose and aggressive aims. Because it is the nature of the beast, and because childhood always presents its full share of trauma, all individuals seek to bolster lingering instabilities of their self-image by means of continuing idealizations. In healthy circumstances, these take the form of idealization of loved ones or of heroes, as well as of human aims for creative, ambitious, or spiritual goals. Some individuals, however, while craving narcissistic gratification, deny any idealizing activity and, with envy and vengeance, doggedly and cynically pursue the task of denigrating all possible models. These are the persons who always find the feet of clay. Unfortunately, in so doing, they deprive themselves of the very self-aggrandizement which they seek.

The capacity for idealization clearly relates to the ability to maintain object relations, and both are related to core aspects of self-image and ego ideal. While these core aspects are relatively resistant to change, it is important to be aware that one's idealizations and hence one's identity or self-image are subject to broad change in ways which are of great significance.

For example, a successful businessman makes a second marriage at the age of 45 to a woman who feels he is capable of higher things in life. When seen again in his early fifties, not only has he been to law school, but he is working for a public service law firm, teaching part-time, and looks different. He is bearded instead of clean-shaven, wears tweeds instead of polyester, smokes a pipe instead of cigarettes, and clearly has an image of himself as some sort of Mr. Chips. While his core identity may not have changed, important values, goals, and aspects of self-image have been greatly altered. On closer examination, it emerges that his earlier identity as a businessman was always conflicted, combining positive identifications with a powerful, successful father and an angry, hidden rebellion against his father with a desire to engage in exactly those activities for which the father had contempt. The relationship with the second wife spurred the previously hidden rebellion and, through idealization of her as a selfless intellectual, he was able to make a significant change in himself.

SUMMARY

The intensive study of narcissism which has proceeded during the past decade has emphasized that aspects of narcissism are both a normal feature of development throughout the life cycle and an aspect of all human behavior. While workers of different theoretical persuasion may cast the propositions in different forms, there is agreement that the achievements of satisfactory self-structure, self-image, and self-esteem are core tasks of development and ongoing processes through the entirety of life. Colarusso and Nemiroff (17) state this eloquently:

We see the attainment of authenticity as a central, dynamic task of adulthood, possible in its fullest sense in adulthood because of the nature of the adult-developmental process. In the healthy adult this process includes normative, intrapsychic conflict involving opposing tendencies to unrealistically inflate or deflate the self. Gradually the narcissistic position of childhood in which the self is characterized as special, unique, and qualitatively superior to all others (Kohut's grandiose self) must be abandoned and replaced by an acceptance of the self as special but not unique, a part of the mosaic of humanity. With the muting of the quest for perfection in the self, in others, and in the external world—a concept rooted in the vicissitudes of the early mother-child dyad—comes gradual acceptance of the self as imperfect.

Authenticity includes the capacity to resist the sometimes powerful middle-aged impulse to search regressively for more complete gratification (infantile perfection) as a defense against the loosening of intrapsychic ties to aging or dead parents and to operate alone (psychologically separated from them) within the limits imposed by an imperfect, partially gratifying, and sometimes hostile world. Initially a source of narcissistic injury, the recognition of these external and internal limitations gradually becomes a source of pleasure and strength as the self accepts and develops the capacity to act independently within the restrictions imposed by the human condition (p.86).

All individuals require constantly renewing sources of gratification of narcissistic needs throughout life in order to maintain self-esteem and stability of their inner self. For all but the most extraordinarily self-sufficient persons, the absence of gratification through object relations has a corrosive effect over time, as that lack is interpreted by the superego as evidence of one's unworthiness and unacceptability to others. The ability to be in love, with all its perils, is still one of the best assurances of the continuing fulfillment of never-ending normal needs for narcissistic sustenance.

The capacities to maintain idealizations and to continue strivings toward work and creativity are vital for most persons in their endless battle to maintain self-esteem. Rare individuals who have the capacity to hold and work towards artistic, intellectual, or spiritual ideals and goals are probably best insulated from the insults and vagaries of the external world. There seems to be no society, however, in which self-esteem is not enhanced by power, by the recognition of one's peers, and by the sense of effectiveness. (Work probably derives from very primitive origins in the feeling of being, oneself, capable both of moving one's body at will and of effecting changes in the world).

One can add to a list of sources of narcissistic gratifications. Perhaps most significant of all is the capacity to maintain, simultaneously, a central core of highly stable identity and values with an adaptive flexibility which enables one to keep alive the relation to objects and the sense of effectiveness in the ongoing struggle to maintain one's integrity. Those are the people we are likely to idealize.

REFERENCES

1. FREUD, S.: Three essays on the theory of sexuality. *Standard Edition,* 7: 125-243. London: Hogarth Press, 1957.
2. ERIKSON, E.: *Childhood and Society,* 2nd ed. New York: W.W. Norton, 1963.

56   *Character Pathology: Theory and Treatment*

3. FREUD, A.: The Concept of developmental lines. *Psychoanal. Study Child,* 18: 246-265, 1963.
4. VAILLANT, G.: *Adaptation to Life.* Boston: Little, Brown, 1977.
5. COOPER, A.M.: Narcissism. In: S. Arieti, H. Keith, H. Brodie (Eds.), *American Handbook of Psychiatry.* New York: Basic Books, 1981.
6. COOPER, A.M.: Narcissistic disorders within psychoanalytic theory. In: L. Grinspoon (Ed.), *Psychiatry 1982: The American Psychiatric Association Annual Review.* Washington, D.C.: American Psychiatric Press, Inc., 1982.
7. PULVER, S.: Narcissism: The term and the concept. *J. Am. Psychoanal. Assoc.,* 18: 319-341, 1970.
8. REICH, W.: *Character Analysis,* 3rd ed. Translated by T.P. Wolfe. New York: Orgone Institute Press, 1949.
9. BETTELHEIM, B.: *Freud and Man's Soul.* New York: Alfred A. Knopf, 1983.
10. LAPLANCHE, J., and PONTALIS, J.B.: *The Language of Psychoanalysis.* New York: W.W. Norton, 1973.
11. KOHUT, H.: *The Restoration of the Self.* New York: International Universities Press, 1977.
12. KERNBERG, O.F.: *Borderline Conditions and Pathological Narcissism.* New York: Jason Aronson, 1975.
13. HORNEY, K.: *New Ways in Psychoanalysis.* New York: W.W. Norton, 1939.
14. WINNICOTT, D.W.: *The Maturational Processes and the Facilitating Environment: Studies in the Theory of Emotional Development.* New York: International Universities Press, 1965.
15. SEARLES, H.: Oedipal love in the counter-transference. *Int. J. Psychoanal.,* 40: 180-190, 1959.
16. ORNSTEIN, P.: Self-psychology and the concept of health. *Bull. Assoc. Psychoanal. Med.,* 19: 14-21, 1979.
17. COLARUSSO, C.A. and NEMIROFF, R.A.: *Adult Development, A New Dimension in Psychodynamic Theory and Practice.* New York: Plenum, 1981.

Part II

PROMINENT SYMPTOMATIC DERIVATIVES

4

Character and Violence

*Shervert H. Frazier, M.D.,
William S. James, M.D.,
and Phillip L. Isenberg, M.D.*

Violent acts occur in persons with or without mental impairment. Certainly neurotics are not frequently violent, although they may occasionally or accidently act out during an extraordinary autonomic storm or in a panic disorder. Rarely, an athlete under severe stress, whose judgment becomes distorted as the result of panic attacks, may appear violent. More commonly than neurotics, but less commonly than those with other illnesses, psychotic persons can become violent. A few manic-depressive patients, while feeling great power or powerlessness, either in manic or severe depressive episodes, have assaulted or killed persons not included in their delusions. More frequently, paranoid schizophrenics have carried out violent acts under delusional ideation toward persons included in their delusions or when they are commanded to do so by hallucinatory voices. Evidence is mounting that premorbid personality, rather than mental illness per se, may determine the propensity to violent behavior (1, 2). Most psychiatrists have seen at least one psychotic patient who made violent threats.

Another group of violent patients are those with organic mental disorders, including mildly demented persons with delusions of marital infidelity leading to murder of the spouse, and amnestic persons with alcohol dependence and vitamin deficiencies who have been observed to assault or kill strangers and have no memory of it.

Another example of violence occurs when a person with organic personality

59

syndrome, after serious and often multiple head trauma, inflicts serious harm. One of the most common causes of violence is intoxication with alcohol and multiple drugs, possibly with alcohol/organic mental disorders. These individuals often become belligerent and assaultive. Other individuals are those with the rare but often described interictal confusional states of violent temporal lobe epilepsy. However, only one percent of temporal lobe epilepsy patients are reported to have been violent, so that the frequency of reports is out of proportion to its significance. Included in the description of the so-called epileptic personality are both the organic deficit and the personality structure concomitant with such a lesion.

The remaining category of disorders in which violence may occur is the characterological disorders or the personality disorders. Character is the essence of the human—what is recognized as deeply ingrained patterning of behavior representing a particular person. Through the years, biological, psychological, and sociocultural elements have been described singly and in various combinations, as contributing to the development of character and of character disorders.

HISTORY

In the early 19th century, Pinel (3) described mania without delirium (*manie sans délire*), and Trelat and Rush (4) and then in 1835 Prichard (5) described the concept of "moral insanity." Violent persons have frequently been classified as criminal personalities. That concept evolved from schools of criminology (Bentham, England, 1748-1832; Beccario, Italy, 1738-1794), law school faculties, and psychiatric institutes (Utrecht, 1934; Leiden, 1936; Graz, 1912). These original sources relied heavily on biological and social sciences. Lombroso (6) (1836-1909), an Italian physician, believed that men were born criminals and were under the influence of genetic factors. He considered them "savages in a civilized world"—biological anomalies, possible because of atavism and degeneracy. He studied thousands of postmortem skulls, from which he claimed observable primitive and pathologic characteristics. Early in this century, a British statistical researcher, Charles Goring (7), attempted to discredit Lombroso's methods, and concluded that, even though criminality did have an hereditary base, mental deficiency should also be considered as a cause.

This concept of constitutional inferiority in criminals has persisted over the years. Hooten (8), in 1939, reported the results of a survey of 17,077 white American prisoners and their physical features—eyebrow thickness, moles and freckles—and determined that criminals are "inferior to civilians in nearly all of their bodily measurements." He concluded that poorer and weaker specimens tended to select themselves for antisocial careers. Sheldon (9) in the 1940s and

1950s described his belief that personality is reflected in observable bodily features, which are hereditary. He correlated temperament and body type. He saw most criminals as mesomorphs destined to follow a criminal path. The Gluecks (10) in 1950 compared 500 delinquents and 500 nondelinquents from similar neighborhoods and also found that the delinquents were mesomorphs. Lindzey (11) in 1973 noted a correlation between mesomorphy and delinquency.

Several investigators (12, 13, 14) have supported the contention that genetic factors predispose offspring of criminals to develop a criminal personality, even if removed from their parents when young. Electroencephalographic differences, low IQs, mesomorphy, possible role of XXY (not XYY) factors, sexual disturbance, hyperactivity, tendencies toward sociopathy and alcoholism in men and hysteria in women are among the "genetically influenced variables" described by Henderson (15), Karpman (16), Trasler (17), Eysenck (18), Rosenthal (19), and Guze and Woodruff (20). Eysenck described an "innate predisposition to form weak and fleeting conditioned responses," possibly due to organic brain lesions. Thompson (21) described the psychopathic personality as the product of "psychogenic factors working upon a previously impaired brain," while White and Watt (22) stated, "Some subtle inadequacy of cerebral tissue might underlie the psychopath's inability to be governed by the standards and restraints of society." Winkler and Kove (23) stated that an organic brain lesion is the "agent which conditions the individual to react with aggressive behavior to environmental pressures." Pontius (24) described a frontal lobe dysfunction due to a "developmental lag and/or neuropathological deficit" as the basis for some forms of juvenile delinquency due to a "genuine neurologically based loss of mastery over one's actions." Lidberg (25) found a greater incidence of brain concussion among 439 Swedish criminals than among a normal control group of Swedish military conscripts.

Continuing biological studies (26) defined the amygdala as the seat of violence, with the procedure amygdalectomy as a possible new treatment. Quay (27) described stimulation-seeking pathology and questioned the possibility of a constitutionally different pattern of reactivity peculiar to psychopaths. Hare (28) studied underresponsivity of the autonomic nervous system to emotionally charged situations in psychopaths. Other hypotheses include facial attractiveness, hypoglycemia, and higher concentrations of neutralizing antibodies to herpes simplex virus. Few are willing totally to exclude organic considerations as causal. As Wattenberg (29) said, "Congenital factors produce vulnerabilities, not inevitabilities."

The IQ question was partially settled by Tulchin (30) in 1939 in a study of more than 10,000 Illinois prisoners. Distribution of intelligence was the same among the prisoner population as among a group of non-criminals drafted into the army. A New York City youth board study in 1960 noted that delinquents are quick to despair of school but quick to learn and question in areas that are real to them. Learning involving words, however, is impaired, thus depriving these students of a valuable means of managing social interactions and delaying impulses. Speech deficits are not uncommon. The difficulty in using words inhibits cognitive development.

Descriptions of criminal behavior as a response to adverse social situations began in the Industrial Revolution and placed the cause of crime outside the individual, rather than inside. Vast amounts of data have been gathered regarding many social variables. One thing is clear: Causation should not be concluded from correlation.

Defining a criminal is difficult. George Bernard Shaw, for example, was quoted as saying, "You go to jail if you steal a loaf of bread, but you go to Parliament if you steal a railroad." Social circumstances of birth can determine whether one is prosecuted as a criminal. The following theories of crime have been elucidated: the contagion theory (a man is influenced by the company he keeps); social, cultural, and economic deprivation; the deprivation of challenge that comes with overabundance; schools as destroyers of self-esteem of lower socioeconomic class students; violence on television encouraging violent forms of behavior; newspaper reporting of crime; pornography; the "sick society"; anomie; alienation; ghettos; and economic recession. At one time or another, each has been declared the central causative factor. An increase in small plane accidents involving one to two passengers occurs in the seven-to-10-day period after a well-publicized incident of violence, as well as newspapers reports of immolation after a late night movie showing immolation. These suggest the possibility of suicidal effects or suicide/homicides. There are generalized societally sanctioned violent climates, such as vendettas in Sardinia or violence in Colombia. It can be said that a multitude of factors causes crime, and the theories are predicated on biopsychosocial approaches. Focusing on causation seems futile—to ask why and how delinquency occurs is like asking why human nature is what it is.

The psychoanalytic approach has included several premises: an unconscious sense of guilt; crime as a need to assert one's sexuality or to compensate for a precarious sexual identity; the need to be punished for unresolved Oedipal guilt; the projection of guilt; exaggerated anal character traits prototypic of a number of antisocial characteristics; hypertrophically developed ego functions applied in the service of the wrong goal; maternal deprivation of young children; prolonged separation of a child from his mother during the first five years of life (Bowlby's [31] stage of detachment); "smother love"; and absence of a father. All have been considered at one time or another. It is clear that cause and effect from a single factor cannot easily be predicted in all cases, but certainly each of these factors may be central in some cases. One problem is the nature of the psychopath. Cleckley (32) lucidly pointed out how easily the psychopath learns the therapist's system and feeds it back to him.

CLINICAL OBSERVATIONS

Violent acts may be considered as symptoms of illnesses such as a character neurosis, paranoid personality disorder, schizoid personality disorder, schizotypal personality disorder, narcissistic personality disorder, or borderline personality disorder. Our experience with nonpsychotic, non-organic-brain-disordered patients who have a history of violent actions leaves us with a clear perception of the mixing of various personality traits and attitudes. There is a prominent lack of emotional feelings for people in the vicinity of the person committing the violent action, along with the perception that he is a freak or that people are calling him a freak. A disturbance in the organization of the person's affect is also noted, with that disturbance of affect reflected in anger, rage, and aggression. The person feels cornered, that everything is closing in and there is no way out. We have also noted the ability of violent persons to dehumanize other persons over time. With such dehumanization, the performance of violence becomes a less meaningful event. The dehumanization frequently begins with a narcissistic injury inflicted by others, often involving the reviving of early intense fears of separation or the reliving of the earlier experience of physical abuse or humiliation.

Rejection, abandonment, separation, and the threats of these may elicit a much lowered self-esteem, a loss of face, especially when the victim-to-be has been idealized. The degree of injury to self-esteem and the consequent degree of narcissistic rage resulting from actions of the vicitm are related to the degree of initial narcissistic vulnerability in the perpetrator. Spouse murders often have such a narcissistic orientation and involve an idealized victim-to-be, with great denial of anger. The murderers must idealize their spouse in order to preserve their own narcissistic image. For the same reason, they must deny anger at the spouse. Rage can then be experienced only explosively.

We have seen these same psychopathological perceptions in familicide. In the paranoid personality, patterns of pathological jealousy often begin in latency and persist into adolescence and adulthood, accompanied by hypervigilance, perceiving hidden motives in various people, including the victim-to-be, connecting events and actions which are not connected except by coincidence, and transient ideas of reference associated with feelings that vulgarities about the patient are being passed around. Tension rises, anxiety heightens, and vulnerability to action increases. These persons often have a history of high alcohol intake and a paranoid cognitive style characterized by guardedness, secretiveness, avoidance of blame, general expectations of someone's playing tricks on them, questioning of friends and acquaintances about loyalty, inability to see the forest for the trees, easiness in taking offense, and humorlessness.

Personality disordered violent persons often show an imbalance of affect control (affect dyscontrol) somewhat different from isolation of affect. Some demonstrate overcontrolled hostility, sadism (nonsexual), and masochism (nonsexual). More than half of our violent population has no major mental illness, i.e., psychosis. Our experience has been with men predominantly at Bridgewater State Hospital for the Criminally Insane. These men feel they are "done in" by women and made to feel shamed by them, deceived by them. They are unable to use words to solve their problems and thus respond to inner cues with action. The woman is perceived to be more powerful than the man and continues her normal behavior, which causes even more fury. She then becomes the victim of physical violence, usually nonsexual. Fatigue, sleep deprivation, and indulgence in alcohol are afterward described as having been present before the violent action. Disclosure of remorse and/or guilt without appropriate emotion is common. We usually do not obtain an early history of physical child abuse, but there is a long-term sense of low self-esteem and a sense of resignation to one's life situation. These patients have poor verbal facility, do not engage in psychotherapy or group therapy, and often resign themselves to waiting out any period of incarceration.

Another subtype of characterologically impaired patients are young adult males who adapt remarkably well to the prison environment and read cues extremely well, always giving physicians and correctional personnel correct and appropriate answers. These patients may have committed horrendous murders, with torture, etc., but feel no guilt or remorse. They usually have a history from age six or eight of petty thievery, larceny, obnoxious behavior, harassment, disturbing the peace, vandalism, sexual misbehavior, lying, truancy, suspension from school, drug use, runaway episodes—all keep on a continuing police blotter record. There is little or no work record or frequent job changes. They show a failure to make long-term relationships and, despite previous punishments, do not seem to learn from experience.

In institutions, these patients have no plans, no goals, and no real friends. They are impulsive and have multiple incident reports for assaults on other patients or corrections personnel. They are the real "con artists," the psychopaths. Their lying, restlessness, lack of time perspective, exaggerated moods and attitudes, history of unsatisfactory sexual performance, and a wide variety of antisocial activities are characteristic of classical psychopathy. They are often bright and talented, do not have thinking disorders, show no signs of psychotic disturbance, and do not respond to psychotherapy, but go along with it. They learn the therapist's language and then they go out and act as they had previously, but with more and better explanations for why they did it.

Yochelson and Samenow (33) have described the psychopathology of this group in quite different terms. They note that, like young children, psychopaths are concrete in operations of thought and interpersonal relations. *Their failure to recognize the similarity between situations* is often characterized as a failure to learn from experience. The concreteness is not due to any known organic deficit or to mental illness, and this is confirmed by the fact that they do well on the "Similarities" subtest of the Wechsler Adult Intelligence Scale. Yochelson and Samenow have also stated that the psychopath lacks concepts of home or family and of reciprocal relationships. There is no concept of integrity or of consistent behavior with an overall goal. Religiosity is a conglomeration of concrete practices and isolated ideas. The psychopath thinks that responsible living entails a set of concrete isolated acts and is not built on ethical or moral standards. People are viewed as basically hostile, and interpersonal relationships are reduced to power struggles. The psychopath thinks all people experience these changes of mind, but others hide them better. True ambivalence may also coexist with fragmentation. Psychotic fragmentation of thinking is not the same. The psychopath knows what he is doing. When he desires excitement, he shifts in his desires. There is no confusion.

Another view of violence and violent acts is that they are integral parts of life experience, resulting from elements in daily living operating from a multideterminant psychological set, with stress as a major precipitant. Such a view postulates a style of life that involves loosely knit large families venting raw emotions openly in a society which condones many aberrant behaviors and actions. There are few and inconsistent prohibitions against such behaviors and relative freedom, often license, to assault or threaten one or a group of persons. The frequency in epidemiologic studies of child abuse, alcohol intoxication, fighting, spouse beating, forced sexual experiences, and frequent intimidations would confirm the importance of such a view. The behaviors are not universal, but sufficiently common to give support to the theory of violence as an integral part of life in some segments of society.

In line with such a view are the frequent reports among violent persons in state psychiatric and correctional facilities of childhood experiences of repeated abuse, incest, and/or sexual molestation. Such persons also report being the victims of extraordinary, but inconsistent, disciplinary punishment. When such victimization is frequent, multiple personalities may develop—a good self, a bad self, or various selves—almost as a defense against being overwhelmed by cruelty and as an attempt at repair with fantasied concepts of another self.

Children respond to severe and cruel punishment with fear of being oneself, feelings of shame and badness, as well as rage at the punishers, with the desire to kill or be killed not rare. The response to continuing emotional deprivation is a disabling deficit in integration of experience, including a faulty sense of self, a lack of ego development, and a failure of development of self-esteem. Development of interpersonal relationships is distorted, leading to cruel indifference to others, withdrawal, or a shallow pseudo-warmth overlying a lack of real involvement with people. Continued neglect of emotional needs is frequently accompanied by nutritional deficits and their biological effect on the development of emotions. Apathy and psychological withdrawal, feelings of futility, deficiencies in development of intelligence, cognitive defects, and failure of socialization are the hallmarks of such children.

Abuse may be summarized as punishment abuse, accident abuse, and neglect abuse, each producing physical and psychological results. Adolescents and older violent persons recalling their adolescent years have characterized their family interactions as:

1) lack of involvement in constructive family functions;
2) defiance against parents;
3) disruptive family behavior with alienation from family, a feeling of future futility, poor planning abilities, and problems with authority.

Superego lacunae (34) were postulated in many families. Children and adolescents with aberration of behavior seemed to act so as to gratify parental expectations vicariously. In these families, the parents' marriage was not satisfactory, and vicarious gratification by the parent was experienced when the child carried out a parent's unacceptable fantasies and impulses.

Adolescents in alcoholic families have suffered all three types of abuse (punishment, accident, and neglect) and have not been guided toward functional autonomy. Rather, they have been neglected to the point of having little social experience other than their unstructured, chaotic environment. Such an adolescent may have an aversion to alcohol, but primitive rage toward uncaring and neglectful family members will fester and eventually erupt.

Various patterns occur in psychotic families, depending on the nature of the psychosis. Adolescent experience is often a continuation of years of aberration in the physical, psychological, and sexual areas. Our only cases of mother-son incest occur in such families, and the adolescents may be transiently psychotic. There are severe boundary problems, and counterfeit communications are common, leading to identity and individuation problems. Behavioral observations of children of psychotic families are not sufficiently recorded. The threats of this chaotic environment wipe out previous relationships. The sons attack the fathers and break a very strong intrapsychic taboo, and the daughters are frequently abused. Absence of family after the early developmental period sometimes leads to multiple tentative interpersonal relationships with depressive periods but without alteration of behavior. Premature separation from the family may lead to affection-seeking behaviors, with frustration and intermittent explosive outbursts of violence, and then settling into a structured environment of the hospital. Isenberg (35) has noted the adaptive generational rearrangement, the telescoping of three generations of a family into two due to the absence of one generation because of abandonment. For example, a grandmother may become a mother of her grandchildren with the frequent loss in adolescence of the middle generation. The children do not have continuing familial support because of the aging and death of grandparents.

It is during adolescence that the solo delinquent becomes differentiated from the group or gang delinquent. Solo or loner actions are the result of fantasy and isolation. The failure of socialization of anger follows, with all-too-frequent patterns of retaliation at absent caretakers and a continuing searching for role models. These loners, after a series of violent acts, respond to the structured environment of the hospital, with its rules, strictures, and authority figures, but upon discharge frequently feel lost and rejected. Previous patterns of striking out in frustration and rage at relatives, neighbors, and strangers then recur. The loner makes no friendships or attachments to moderate his impulses and support his reality-testing. Organized group sanctions may allow poorly integrated social isolates a "community of support" with identity and goals albeit violent ones. When these isolates join, they often associate with spontaneously organized groups such as mobs, vacillating from cause to cause, enjoying the relief of frustration in violent assaults, but ending in isolation or as a victim of violence.

Early adulthood is a difficult time when adolescence has not been completed and role models are not incorporated. Insecurities still exist with unemployment and multiple job rejections following previous school failure. This inevitably leads to comparing oneself with others and envying those who have succeeded. Drugs, alcohol and fantasy (visions of TV models of American young adults with everything) are methods of support of their self-concept.

At this point, family transitions may be especially difficult emotionally. The mother is exhausted, housing is inadequate, father is absent, and the young adult is excluded and extruded. He is interfering with whatever stability is left and with the rights of the younger siblings. Self-contempt and previous family disruptions have made other relatives unavailable.

The burdens of young females are increased by single parenthood. Feelings of social failure, of being an inadequate parent, and of humilation when idealized images of parenthood held internally are not met often lead to the initial crossing of the personal assault line. The victim is usually a young child. In young men, the search for power and dependency satisfaction may lead to fears of homosexuality and failure to meet a previously held image of masculinity. Thus, the young adult may be deprived of involvement in the societal structures of work, of economic reward, and of family and parental role, all of which normally inhibit violent outlets.

In addition, the changing patterns of dealing with emotionally disturbed and mentally ill persons have taken their toll, especially when expected resources have changed. The inadequacies of child intervention, family, and educational programs to handle this enormous need have resulted in the criminal justice system's becoming the net that catches the people who fall between the programs.

It is clear that we have vast areas of ignorance regarding the causes of violence. We unwittingly defeat our own progress by ignoring violence because of our fear of becoming its victim. Our feeling of helplessness in the face of the magnitude and horror of the problem must be confronted and the issues addressed, or we will remain victimized by the alternative.

REFERENCES

1. ROBINS, L.N.: *Deviant Children Grown Up.* Baltimore: Williams & Wilkins, 1966.
2. STEADMAN, H.J., and VANDERWYST, D., and RIBNER, S.: Comparing the arrest rates of mental patients and offenders. *Am. J. Psychiat.,* 135: 1218-1220, 1978.
3. PINEL, P.: In: G. Zilboorg (Ed.), *A History of Medical Psychology.* New York: W.W. Norton, 1941.
4. TRELAT, O.: *Recherches Historiques sur la Folie.* Paris: 1835, p. 12. Rush, B.: In: B. Zilboorg (Ed.), *A History of Medical Psychology.* New York: W.W. Norton, 1941.
5. PRICHARD, J.C.: In: G. Zilboorg (Ed.), *A History of Medical Psychology.* New York: W.W. Norton, 1941.
6. LOMBROSO, C.: *After Death What?* Boston: Small, Meynard & Co., 1909.
7. GORING, C.: In: E.A. Hooten (Ed.), *Crime and the Man.* Cambridge, MA.: Harvard University Press, 1939.
8. HOOTEN, E.A. (Ed.): *Crime and the Man.* Cambridge, MA.: Harvard University Press, 1939.
9. SHELDON, W.H.: *Atlas of Men.* New York: Harper & Bros., 1954.
10. GLUECK, S., and GLUECK, E.: *Unraveling Juvenile Delinquency.* New York: Commonwealth Fund, 1950.
11. LINDZEY, G.: *Morphology & Behavior.* In: G. Lindzey, et al. (Eds.), *Theories of Personality, Primary Sources & Research.* New York: J. Wiley, 1973.
12. NEWKIRK, P.R.: Psychopathic traits are inheritable. *Dis. Nerv. Syst.,* 18: 52-60, 1957.
13. CROWE, R.R.: The adopted offspring of women criminal offenders. *Arch. Gen. Psychiat.,* 27: 600-603, 1972.
14. SCHULSINGER, F.: Psychopathology: hereditary and environment. *Int. J. Ment. Health,* 190-197, 1972.
15. HENDERSON, D.K.: *Psychopathic States.* New York: W.W. Norton, 1939.
16. KARPMAN, B.: The structure of neurosis. *Arch. Crim. Psychodyn.,* 4: 599-646, 1961.
17. TRASLER, G.: *The Explanation of Criminality.* London: Roultedge & Kegan Paul, 1962.

18. EYSENCK, H.J.: *Crime and Personality*. Boulder, CO: Paladin, 1973.
19. ROSENTHAL, D.: Heredity in criminality. Reprint Address, AAAS. Dec. 27, 1972.
20. GUZE, S.B., and WOODRUFF, R.A.: *Psychiatric Diagnosis*. Oxford University Press, 1974.
21. THOMPSON, G.N.: *Psychopathic Delinquent and Criminality*. Springfield, IL.: Charles C Thomas, 1953.
22. WHITE, R.W., and WATT, N.F.: *The Abnormal Personality*, 4th ed. New Haven: Yale University Press, 1953.
23. WINKLER, G.E., and KOVE, S.S.: The implications of EEG abnormalities in homicide. *J. Neuropsych.*, 3: 322-331, 1962.
24. PONTIUS, A.: Neurological aspects in some type of delinquency, especially among juveniles. *Adolescence*, 7: 289-308, 1972.
25. LIDBERG, L.: Frequency of concussion and type of criminality. *Acta Psychiat. Scand.*, 47: 452-456, 1971.
26. MARK, V.H., and ERWIN, F.P.: *Violence and the Brain*. New York: Harper & Row, 1970.
27. QUAY, H.C.: Psychopathic personality as pathological stimulation seeking. *Am. J. Psychiat.*, 122: 180-183, 1965.
28. HARE, R.D.: *Psychopathy, Theory and Research*. New York: J. Wiley, 1970.
29. WATTENBERG, W.W.: *The Adolescent Years*. New York: Harcourt Press, 1973.
30. TULCHIN, S.H.: *Intelligence and Crime*. Chicago: University of Chicago Press, 1939.
31. BOWLBY, J.: *Attachment and Loss*. Vol. 1. New York: Basic Books, 1969.
32. CLECKLEY, H.M.: *The Mask of Sanity*, 5th ed. St. Louis: C. V. Mosby, 1964.
33. YOCHELSON, S., and SAMENOW, S.E.: *The Criminal Personality*. Vols. 1 and 2. New York: Jason Aronson, 1976.
34. JOHNSON, A.M., and SZUREK, S.: The genesis of antisocial acting out in children and adults. *Psychoanl. Quart.*, 21: 323-343, 1952.
35. ISENBERG, P.: Personal communications, 1983.

5

Biopsychosocial Correlates of Conduct Disorders in Children and Adolescents

Dorothy Otnow Lewis, M.D.

For the past 40 years, most efforts to understand and classify behaviorally disordered youngsters have rested on the assumptions: 1) that an unjust society was the basic cause of children's antisocial acts; and 2) that delinquent children were essentially characterologically impaired. The most influential of the sociological studies hypothesized that delinquent behavior was the response of individuals who could not achieve social or economic success through socially sanctioned methods and therefore had to resort to antisocial means to achieve their goals (1-3). Another influential sociological theory (3) hypothesized a delinquent "subculture." Under deprived socioeconomic conditions, delinquent behavior was normal and unrelated to psychopathology. Stealing was simply a way of life; violence was understandable in the context of discrimination and deprivation.

Almost simultaneous with these sociological theories came the characterological theories of Hewitt and Jenkins (4). In the 1940s they set out "to verify the existence, in a clinic population of 500 cases from the Michigan Child Guidance Institute, of three types of delinquents" (5). Jenkins' initial groupings were "done not by statistical method, but 'free-hand' by clinical judgment somewhat guided by the degree of association between *selected traits*" (italics added). This difficult, time-consuming procedure led to the conceptualization of three types of behaviorally disturbed youngsters: the socialized delinquent; the unsocialized aggressive delinquent; and the overinhibited delinquent. It led subsequently to the conceptualization of two additional types of delinquents, the "schizoid" and the "brain injured" or "hyperkinetic." It is probably fair to say that our relative ignorance of the neuropsychiatric factors underlying mal-

70

adaptive antisocial behaviors is the direct result of those "selected traits" Jenkins chose to study and, more importantly, those he chose to ignore.

Jenkins (6) selected to study manifest behaviors (e.g., cooperative stealing, aggressive stealing, temper tantrums, running away, cruelty, obscenity, and profanity). Other traits he considered were general and based on subjective judgment (e.g., emotional immaturity, submissiveness, overdependence, awkwardness, revengefulness).

What kinds of factors were ignored? For the most part, he ignored the kinds of information that can be elicited from careful neuropsychiatric, psychoeducational, and pediatric assessments. Thus, such factors as hallucinations, loose illogical thought processes, impaired short-term memory, major and minor neurological signs, perceptual motor impairment, and specific learning disabilities were not studied systematically.

In the 1960s and 1970s, other investigators, using sophisticated multivariate statistical methods made possible by computer technology, came to conclusions similar to Jenkins' (7-13). However, a review of the traits coded by such modern social scientists as Quay (8) indicates that he selected the same kinds of factors as Jenkins (e.g., bad companions, truancy, little concern for others, inadequate guilty feelings), and overlooked the same kinds of neuropsychiatric and psychoeducational factors overlooked by Jenkins. Thus, it is no wonder that Quay and others found delinquent groupings similar to Jenkins' categories.

It is clear that the DSM-III (14) definition of conduct disorder, "a repetitive and persistent pattern of conduct in which either the basic rights of others or major age appropriate societal norms or rules are violated" (p. 15), with its aggressive-nonaggressive, socialized-unsocialized subtypes and its minimizing of neuropsychiatric factors, is a direct descendant of the Jenkins-Quay classification.

As a result of this kind of conceptualization of deviant behaviors, most youngsters manifesting serious behavioral problems tend to be dismissed as characterologically impaired, and little effort is made to search for possible underlying medical, psychological, or psychoeducational factors influencing their behaviors. The purpose of this chapter is to present recent studies that focus on those often overlooked factors, neurological and psychiatric, that now seem so closely associated with severe behavior problems and that call into question the very diagnosis "conduct disorder" as an entity. It will present an overview of the work of a small team of researchers over the past decade.

RESEARCH ON BIOPSYCHOSOCIAL CORRELATES OF CONDUCT DISORDERS

The work began at the first juvenile court clinic in Connecticut. In the course of ordinary clinical work, performing comprehensive psychiatric and psychological assessments, the team discovered that, contrary to the prevailing sociological literature, approximately 25 percent of the delinquent children referred for evaluation manifested psychotic symptomatology. This was reported in a brief clinical paper (15). Futhermore, medical histories elicited from children and their families indicated that many of the children had suffered severe accidents, injuries, and illnesses.

Medical Histories of Delinquent Children

Were the medical histories of the children evaluated peculiar to those youngsters referred for evaluation or were they characteristic of most delinquents coming through the courts? An epidemiological study followed, comparing the medical histories of a random sample of 109 delinquents with a sample of 109 nondelinquents from the same geographic area, matched for age, sex, race, and approximate socioeconomic status (16). The source of data was the medical record of each child as reflected in his hospital chart from the large general hospital serving this population as its major source of primary care.

Epidemiological findings confirmed clinical impressions. That is, throughout childhood, from birth through age 16, delinquent children had more hospital contacts than nondelinquents. Not only did they have greater numbers of emergency room, clinic, and ward admissions, but they also had greater numbers of illnesses, accidents, and injuries, especially head and face injuries.

Was a child's degree of violence related to his medical history? The next epidemiological study compared the medical histories of incarcerated delinquents with those of less seriously antisocial, nonincarcerated delinquents (17). Although numbers of hospital contacts did not distinguish between these two groups significantly, the reasons for hospital contacts did distinguish them from each other. The incarcerated delinquents had significantly more perinatal difficulties and suffered significantly more head and face injuries. Moreover, physical abuse was documented somewhat more frequently in the hospital charts. It only later became apparent, during a clinical study of the neuropsychiatric status of incarcerated delinquents, how underreported physical abuse was in the hospital records of delinquents. (See Figure 1.)

Violent Incarcerated Delinquents

Attention next focused on a clinical study of seriously violent incarcerated delinquents at the only correctional school serving Connecticut (18). There comprehensive psychiatric, neurological, and psychoeducational assessments of 97 boys were performed. The investigators also had access to a wealth of clinical and social material about each boy, since most had received evaluations prior to incarceration, and approximately 60 percent of them had been in psychiatric

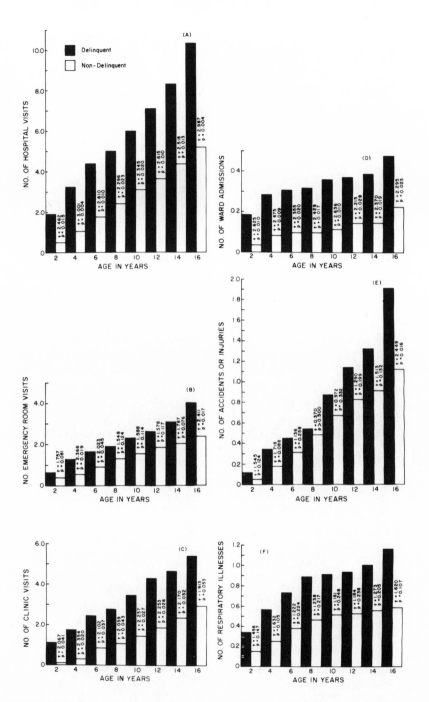

FIGURE 1. Cumulative Hospital Contacts and Medical Problems of Delinquent and Nondelinquent Children Throughout Childhood.

hospitals and/or residential psychiatric treatment centers prior to incarceration (19).

At the time of the study, finding themselves unable to clinically evaluate a comparable sample of nondelinquent boys, the research team devised a method of rating each subject on a scale of violence (18) in order to be able to compare the more aggressive incarcerated delinquents with their less aggressive incarcerated peers.

Psychiatric Factors

When the more violent boys were compared with their less violent peers, certain psychiatric, neurological, educational, and experiential factors distinguished the groups from each other. Looking first at the psychiatric variables, psychotic symptomatology (i.e., hallucinations, paranoid ideation, and loose, illogical thought processes) was more prevalent in the more violent group. The most significant psychotic symptom distinguishing the violent group was paranoid ideation. That is, over 80 percent of the more violent group manifested paranoid ideation, in contrast to approximately 17 percent of the less violent group. The more violent group was also significantly more likely to manifest loose, rambling, and illogical thought processes. The majority of the more violent group was unable to subtract serial 7's (69.5 percent vs. 33.3 percent) and was significantly less likely to be able to recall four digits backward (60.8 percent vs. 33.3 percent). (See Table 1.)

Neurological Factors

When neurological status was considered, again the more violent group was significantly more impaired than the less violent group. That is, 46.3 percent

TABLE 1
More Violent vs. Less Violent Delinquents

Psychiatric Factors	More #	Violent %*	Less #	Violent %*	X^2_y	p Value
Depressive symptoms	23	65.7	11	84.6	0.852	.356
Visual hallucinations	18	30.0	2	11.1	1.695	.193
Auditory hallucinations	28	43.3	3	17.6	2.704	.101
Olfactory hallucinations	11	15.1	0	0	2.126	.145
Paranoid symptomatology	54	81.8	3	16.7	24.618	<.001
Loose, rambling, illogical	28	59.6	4	23.5	5.126	.024

* Percentages are based upon the actual number of subjects on whom information was available for each category.

TABLE 2
More Violent vs. Less Violent Delinquents

Neurological Factors	More Violent #	More Violent %*	Less Violent #	Less Violent %*	X^2	p Value
Major Neurological Signs	31	46.3	1	6.7	6.499	.011
Abnormal EEG	19	29.7	0	0	2.590	.108
Positive Babinski	11	15.9	1	5.6	.569	>.5
Minor Neurological signs	71	98.6	12	66.7	16.275	.001
Inability to skip	26	43.3	2	11.1	4.926	.027
Choreiform movements	40	60.6	5	31.1	3.375	.067
Psychomotor symptomatology	46	71.9	6	37.5	5.223	.023
No Serial 7's	41	69.5	6	33.3	6.138	.014
No 4 Digits backwards	31	60.8	2	13.3	8.627	.004

* Percentages are based upon the actual number of subjects on whom information was available for each category.

had one or more major neurological signs (i.e., abnormal EEG or seizures, Babinski sign, or head circumference 2 or more standard deviations from the mean), compared with only 6.7 percent of the less violent group. Minor neurological signs were also significantly more common in the more violent group, as can be seen in Table 2.

Psychoeducational Factors

Of note, psychometric testing indicated that the two groups were remarkably similar intellectually. The more violent group, however, scored somewhat lower on the verbal section of the WISC, the greatest and only significant difference in average scores occurring on the arithmetic subtest.

In contrast to the results of the intelligence testing, educational assessments did reveal an important difference between the two groups. The more violent group was significantly more handicapped in terms of reading skills. In fact, on the average, the more violent group read 4.4 years below their expected grade

TABLE 3
More Violent vs. Less Violent Delinquents

Psychological Factors	More Violent	Less Violent	t-Test	p Value
Average full-scale IQ WISC	86.459	93.000	1.943	.056
WISC Verbal score	82.597	88.812	1.978	.052
WISC Performance score	92.875	98.875	1.507	.136

TABLE 4
More Violent vs. Less Violent Delinquents

Educational Factors	More Violent	Less Violent	t-Test	p Value
Reading grade discrepancy	4.4	2.3	2.148	.037
Math grade discrepancy	3.4	2.2	1.602	.115

level for age, in contrast to the less violent group that read 2.3 years below their expected level. Thus, evidence derived from both the WISC and the educational assessment indicated that the more violent group was less competent verbally than the less violent group.

Although the more violent group was found to be more psychiatrically, neurologically, and psychoeducationally impaired than their less violent peers, these differences did not account in full for their more aggressive behaviors. Clearly, most psychotic children, most neurologically impaired children, and most learning disabled children are not violent. What other kinds of factors might account for the behavioral differences between the two groups?

Abuse Factors

Attention focused on the experience of violence itself, that is, issues of physical abuse and violence in the home. For purposes of this study, beatings on the buttocks with a strap, switch, or bare hand were not considered to constitute physical abuse. In order that a child be rated as having been physically abused, he would have to have been punched, beaten with a stick, board, pipe, or belt buckle, or beaten with a switch or belt other than on the buttocks. He was also considered to have been abused if he had been deliberately cut, burned, or thrown downstairs or across the room.

As can be seen in Table 5, the more violent youngsters were significantly more likely to have been severely physically abused than the less violent youngsters. The degree of abuse they experienced was extraordinary. One psychotic father beat his epileptic son unmercifully to ''exorcise the devil''; another threw his infant son across the room; another chained and burned his son's feet; and another threw his son downstairs, injuring his head, following which the boy had seizures.

Mothers, too, were abusive. One psychotic mother broke all of her son's fingers; another broke her son's leg with a broom handle; and one psychotic aunt (guardian of a boy whose mother had died) had her boyfriends hold the boy's arms and legs while she wet down his back and beat him with an extension cord ''because it hurt more if you wet down the back.''

In addition to having been beaten, the majority of the more violent boys had witnessed extraordinary violence. They had seen fathers slash mothers and mothers knife fathers. They had seen fathers threaten with loaded guns, and often they had tried to come to the rescue of mothers by holding off their attackers.

How can one understand the effects of such abuse on the development of violent behaviors? First, physical abuse often leads to central nervous system injury. Such injury is often associated with impulsivity and difficulty concentrating (20). Moreover, it may contribute to the kinds of learning disabilities documented. Second, witnessing and being the victim of violence invites imitation. Whether one conceptualizes such mimicry psychoanalytically as "identification with the aggressor," or psychologically as "modeling," one knows that parental behaviors tend to be copied by children. Finally, it is reasonable to suppose that this brutal, abusive behavior within the family engenders rage in the child, rage that subsequently is displaced onto others in the child's environment. This chain of reactions probably explains in great measure the difficulties these delinquent children experience when dealing with authority figures of any kind, including teachers and police officers.

It is important to emphasize here again that the kinds of neuropsychiatric vulnerabilities documented in violent children do not in and of themselves cause violence. Neither psychosis alone, brain injury alone, seizures alone, nor hyperactivity alone causes violence. Most children with these kinds of vulnerabilities are not violent. The findings suggest, however, that when one of these vulnerabilities or a combination of them is coupled with the experience of having witnessed extreme violence and having been brutally physically abused, this constellation of psychobiological and experiential factors does engender violence. Unfortunately, this constellation of adverse factors is common in our society today.

TABLE 5
More Violent vs. Less Violent Delinquents

History of Abuse	More Violent		Less Violent		X^2_y	p Value
	#	%*	#	%*		
Abused by mother	21	43.8	2	14.3	2.869	.091
Abused by father	29	54.7	5	29.4	2.364	.125
Abused by others	23	45.1	2	14.3	3.200	.074
Ever abused	52	75.4	6	33.3	9.535	.003
Witness to extreme violence	44	78.6	3	20.0	15.615	<.001

* Percentages are based upon the actual numbers of subjects on whom information was available for each category.

Racial Factors

The degree of neuropsychopathology documented in these clinical studies caused the team to wonder whether the incarcerated adolescents differed in any special way from psychiatrically hospitalized adolescents. Clinically, they closely resembled their hospitalized counterparts. Perhaps adolescents sent to correctional facilities were as psychiatrically impaired as their hospitalized peers but were more violent.

Questions regarding the similarities and differences between psychiatrically hospitalized and incarcerated adolescents led to the following study (21). The psychiatric hospital records and correctional school records of an entire sample of all adolescents in a single given year from a small city in Connecticut who were sent either to corrections or to the only state hospital adolescent inpatient unit serving the designated town were studied.

The team hypothesized that similarly severe psychopathology would be found in the two groups, but that the incarcerated group would be found to have been more violent. This hypothesis was wrong. True, both groups had similar prevalences of psychotic and organic symptomatology. Except for a small number of floridly psychotic youngsters in the hospital group, the two groups were essentially similar clinically. Of considerable surprise, however, was the finding that the hospitalized adolescents were as violent as their incarcerated counterparts. Similar proportions in the two groups had been involved in such aggressive acts as robbing, sexual assault, and assault with a weapon. None in either group had committed murder.

When the data were further analyzed, certain important differences between the groups did emerge. The most important factor distinguishing the groups was race. If an adolescent was white and violent and psychiatrically ill, he was significantly more likely to be sent to the hospital. If, on the other hand, he was black and violent and psychiatrically ill, he was significantly more likely to be incarcerated in a correctional institution. Also, disturbed violent girls were more likely to be hospitalized than disturbed violent boys.

Having documented similarities between psychiatrically hospitalized adolescents and incarcerated adolescents in Connecticut, the question arose whether delinquents from other states were as neuropsychiatrically impaired as those in Connecticut. Perhaps antisocial individuals from urban environments such as New York City were tougher, more antisocial, and less impaired than those from New England. Current studies (22) of young adult prisoners in New York City suggest that this sample of young prisoners is neuropsychiatrically very similar to the New Haven sample of incarcerated adolescents. Furthermore, preliminary data suggest that similarly high proportions in both groups had been severely physically abused.

Throughout the course of the clinical studies of violent individuals, the team was impressed by the frequency with which severely disturbed, often psychotic delinquents and criminals had been diagnosed "conduct disorder" or one of its synonyms (e.g., unsocialized aggressive reaction, antisocial personality, sociopathic character disorder). Therefore, attention was turned toward the study of a sample of psychiatrically hospitalized adolescents, their signs, symptoms, diagnoses, and treatment.

Clinically, it seemed that most of the adolescents on an inpatient psychiatric service who were discharged with the diagnosis of conduct disorder had previously been diagnosed as suffering from other kinds of disorders, such as schizophrenia, attention deficit disorder, and retardation. Moreover, it seemed common to discover that adolescents discharged with a diagnosis of psychosis (e.g., schizophrenia) had on previous evaluations been diagnosed conduct disorder. Did adolescents receiving a diagnosis of conduct disorder differ in any way from those given other diagnoses?

The psychiatric records of a one-year sample of all male adolescents admitted to the adolescent inpatient service of a teaching hospital at a time when DSM-III criteria were in use (N = 66) became the database for the next study (23). Adolescents who had ever, at any time, received the diagnosis conduct disorder (N = 34) were compared with those never having received that diagnosis (N = 32). There were no significant symptomatic differences between the two groups. Similarly high proportions in each group had psychotic symptomatology, such as hallucinations and delusions, noted in their charts. In fact, over 50 percent of adolescents in each group had at one time been diagnosed psychotic. Ironically, those ever diagnosed conduct disorder were significantly more likely to have been treated with antipsychotic medication. They were also significantly more likely to have been in foster or group homes and somewhat more likely to have been psychiatrically hospitalized. (See Table 6.)

Furthermore, the mothers of children diagnosed conduct disorder were significantly more likely to have been psychiatrically hospitalized. All of these factors (i.e., previous psychiatric hospitalization, psychotic symptomatology, severe maternal psychopathology) suggested that children diagnosed conduct disorder suffered from more serious impairment than character pathology.

There was a similarly low prevalence of enuresis, firesetting, and cruelty to animals in the two groups. The most significant factor distinguishing the groups was violence. Those diagnosed conduct disorder were significantly more likely to have been seriously assaultive than those never having received the diagnosis.

Of the 34 boys who had at some time received a conduct disorder diagnosis, only 15 were discharged from the hospitalization in question with that diagnosis. In 19 cases, the diagnosis was changed, and in over half of these cases the diagnosis was changed to schizophrenia.

TABLE 6
Comparison of City Hospital Boys Ever Diagnosed Conduct Disorder with
Those Never Diagnosed Conduct Disorder: Diagnostic and Symptomatic
Variables

Other Diagnoses Received and Symptoms Documented	Ever Diagnosed Conduct Disorder		Never Diagnosed Conduct Disorder	
	#	%[a]	#	%[a]
Psychotic	19	55.9	18	62.1
ADD	12	35.3	4	12.5★
Epileptic	1	2.9	4	12.9
Retarded	9	26.5	5	15.6
Neurotic or adj. rxn.	15	45.5	16	51.6
Learning disabled	19	61.3	13	43.3
Visual hallucinations	9	26.5	11	34.4
Auditory hallucinations	16	48.5	14	46.7
Loose rambling or illogical	8	23.5	13	41.9
Paranoid ideation	17	50.0	10	33.3
Other delusions	10	30.3	9	29.0
Isolation or withdrawal	8	24.2	10	31.3
Sleep problems	12	35.3	13	40.6
Sadness or crying	6	17.6	3	9.7
Having had a seizure	3	9.7	5	16.7
Neurological soft signs	19	57.6	12	40.0

[a] Percentages are calculated according to the number of subjects for whom data in each category were available, using Yates corrected X^2_y
★ = p<.10

When the 15 boys discharged conduct disorder were compared with those 19 whose diagnoses were changed, they were symptomatically and behaviorally similar. The only symptom more characteristic of those whose diagnosis was changed was auditory hallucinations. Behaviorally, high percentages of both groups were extremely violent (i.e., 76.9 percent discharged conduct disorder vs. 82.4 percent with changed diagnoses).

Was the apparent diagnostic inexactitude regarding conduct disorder peculiar to the city hospital in question or was it characteristic of other psychiatric institutions? To answer this question, the study was repeated on a random sample of adolescent boys (N = 48) hospitalized at a voluntary psychiatric hospital in New York City. When those ever diagnosed conduct disorder (N = 17) were compared with those never so diagnosed, there were many similarities and few differences. For example, the prevalence of psychotic symptomatology and organic symptomatology did not distinguish the two groups. In fact, the only symptoms more characteristic of those never diagnosed conduct disorder were isolation and withdrawal. Similar to the earlier study the behavioral prevalence of enuresis, firesetting, and cruelty to animals was low in the two groups.

Again, however, the most significant factor distinguishing those ever diagnosed conduct disorder from those never so diagnosed was violence (56.3 percent vs. 7.7 percent, $X^2_y = 9.700$, p = .002). And again, those ever diagnosed conduct disorder were significantly more likely to have been in foster or group home placement (62.5 percent vs. 25.9 percent, $X^2_y = 4.196$, p = .04).

Of the 17 voluntary hospital boys who had at one time been diagnosed conduct disorder, 10 retained the diagnosis on discharge, while seven had their diagnosis changed. When these two groups were compared, specific psychotic symptoms (e.g., hallucinations, delusions, looseness of associations) were similarly prevalent in both groups, but the seven whose diagnoses were changed averaged greater numbers of psychotic symptoms (2.286 vs. 1.000, t = 2.757, p = .015). Of note, these seven psychotic youngsters also tended to be more violent.

TREATMENT IMPLICATIONS

These findings demonstrate clearly that youngsters diagnosed conduct disorder have a multiplicity of signs and symptoms characteristic of other diagnoses. They seem to fall on the border of, or within the spectrum of other diagnostic categories, specifically psychosis and retardation. The most important characteristic that distinguishes them from youngsters receiving other diagnoses is violence. These findings also suggest that conduct disorder is often an interim designation on the way to a more rigorous diagnosis. When signs of psychosis or intellectual impairment become more obvious, many youngsters are removed from the catch-all category of conduct disorder. Unfortunately, often the signs and symptoms of psychosis, retardation, and organic dysfunction remain hidden, and youngsters dubbed conduct disorder graduate to the adult diagnosis of antisocial personality, thus further diminishing any chance for appropriate treatment.

Given ample evidence of severe psychopathology in both incarcerated delinquent youngsters and psychiatrically hospitalized youngsters diagnosed conduct disorder, one must wonder why we often fail to recognize, or we simply ignore, evidence of potentially treatable psychotic and organic impairment. There are probably several explanations for this practice. First, the severely disturbed adolescents described here have been violent. This characteristic alone is often sufficient to alienate clinicians and lead to a superficial, brief assessment. Second, the parents of these youngsters are themselves often seriously psychiatrically impaired, hence their children's multiple placements. The parents are, therefore, frequently unavailable for purposes of providing an accurate developmental, medical, family, and behavioral history. Clinical histories often must be obtained from foster parents or group home staff, who are able only to provide a history of the behaviors of the adolescent that have led to his extrusion from the placement. In brief, the aggressive adolescent tends to lack an informed advocate who can shed light on the factors contributing to his frightening behaviors.

Finally, the mythology surrounding antisocial aggressive youngsters is that they are different from other psychiatrically ill children and that there is no effective treatment for their disorder. They are assumed to be characterologically impaired and beyond ordinary available psychiatric help. This pessimistic attitude often leads us to give up on these young people before we complete the kind of thorough diagnostic assessment that would bring to light potentially treatable vulnerabilities contributing to aggressive behaviors.

Unfortunately, even when a thorough assessment brings to light psychotic, organic, or psychoeducational factors, the clinician is faced with such a dearth of family and societal supports that he may wish he had never uncovered the multiple vulnerabilities in the first place.

Does it matter that we overlook evidence of severe psychopathology in children called delinquent and/or diagnosed "conduct disorder"? Some might argue that it is in a child's best interest to be diagnosed "conduct disorder" rather than labeled psychotic or organically impaired. Is it not better to have a character disorder than a psychosis? In order to understand why this practice is malignant, we must focus on the purpose of categorization (i.e., diagnosis) in the first place.

Whenever we categorize, we attempt to focus on important commonalities and ignore only relatively unimportant differences. When we categorize psychopathology, we do so for purposes of treatment and try not to eliminate from our diagnoses signs and symptoms with important treatment implications. As these studies of incarcerated and psychiatrically hospitalized adolescents show, the designation "conduct disorder" obfuscates important potentially treatable neuropsychiatric signs and symptoms. The disorders most frequently masked are psychosis, organic dysfunction, severe learning disabilities, and intellectual impairment.

Given the scientific and therapeutic disadvantages of the dead end diagnosis "conduct disorder," it is suggested, based on the studies reported here, that it be eliminated from the nomenclature of child psychiatry. One can only wonder whether or not similar studies of adult offenders diagnosed "antisocial personality" might lead to the elimination of that diagnosis as well.

REFERENCES

1. MERTON, R.: *Social Theory and Social Structure*. New York: Free Press, 1957.
2. CLOWARD, R.A., and OHLIN, L.E.: *Delinquency and Opportunity: A Theory of Delinquent Gangs*. New York: Free Press, 1961.

3. COHEN, A.K.: *Delinquent Boys: The Culture of the Gang.* New York: Free Press, 1955.
4. HEWITT, L., and JENKINS, R.L.: *Fundamental Patterns of Maladjustment: Their Dynamics and Their Origin.* Springfield, IL.: State of Illinois, 1946.
5. JENKINS, R.L.: *Behavior Disorders of Childhood and Adolescence.* Springfield, IL: Charles C Thomas, 1973.
6. JENKINS, R.L., and BOYERS, A.: Types of delinquent behavior and background factors. *Int. J. Soc. Psychiat.,* 14: 65-76, 1967.
7. RODMAN, H., and GRAMS, P.: Juvenile delinquency and the family: A review and discussion. In: *Juvenile Delinquency and Youth Crime.* Washington, D.C.: U.S. Government Printing Office, 1967.
8. QUAY, H.C.: Dimensions of personality in delinquent boys as inferred from factor analysis of case history data. *Child Dev.,* 35: 479-484, 1964.
9. QUAY, H.C.: Personality dimensions in delinquent males as inferred from the factor analysis of behavior ratings. *J. Res. Crime Delinq.,* 1: 33-37, 1964.
10. QUAY, H.C.: Personality patterns in preadolescent delinquent boys. *Educ. Psychol. Measurement,* 26: 99-110, 1966.
11. QUAY, H.C.: Classification in the treatment of delinquency and antisocial behavior. In: N. Hobbs (Ed.), *Issues on the Classification of Children, Volume 1.* San Francisco: Jossey-Bass, 1975.
12. PETERSON, D.R., QUAY, H.C., and CAMERON, G.R.: Personality and background factors in juvenile delinquency as inferred from questionnaire responses. *J. Consult. Psychol.,* 23: 395-399, 1959.
13. PETERSON, D.R., QUAY, H.C., and TIFFANY, T.L.: Personality factors related to juvenile delinquency. *Child Dev.,* 32: 355-372, 1961.
14. *Diagnostic and Statistical Manual of Mental Disorders,* Third Edition. Washington, D.C.: American Psychiatric Association, 1980.
15. LEWIS, D.O., BALLA, D.A., SACKS, H., and JEKEL, J.: Psychotic symptomatology in a juvenile court clinic population. *J. Am. Acad. Child Psychiat.,* 12: 660-675, 1973.
16. LEWIS, D.O., and SHANOK, S.S.: Medical histories of delinquent and nondelinquent children: An epidemiological study. *Am. J. Psychiat.,* 134: 1020-1025, 1977.
17. LEWIS, D.O., SHANOK, S.S., and BALLA, D.A.: Perinatal difficulties, head and face trauma, and child abuse in the medical histories of seriously delinquent children. *Am. J. Psychiat.,* 136: 419-423, 1979.
18. LEWIS, D.O., SHANOK, S.S., PINCUS, J.H., and GLASER, G.H.: Violent juvenile delinquents: Psychiatric, neurological, psychological, and abuse factors. *J. Am. Acad. Child Psychiat.,* 18: 307-319, 1979.
19. LEWIS, D.O., and SHANOK, S.S.: The use of a correctional setting for follow-up care of psychiatrically disturbed adolescents. *Am. J. Psychiat.,* 137: 953-955, 1980.
20. CANTWELL, D.P.: *The Hyperactive Child.* New York: Spectrum Publications, 1975.
21. LEWIS, D.O., SHANOK, S.S., COHEN, R.J., KLIGFELD, M., and FRISONE, G.: Race bias in the diagnosis and disposition of violent adolescents. *Am. J. Psychiat.,* 137: 1211-1216, 1980.
22. LEWIS, D.O.: A study of the neuropsychiatric status of urban violent juveniles. *Report to the Ford Foundation,* February 25, 1982.
23. LEWIS, O.D., SHANOK, S.S., LEWIS, M., UNGER, L., and GOLDMAN, C.: Conduct disorder and its synonyms: Diagnoses of dubious validity and usefulness. *Am. J. Psychiat.,* (in press).

6

Types of Alcoholism Reflective of Character Disorders

E. Mansell Pattison, M.D.

The relationship between alcoholism, personality structure, and character disorders has a checkered history of conflict and confusion. I intend to survey these debated themes in order to dissect out the sources of conflicting empirical data, contradictory clinical opinion, and competing psychodynamic theories. I shall conclude with a synthesizing model of alcoholism syndromes aligned in developmental sequence in accord with self psychology and object-relations theory.

THE ALCOHOLIC PERSONALITY

There is no doubt that human societies have always recognized and labeled certain persons as alcoholic. The "face validity" of the social reality-testing leads us to consensually agree on certain common traits of the "drunkard." Such a man is preoccupied with his drinking, his life deteriorates, and adverse personality traits are accentuated. The Old Testament gives a portrait of the alcoholic personality:

> Our son is stubborn and rebellious, he will not obey our voice; he is a glutton and a drunkard (Deuteronomy, 21:20).
> The drunkard and the glutton shall come to poverty; and drowsiness shall clothe a man in rags. Who hath woe? Who hath sorrow? Who hath contentions? Who hath babbling? Who hath wounds without cause? Who hath redness of eyes? They that tarry long at the wine (Proverbs, 23:21-30).

Woe to the crown of pride, to the drunkards . . . whose glorious beauty
is a fading flower (Isaiah, 28:1).

It is easy to see why the early psychologists and psychoanalytic pioneers
postulated a core developmental conflict, with the subsequent development of
a characteristic flawed alcoholic personality disorder. A corollary (but logically
not necessary) was the claim that the developmental conflict or fixation was the
primary *etiological factor* in the development of alcoholism.

A counterreaction has been created by the accumulation of empirical data,
both psychometric and clinical, which *failed* to demonstrate common personality
conflicts or traits among alcoholics, but did demonstrate the *non-uniqueness* of
alcoholics, who shared common core conflicts, common developmental problems, and common personality traits with non-alcoholic control samples. Major
reviews in the 1950s by Sutherland et al. (1) and by Syme (2) repudiated the
concept of an alcoholic personality and by inference rejected the concept of
predisposing or etiologic character variables.

Despite the demise of the ''alcoholic personality,'' a number of reformulations
have been offered. In Table 1, I have collated current competing theories. A
brief synoptic review presents *my* inferences and interpretations. My intent is
to sharpen the *implications* of each position, which means that I will not do
justice to many variations within each theory.

Classic Psychoanalytic Theory

The early psychoanalytic pioneers—Freud, Abraham, Tausk, Schilder, Hartmann, Brill, Jelliffe, Oberndorf, Simmel, etc.—conceived alcoholism in terms
of instinctual conflict and drive reduction. They stressed the etiological importance of the erotogenic oral zone and a close relationship to homosexuality.
Freud alluded to alcohol as a substitute symptom for sexual impulse gratification.
Abraham elaborated this in the concept of the ''oral-dependent'' personality.
Fenichel (3, p.379) put it clearly: ''specific oral frustrations . . . gave rise to
oral fixations, with all the consequences of such fixations for the structure of
personality.'' It was the 1933 paper by Rado (4), however, which proved most
influential. He proposed that the addiction to alcohol was unrelated to its pharmacologic effect, but rested in the unconscious symbolic meaning of the drug.
Hence, the pleasure effect of the drug was ''brought about by the ego itself,''
to use his words. This process he termed ''pharmacothymia'' to indicate that the
primary addiction is solely a psychological disorder of psychosexual fixation.
He considered the reactive and adaptive ego responses to drug effects to be
secondary symptoms.

This theory gave rise to the famous psychic equation that *bottle equals breast.*

TABLE 1
Theoretical Views on Alcoholic Personality

Types of Theory	Uniform Alcoholic Personality	Core Instinct-Drive Conflict	Core Structural Fault	Uniform Psychodynamics	Pharmacologic Effect of Alcohol
Classic Psychoanalytic (Rado, Fenichel)	Yes (oral dependent)	Yes	Yes (2°)	Yes (fixated)	None 2° symptoms
Psychoanalytic Structural (Kernberg, Kohut)	Yes (borderline, narcissist)	No	Yes (1°)	Yes (fixated ego processes)	None 2° symptoms
Psychoanalytic Ego Psychology (Mack, Khantzian)	No - initially Yes - regression	No	No	Yes (regressive ego processes)	2° effect on ego processing
Pharmaco-Dynamic Psychology (Bean, Vaillant, Zimberg)	No	No	No	Yes (adaptational ego processes)	1° effect on ego processing
Social Learning Theory	No	No	No	No	2° reinforcement variable on ego processing
Pharmacologic Theory	No	No	No	No	1° effect on brain processing

Drinking is a primary process event of infantile incorporation of the symbiotic mother.

Some patients do present clinical confirmation of the bottle-breast equation. However, is this true of all alcoholics? Chein et al. (5) noted that:

> By and large, those patients who directly associate their addiction experiences with these oral concepts have the most clinically evident ego disturbances; they suffer from anxiety verging on panic or are overtly psychotic. They are least able to repress or otherwise defend themselves against the perception of such ideas and images, and they are thus able to directly verbalize what may only be inferred from the symbolic communications of others (p. 232).

My clinical observations sustain the Chein position, namely that erotic-oral-breast symbolism can be elicited from schizophrenic or manic-depressive patients, from "primitive-inadequate" character disorders, from patients with substantial regression during a long drinking career, and from alcoholics in intensive psychoanalytic therapy. However, in nonregressed alcoholics and in many types of neurotic alcoholics I have *not* found clinical evidence of either an oral-dependent character structure or a primary oral-maternal symbolism.

This is not to say that elements of oral-maternal symbolism are not present in us all and cannot be found with some representation in many of our own everyday behaviors. Rather, the question is: Can such symbolism be considered etiologic in all alcoholics, or how important is such primary unconscious oral symbolism? Again Chein et al. (5) spoke directly to this issue:

> Unconscious symbolism of this sort occurs in addiction. The question is, "What role does it play in addiction?" Obviously, no one takes drugs for the first time with such ideas in mind as that the syringe is a breast. . . . No one becomes an addict simply because he is laden with unconscious oral fantasies and cravings for breasts, sustenance, and warmth . . . these unconscious symbolizations are less weighty in the motivations for becoming an addict than are the forces of conscious experience . . . they probably do contribute importantly to the appetite for drug use (p. 234).

A final question is: Why should alcohol be chosen for psychic investment with breast-mother symbolism? Cross-cultural evidence suggests that when other drugs of addiction are legally and readily available, alcohol is almost always the preferred drug (6). Some abstinent alcoholics "transfer" their psychic symbolism rapidly to other drugs, including sedatives, hypnotics, or minor tranquilizers. It would appear that the alcohol-induced psychic experience itself is a potent reinforcer that interacts with the "psychic need" to produce the symbolic value attached to alcohol. Pharmacologic effects of alcohol may reinforce continued alcohol use, without having to posit either an oral-dependent fixation or a specific symbolic meaning to alcohol. In a word, we can have *non-symbolic alcoholism*.

Evaluation

First, the evidence does not sustain a universal oral-dependent personality, or a primary psychosexual conflict, or a primitive fixated character development in *all* alcoholics.

Second, the evidence does not support the assertion that unconscious symbolism is a primary or sole etiological variable in the genesis of alcoholism.

Third, it does appear plausible that some alcoholics with primitive, almost autistic, character development *do* demonstrate fixation at the pre-12-month age of symbiotic fusion with a maternal object, or that, while regressed, psychotics and/or borderline and narcissistic character disorders all demonstrate significant elements of unconscious symbolic use of alcohol.

Fourth, such unconscious symbolization may contribute to the etiology of alcoholism in these character disorders more often than in more mature character structures.

Fifth, we need more systematic clinical data to determine how much of a motivating force such unconscious symbolism may play in alcoholics who do *not* demonstrate regression and/or have more mature character structure.

Psychoanalytic Structural Theory

Although the classic psychoanalytic version of an alcoholic personality is not generally accepted, a new psychoanalytic theory based on object-relations theory and self psychology has emerged. Its genesis is in the work of Robert Knight (7), who described an "essential alcoholic" personality with flaws in ego formation. Balint (8) termed this a "basic fault" in the infant-mother relationship. Subsequently, Kernberg (9) and Kohut (10) postulated a structural personality flaw as the substrate for alcoholism. For Kernberg the flawed structure is the borderline character, while for Kohut it is the narcissistic character. Neither of these latter theorists explored the clinical phenomenon of alcoholism in detail, but it has been explicated by their expositors (11, 12, 13).

This theory posits a developmental fixation between 15 and 36 months of age. We then infer a psychic symbolic use of alcohol as a "transitional object" by the borderline or as an "object" representation in the narcissist. Alcohol use is therefore a psychic maneuver used in an attempt at "self-repair" of the structural self-object flaw in the personality of the alcoholic.

Evaluation

First, the empirical data on both premorbid and morbid personalities of alcoholics do *not* demonstrate the consistent or even typical presence of a borderline or narcissistic character disorder.

Second, some alcoholics demonstrate borderline or narcissistic behavior typical of those character disorders; however, this may result from pharmacologic effects on ego operations and/or regressive behavior in a career of alcoholism, rather than a fixated character disorder.

Third, some alcoholics do demonstrate borderline and narcissistic character disorders, which make them at higher risk to become alcoholic—although that remains to be empirically demonstrated.

Fourth, although alcohol does *at times* assume the psychic function of a transitional object and/or object representation, we lack systematic clinical evidence that such symbolic meaning or use of alcohol is *necessarily* present even in alcoholics with borderline or narcissistic character disorders.

Psychoanalytic Ego Psychology

This perspective, represented by Mack (14) and Khantzian (15), focuses on deficits in ego operation. They emphasize the inability of ego operations to sustain adequate "self-care" functions. They do not assume structural fixation, but emphasize the deficits in the ego operations of affect regulations, maintenance of self-object stability, and defects in reality-testing, judgment, and ego synthesis.

This group acknowledges important developmental weaknesses in character development, but gives primary emphasis to the vulnerability of the premorbid ego processes of the alcoholic. They interpret the primitive character operations of the alcoholic as a regressive phenomenon, as the ego is overwhelmed by the process of alcoholic deterioration. This group does *not* assert a uniform fixated character structure, but would suggest a *uniform personality* pattern resulting from a common regression process.

Evaluation

First, this position is more compatible with longitudinal personality studies which suggest that personality regression is more common among alcoholics than character fixation.

Second, this position is compatible with the posttreatment data that successful outcome alcoholics regain mature and effective ego operations.

Third, this position is compatible with the observation that long-time sober alcoholics demonstrate effective ego operations, yet may at the same time demonstrate narcissistic character structure.

Fourth, this position still posits a common psychodynamic personality profile, which is contravened by data on acute alcoholics which fail to validate common personality profiles. Thus, the proposed common pattern of regression in ego operations appears plausible for only certain alcoholics. *Not all* alcoholics demonstrate such regression in ego operations.

Pharmacodynamic Psychology

This group, represented by Bean (16), Vaillant (17), and Zimberg (18), places even less emphasis on premorbid character development. They argue that there are common *psychodynamic patterns* observed in alcoholics, but *not* a common personality or character. These common psychodynamics result primarily from the pharmacologic effects upon ego operations which result in degradation or deterioration of ego functions combined with neurotic and/or quasi-adaptive ego responses to these deficits and the associated alcoholic lifestyle. They acknowledge a common pattern of regression in ego operations; however, rather than attributing such regression to premorbid flaws in ego operations, they attribute the regression to pharmacologic and reactive disorganization of ego functions.

Evaluation

First, this position is congruent with neuropsychological data which demonstrate short-term and long-term degradation of ego functions directly due to the pharmacologic effects of alcohol on the brain.

Second, this position is congruent with neuropsychological data on follow-up of abstinent alcoholics who regain effective ego operations during abstinence, regardless of any psychotherapeutic intervention.

Third, this position is compatible with the empirical demonstration of mature personality organization and ego function in premorbid alcoholics, without evidence of manifest character fixation or ego deficits.

Fourth, this position appears to ignore the evidence of character development fixation, high-risk character disorders, and premorbid ego deficits in *some* alcoholics.

Fifth, this position ignores the fact that some alcoholics maintain high level ego operations despite heavy alcoholic intake and do not demonstrate deterioration of ego functions.

Social Learning Theory

This is a persuasive and powerful theoretical position, based on the most solid stratum of empirical research (19). It posits that there may be a high-risk personality structure or high-risk ego-deficit persons. Nevertheless, such characterologic features are not etiologic. Rather, alcoholism is a conditioned learned behavior, produced by interaction with environmental variables associated with the consumption of alcohol. In brief, alcoholism is a "bad habit." No common psychodynamics would be acknowledged, since psychodynamic processes are not a primary element of analysis. Instead, there are common behavioral patterns, which may include a variety of psychodynamics.

Evaluation

First, this position may be behaviorally reductionistic and ignore the relevance of psychodynamic data, although not necessarily so.

Second, this position at times ignores the pharmacologic effects of alcohol on psychic function, but again, not necessarily so.

Third, this position is compatible with all of the psychodynamic theories discussed above, although not usually acknowledged by behaviorists. The major point of difference would be on the etiologic weight given to developmental or ego operation variables in the genesis of an alcoholic career.

Fourth, social learning theory provides a necessary variable to account for variation in personalities and character structure among alcoholics, for adverse drinking behavior in persons without significant regression of ego operations, and for cross-cultural variations in alcohol syndromes.

Pharmacologic Theory

This theory essentially ignores psychodynamic factors. It would posit that psychological disturbances in the alcoholic are the effects of pharmacologic disruption of brain processes (20). This position would assume no common personality disorder, no common development vulnerabilities, and no common psychodynamics, except as sequelae of brain dysfunction.

Evaluation

First, this is a grossly reductionistic theory that ignores the relevance of psychodynamic data to addictive behavior.

Second, this theory does not account for drug-seeking behavior without the consumption of alcohol and/or after years of sobriety.

Overall Evaluation

My synoptic view of these major theories is that each contributes a vital and essential piece to the puzzle of alcoholism. None fails to describe some element in the genesis and maintenance of alcoholism, yet each describes only one type of alcoholic or accounts for only one aspect of behavior associated with alcoholism.

ELEMENTS FOR A DATABASE

In this section, I plan to briefly recount some of the major trends in alcoholism research bearing on personality and character structure and present their implications for analysis.

Cross-cultural Data

Ethnographic data are relatively barren of comparative personality studies. Nevertheless, in the study of small preliterate societies and subcultural groups, the anthropologic data suggest that social norms of drinking are far more determinative of alcoholism than individual personality traits (6). For example, Bacon (21) reports that of preliterate societies where alcohol has been introduced in the past 100 years by Western society, fully 92.5 percent have ubiquitous uncontrolled alcoholism with lack of effective drinking norms. Even more instructive is a recent study of Northern Alaska Eskimo communities which use alcohol. Here the introduction of the arctic oil economy disrupted the Eskimo social structure and within five years 72 percent of the population exhibited symptomatic alcoholism (22).

Even within relatively homogeneous American populations we find substantially different patterns of alcohol use and associated alcoholism syndromes. For example, in a recent comparison of five white urban populations of different ethnicity, Greeley et al. (23) reported substantially different ordering of the population who drank, the frequency and amount of drinking, and the associated degree of alcoholism problems. Although the English and Irish had fewer drinkers, they had far more alcoholism, while the Italians and Jews had mostly drinkers and a very low rate of alcoholism, as shown in Table 2.

TABLE 2
U.S. White Population Drinking Patterns

	% Non-Abstainers	Frequency of Drinking	Number Drinks/Event	% Drinkers w/ problem	% Drinkers w/ Adverse Consequence
High	Irish	Irish	Irish	English	English
	Jewish	English	English	Irish	Irish
	Italian	Slavic	Slavic	Slavic	Slavic
	Slavic	Italian	Italian	Jewish	Italian
Low	English	Jewish	Jewish	Italian	Jewish

Modified from Greeley et al. (23).

Implications

These types of cross-cultural data indicate that with cultural disorganization a type of "normless alcoholism" can become endemic to a population, and that socialization and family process substantially alter the development of alcoholism, despite widespread population exposure to and use of alcohol. It suggests that the development of alcoholism is substantially related to sociocultural norming processes. The theory that some basic personality type is primarily responsible for the development of alcoholism seems implausible in the face of these data.

Social Psychology Data

Here I refer to behavioral drinking studies which observe alcoholics under experimental conditions where they have free access to alcohol or can earn alcohol. In either case, alcoholics do *not* drink indiscriminately, indefinitely, or continuously. Rather, alcoholics drink in response to definable and predictable environmental stimuli and cues (24-26).

Related survey data on variables correlated with problem drinking demonstrate that personality variables are *not* correlated with drinking, but social relationship variables are the most potent predictors of problem drinking (27), as shown in Table 3.

Implications

These data support the contention that alcoholism is significantly determined

TABLE 3

Social-Psychological Correlates of Alcoholism

(6 Most Significant of 51 Variables)

Intervening Variable	Multiple Correlation	Partial Correlation	Simple Correlation (Pearson r)
Drinking by significant other	0.26	0.15	.26
Tolerance of deviance	0.33	0.13	.22
Own attitude toward drinking	0.37	0.18	.26
Index of social position	0.41	0.11	.16
Black	0.42	0.09	.15
Non-helpfulness of others	0.43	0.06	.16

Modified from Cahalan & Cisin (27).

TABLE 4

A Drinking Pattern - Personality Typology

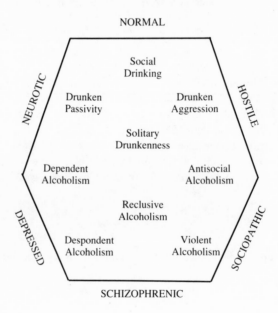

Modified from Barry (31).

by social learning, reinforced and maintained by social relations, and that drinking behavior serves social adaptational needs, rather than unconscious or structural psychodynamic needs.

Personality Typologies

After the search for a typical alcoholic personality was abandoned in the 1950s, psychologists turned to comparative personality studies. This research confirms the earlier conclusion that no common or unique set of personality traits obtains for alcoholics (28-30). At the same time, several different data reduction techniques have been used to parse out phenotypical typologies of alcoholic personalities. For example, Barry (31) has organized a personality typology based on drinking patterns, as shown in Table 4, whereas Costello (32) has derived an object-relations theory based distribution profiles of personality types, as shown in Table 5.

Implications

These data demonstrate that repeated research fails to support the idea of a common personality and/or character disorder among alcoholics. Sophisticated data analysis does demonstrate phenomenologic and psychodynamic variation in alcoholics.

TABLE 5
A Self Psychology Typology Distribution
of
120 Alcoholics

Rigid

I 2	II 12	III 3		
IV 6	V 12	VI 11	Activated	Self-in-Relationship to-Others
VII 14	VIII 49	IX 11		

Withdrawn (left of the grid)

Labile
Self-as-Object

Modified from Costello (32).

Premorbid Personality Data

There are few longitudinal studies of alcoholics *before* they became alcoholics. Kammeier et al. (33) reported that premorbid MMPI profiles of alcoholics were normal. McCord and McCord (34) and Robins (35) found that premorbid characteristics of alcoholic versus non-alcoholic samples did not differ in childhood behavior or development. Vaillant (36) reported that blind assessment of the childhood of pre-alcoholics did not differentiate them from non-alcoholics.

Implications

These data do not support the theory that alcoholism necessarily or primarily originates in fixed character disorders.

Acute Alcoholic Populations

Comparative studies of alcoholism treatment facilities reveals that different types of alcoholic populations present at different treatment facilities. Thus, any one facility is likely to encounter one consistent type of alcoholic, but not encounter other types of alcoholics (37). Acute alcoholics differ substantially in their presenting personality organization. For example, Table 6 presents the

TABLE 6

MMPI Personality Profiles of

Acute Alcoholics at Four Different Treatment Facilities

	F	K	Hy	Pd	Ma	Si	MacAndrew Alcoholism Scale
ACH	59.4	55.0	66.4	67.1	61.9	53.2	25.3
OPC	64.1	52.0	67.1	74.5	60.1	59.0	26.3
HWH	67.1	49.2	64.8	76.8	69.9	54.9	30.6
PWC	62.9	49.6	61.1	75.1	60.8	60.2	28.3

Significant Differences Between Populations

(p Values, Duncan Multiple Range Test)

	F	K	Hy	Pd	Ma	Si	MacAndrew Alcoholism Scale
ACH X OPC				<.01		<.05	
ACH X HWH	<.01	<.05		<.01	<.01		<.01
ACH X PWC		<.05	<.05	<.01		<.05	
OPC X HWH					<.01		<.01
OPC X PWC			<.05				<.01
HWH X PWC					<.01		

Modified from Pattison et al. (38).

MMPI profiles for acute alcoholic populations at four different facilities, as reported by Pattison et al. (38). In brief, the Alcoholism Aversion Conditioning Hospital population (ACH) showed no regression with intact narcissistic character structure; the Outpatient Clinic population (OPC) showed no regression with immature neurotic defenses; the Halfway House population (HWH) showed massive regression in immature character disorders; while the Prison Work Camp population (PWC) demonstrated no regression but fixated primitive character structure.

Implications

These studies demonstrate that even among acute alcoholics there is substantial variation. Some show regression; some do not. Futher, there is *no clear relationship* between regressive behavior and the presence of a character disorder. They are not necessarily related.

Developmental Assessment

Although there are clinical reports on the developmental levels of alcoholics, there are almost no empirical data. One intriguing study by Thornton et al. (39) assessed a group of acute alcoholics in terms of ego development and ego strength. They divided the alcoholics into high ego development (HDL), medium ego development (MDL), and low ego development (LDL). At admission all three groups had similar MMPI profiles, except that the high group (HDL) showed no manic or psychopathic qualities. After six weeks the HDL group demonstrated the most significant improvement and had normalized on their MMPI profiles, as shown in Table 7.

In a recent review of recent studies of childhood development and drinking behavior, Zucker (40) has shown two different patterns of youthful development of alcoholism: *embryonic* and *hierarchical*. The embryonic pattern reflects maturational defects and failure to successfully achieve developmental landmarks, which are associated with early and progressive alcoholismic drinking patterns. On the other hand, in the hierarchical pattern there is normal maturation and development. Here drinking is not immediately or necessarily alcoholismic, but regressive alcoholic behavior may ensue.

Implications

This work suggests that we can empirically profile levels of ego development which may be correlated with types of alcoholism. Of theoretical importance is the inference that the HDL group had a capacity for mature (hierarchical) ego

TABLE 7
Relationship of Ego Development Level
to Pre and Post Treatment MMPI Profiles

MMPI	HDL		MDL		LDL	
Scale	Week 1	Week 6	Week 1	Week 6	Week 1	Week 6
Hypochondriasis (Hs)	59.6	55.2	61.5	60.8	64.3	61.6
Depression (D)	75.8	68.0	72.2	70.2	74.7	69.4
Hysteria (Hy)	62.5	58.9	61.8	61.2	62.6	59.8
Psychopathic Deviance (Pd)	75.9	72.5	77.1	75.4	77.6	74.7
Paranoia (Pa)	64.5	61.9	63.7	64.0	65.0	67.5
Psychasthenia (Pt)	69.6	65.3	70.4	68.4	74.1	69.9
Schizophrenia (Sc)	69.8	67.5	73.6	72.2	76.7	74.6
Mania (Ma)	63.8	66.5	72.0	72.1	71.3	70.9
MacAndrew (Mac)	28.7	28.7	28.8	29.3	29.8	29.9
Ego Strength (ES)	41.3	44.0	45.6	47.2	39.5	41.3

HDL = high ego development
MDL = medium ego development
LDL = low ego development

From Thornton et al. (39).

operations, but had experienced regression in ego operations. At the same time the LDL group represents fixated ego development (embryonic).

Neuropsychopharmacologic Data

Here we are concerned with the effect of alcohol as a pharmacologic agent upon brain operation and attendant ego operations. Mello (41) has described differential effects of low dose versus high dose alcohol ingestion. Specific effects of alcohol are altered at different dose levels, and not all in the same direction. Further, longitudinal neuropsychological studies reveal that affective and cognitive processes are severely disrupted during and after heavy alcohol ingestion, with impairment that may last up to six months. Under conditions of continued alcohol ingestion, the brain and, therefore, ego functions are chronically organically impaired (42).

Recent worldwide surveys of alcohol consumption and the epidemiology of alcoholism problems demonstrate general correlations. That is, more frequent and heavier alcohol consumption is consistently associated with rising rates of general alcoholism problems (43, 44).

Implications

These data strongly support the theory that alcoholics experience regression in ego operations due to the pharmacologic effect of alcohol. Much of the common alcoholic personality observed may be due to a common pattern of alcoholic organicity and the compensatory ego responses to those deficits. As a corollary, these same studies demonstrate a return to normalized ego operations and mature personality organization after substantial periods of sobriety.

Psychological Effects of Drinking

Here we are concerned with how the personality and/or the behavior of the alcoholic changes when drinking. In a word, there is *no uniform* psychological response to drinking. The 1979 report on alcoholism of the British Royal College of Psychiatrists (45) gives a clear account of the variant, opposing, and paradoxical effects of alcohol on affect, cognition, and personality. Some people become less anxious, some more. Some people feel less depressed, some more. Some people become more vivacious, some more withdrawn, etc.

Implications

To posit some universal psychodynamic meaning or common psychodynamic response to the ingestion of alcohol does not square with reported clinical observation. The clinical data suggest that alcohol can serve many different psychodynamic needs and evoke many different psychodynamic responses.

The Pharmacologic-Cognitive Paradigm

Over the past 15 years a number of experimental studies have attempted to differentiate the pharmacologic effect of alcohol on behavior from the psychodynamic meaning of ingesting alcohol. The basic 2 × 2 experimental design is shown in Table 8.

In these experiments we compare alcoholics and normal drinkers as they respond to four different conditions.

In Cell I, subjects are told they will drink alcohol and are given alcohol. Alcoholics respond positively to the drink as a rewarding psychic experience; normals will acknowledge drinking alcohol but not report a positive alcohol effect at a low dose. At a high dose, alcoholics report an accentuation of the positive effect, while normals will report noticing an alcohol effect.

In Cell II, subjects are told they will drink placebo, but are actually given alcohol. At low doses, alcoholics and normals will both report minimal or no response to drinking the alcohol-laden placebo.

In Cell III, subjects are told they will drink alcohol, but in fact are given placebo. Here alcoholics respond as if they had drunk alcohol. Normals report no effect.

TABLE 8
The Pharmacologic-Cognitive Research Paradigm
(Low-Dose Ethanol Condition)

	Told Alcohol	Told Placebo
Given Alcohol	I Alcoholic (+ +) Normal (0)	II Alcoholic (±) Normal (0)
Given Placebo	III Alcoholic (+ +) Normal (0)	IV Alcoholic (0) Normal (0)

(+) = perceived rewarding alcohol drinking experience
(0) = no perceived effect

In Cell IV, subjects are told they will drink placebo and are given placebo. Neither the alcoholics nor normals report an effect.

Implications

This type of experimental data demonstrates that the normal drinker gives little symbolic or connotative meaning to alcohol, whereas the alcoholic is more sensitive to small pharmacologic effects of alcohol which are enhanced by the symbolic meaning of drinking. Further, the alcoholic will experience the same immediate psychic reward from drinking in the absense of actual alcohol. The alcoholic differs from the normal in that the alcoholic has a *dual* accentuated pharmacologic and psychologic response to drinking. We may infer from this that alcoholismic drinking is maintained by both the pharmacologic and symbolic psychologic effects of drinking.

Overall Summary Evaluation

The available empirical data do *not* support the contention that there is a uniform alcoholic personality, or a common character disorder, or a uniform pattern of fixation or regression, or a uniform pattern of psychodynamics. There are apparently different psychodynamic uses of and responses to alcohol ingestion.

SOURCES OF CONFUSION

As we have seen, the several clinical theories present widely divergent conclusions about the personality of the alcoholic. At the same time, the empirical database does not support any one theory, although each theory has some relevant empirical support. So let us review three major sources of confusion in theory building: a) clinical data interpretation; b) definitions of alcoholism, and c) definitions of personality/character disorder.

Clinical Data Interpretation

Here I refer to who the clinician observes, what is observed or not observed, and what interpretations are made of the clinical observations.

First, alcoholism has not been a major domain of interest to psychiatry, either clinically or theoretically. Freud made six passing allusions to alcoholism in his collected works—no definitive statements. The clinical base in psychiatry has been developed only over the past 20 years and it is a limited data set.

Second, most alcoholics are not amenable to classic and traditional forms of psychotherapy and psychoanalysis. This has had a twofold effect: 1) The major clinical theorists have often treated few alcoholics from which to generate clinical theory; 2) the alcoholics seen in psychodynamic psychotherapy are an atypical, biased, and skewed sample of all alcoholics, leading to spurious theoretical dynamic formulations not generalizable to all alcoholic subpopulations.

Third, alcoholics are often seen in psychotherapy, but the therapist does not identify the alcoholism problem and consequently fails to acquire clinical data on the psychodynamics of alcoholism. In a 1979 survey of a metropolitan mental health center, 23 percent of a random sample of psychotherapy patients had substantial drug or alcohol abuse, yet only 3.5 percent of these were identified by their own therapist (46).

Example: A world famous musician was referred to me by a psychoanalyst in another city when the patient moved to my town. The patient arrived in my office complaining of inability to perform because he became too drunk to play. He had been in analysis for five years for a performance phobia, of which he had been cured, but his alcoholism had become progressively worse during the analysis. When I asked him how his analyst interpreted this progressive alcoholism, he informed me that his analyst never knew he drank any alcohol!

Fourth, there is a large information gap between the researchers and the clinicians in the field of alcoholism. Neither camp of theorists reads the literature of the other, if we go by the discussion and literature citations. They remain isolated theoretical domains without substantial cross-fertilization, much less communications.

Fifth, psychiatry has tended to consider alcoholism as a symptom of some other psychiatric disorder and has thereby overlooked the existence of alcoholism as a distinct mental disorder. DSM-III, for the first time, clearly defines and classifies alcoholism apart from any necessary association with another psychiatric disorder (47). In his review of the relationship between alcoholism and psychiatric disorder, Solomon (48) recently concluded: "There is no evidence to substantiate a general theory of alcoholism and psychiatric disorders. Alcoholism can mask, mimic, precipitate, or independently coexist with the gamut of psychiatric disorders" (p. 65).

Sixth, the clinician usually encounters the alcoholic somewhat far along an alcoholismic career; often the patient is drunk, drinking, or suffering chronic neuropsychologic deficits from drinking. The cross-sectional view of the alcoholic gives a spurious psychodynamic picture of the alcoholic as compared to longitudinal data on alcoholic personality and psychodynamics.

Seventh, the cross-sectional clinical view of the acute alcoholic—a clinical picture which may persist for six months—is a contaminated clinical database. We cannot accurately separate out pharmacologic effects from psychologic effects; we cannot differentiate clearly between clinical features due to character fixation or character regression. The misleading nature of the acute morbid state of the alcoholic is demonstrated by Vaillant and Milofsky (49), who found that the severity of acute clinical features was *not* predictive of treatment response or clinical outcome. This has been substantiated independently by Costello (50) and Moos et al. (51).

Eighth, in the clinical arena it is difficult to separate the pharmacologic effects of alcohol on psychic operation, the symbolic and connotative meanings of alcohol ingestion, the psychodynamic adaptational uses of alcohol, and the reactive psychic adaptions to an alcoholismic lifestyle in one's environment. Evaluation of each requires analysis in a "quasi-experimental" matrix of multi-trait and multi-method sets of data (52, 53).

Ninth, the clinician is vulnerable to misinterpretation of cause and effect when he observes a clinical *correlation*. For example, most acute alcoholics are clinically depressed. There is a high correlation. This does not mean that depression is the cause of alcoholism. In the United States there is a high significant correlation between alcoholism and criminality. For example, Anglin (54) notes: "A strong correlation exists between alcohol use and crime . . . but they are not causally related . . . the association is through a common cause . . . under circumstances of culture, person, place, and situation'' (p. 392). The same is true of homosexuality. There is an increased incidence of alcohol abuse among homosexuals, but not homosexuality among alcoholics. Here the alcohol abuse appears related to special adaptational uses of alcohol in the social processes of a homosexual lifestyle (55).

Tenth, the clinician and the alcoholic patient may be prone to *explain* current psychodynamic and clinical features in terms of early development and character traits. As Vaillant (17) astutely comments:

> What alcoholics tell us and what actually transpires are not congruent. In *retrospect* the alcoholic's use of alcohol seems symptomatic of disordered personality, childhood pain, and the need for a chemical anodyne. But when studied *prospectively*, the loss of control over alcohol comes first and the alcoholic's explanations seem like mere rationalizations (p. 40).

To this I would add that the clinician may also engage in retrospective rationalization as explanation. This presents a major problem in the *logic of clinical inference*. The presence of a fixated character disorder, of childhood developmental conflict, and unconscious symbolism may have *some correlation* with *some types* of alcoholics. But logically that does not imply etiologic significance or define the *degree* of etiologic significance. These factors may be contributory to *risk* or *vulnerability*, but may be logically *neither necessary nor sufficient casual variables*.

Eleventh, both the clinician and the experimentalist collect data on biased population samples. As described earlier, one type of alcoholic is likely to appear at a given type of clinical facility. Therefore, clinical or experimental observations will be biased by virtue of that singular population base. And again, even in the United States our samples are culturally rather homogeneous. When we expand our observations to cross-cultural samples, we encounter substantially different patterns of alcoholism. Thus, our current American theory-building is culturally biased and skewed (56).

Definitions of Alcoholism

The second major source of confusion lies in conceptual debate about what constitutes alcoholism or, more technically, what is the criterion set which shall constitute a diagnosis of alcoholism? Thirty years ago, Jellinek, the pioneer in alcoholism diagnosis, noted the limits to a purely descriptive diagnosis and warned of the need to operationally circumscribe the denotation of "alcoholism." Said Jellinek (57):

The lay public uses the term "alcoholism" as a designation for any form of excessive drinking, instead of a label for a limited and well-defined area of excessive drinking behavior. Automatically, the disease concept of alcoholism becomes extended to all excessive drinking, irrespective of whether or not there is any physical or psychological pathology involved in the drinking behavior. Such an unwarranted extension of the disease conception can only be harmful because, sooner or later, the misapplication will reflect on the legitimate use too and, more importantly, will tend to weaken the social sanctions against drunkenness (p. 24).

But the issue remains with us after 30 years. The 1979 Report on Alcohol and Alcoholism by the Royal College of Psychiatrists (45) states:

The word "alcoholism" is in common use, but at the same time there is general uncertainty about its meaning. Where is the dividing line between heavy drinking and this "illness"? Is it a matter of quantity drunk or damage sustained, or what else besides? This confusion is not limited to the layman, for final clarification has eluded the many experts and expert committees that have grappled with the terms to be used about drinking problems (p. 7).

Among most alcohol research experts today there is general agreement that there is no "unitary" entity of alcoholism. Rather, alcoholism is a "multivariate syndrome" (58-61). That is, there are persons with different personality and character features who use, misuse, and abuse alcohol in different patterns, that result in different patterns of adverse consequences. There is *no one* alcoholism syndrome, but *multiple* alcoholism syndromes, ranging from mild to severe, from acute to chronic, from simple to complex. Pattison et al. (62) have devoted a book to an analysis of the empirical data and theoretical formulation of alcoholism as a multivariate syndrome.

Obviously, this conceptual and definitional problem is clinically important. All of our current diagnostic criteria for the diagnosis of alcoholism (DSM-III, NCA, MAST, BMAST, etc.) are *binary* diagnostic instruments. That is, they lead to only one diagnostic conclusion: the person is or is not alcoholic. The limits of diagnosis of an alcoholic are therefore imbedded in the criterion items of each instrument, which vary, and hence the "sample" who will be diagnosed as alcoholic varies with each instrument (63). Therefore, *binary* diagnosis is not particularly useful for clinical research. As Miller (64) has observed, the utility of an alcoholism diagnosis is the definition of clusters of consistently inter-correlated sets of symptoms (subtypes), with associated implications for etiology, prognosis, treatment, and prevention. Miller concludes: "A large amount of information is lost when the data regarding various aspects of the problem are

TABLE 9
Pattison Ten-Factor Alcoholism Profile

Factor 1.	Alcohol Consumption
Factor 2.	Drinking Behavior
Factor 3.	Psychic Dependence
Factor 4.	Physical Dependence
Factor 5.	Physical Consequences
Factor 6.	Emotional Consequences
Factor 7.	Interpersonal Consequences
Factor 8.	Vocational Consequences
Factor 9.	Informal Social Consequences
Factor 10.	Formal Legal Consequences

reduced to a binary nomenclature. Certainly this cannot improve our prediction of such complex events as treatment outcome'' (p. 667).

The need for a multivariate diagnostic approach to alcoholism has spawned a number of attempts to construct diagnostic typologies, none of which has received wide acceptance or use to date. For illustration, I have constructed the 10-factor diagnostic profile of alcoholism shown in Table 9. Each factor represents one dimension of alcoholism. Any specific alcoholic might have a combination of different factor loadings, producing a "syndrome profile," much like an MMPI profile. Given such a profile, we ask the empirical research question: What is the relationship between a specific alcoholism syndrome profile and personality/character disorder?

In summary, the day is past to look for simple associations between alcoholism and character disorder because there are many types of alcoholism. The relationship must be explored in terms of specific alcoholic syndromes.

Definition of Personality Disorders

The other side of the equation is the nature of personality disorders. This is equally a conceptual quagmire.

In DSM-III we have a multiaxial diagnostic process. On Axis II we are offered 11 Personality Disorder diagnoses. It is tempting to immediately proceed to investigate the relationship between alcoholism syndromes and each of these 11 Personality Disorders; however, I doubt the wisdom or utility of such a research strategy because it is not clear just what the 11 categories represent.

In their classic textbook on personality theory, Hall and Lindzey (65) note that personality theory stands apart from experimental psychology: It is functional in orientation; it assigns a crucial role to motivational processes and usually to selfpsychology; it involves a study of the whole person, and, above all, it stands as an *integrative theory of human behavior.*

In contrast, DSM-III approaches personality apart from theory. It speaks of personality *traits* as styles of interaction with the environment and with oneself. When such traits are maladaptive and/or dysfunctional, then the traits are said to constitute a personality *disorder*. In DSM-III the 11 disorders represent a descriptive collation of phenotypical behavior.

This raises important questions. Are the 11 DSM-III personality disorders an adequate and coherent set of diagnostic categories? Or are they classes of convenience or familiarity? Is there any theoretical coherence to DSM-III Axis II that relates the diagnosis of personality disorder to personality theory? Millon, who served on the Axis II task force, has written a remarkable book on these issues (66), which shows that each Axis II personality disorder can coexist or combine with several Axis I or Axis II disorders, resulting in over 100 intact, clinically distinct pictures! At the same time Millon shows that, although the DSM-III classification of personality disorders lacks theoretical or conceptual coherence, it is possible to theoretically organize personality theory in relation to psychopathology, with due credence to empirical and clinical data.

I cannot address the problems of personality diagnosis here, but merely indicate the substantial inadequacy of the DSM-III format. Therefore, we need to pursue a more rigorous conceptual framework of personality theory if we are to link other clinical phenomena, such as alcoholism, to personality variables.

TOWARD A SYNTHESIS OF ALCOHOLISM AND PERSONALITY

To this point, we have reviewed all of the problems associated with a *simple* or *single* relationship between alcoholism and personality. Nevertheless, our data do support the notion that there are *multiple* and *complex* relationships.

There is much current interest in the attempt to conceptually link clinical personality classes with psychodevelopmental levels, structural psychic organization, and attendant ego processes. Following along the lines proposed by Rinsley (67), I should like to present a clinical formulation of alcoholism syndromes correlated with developmental self psychology and object-relations theory, as shown in Table 10. I shall offer clinical vignettes of these relationships. In this format I have first listed the developmental age level, then diagrammed the object relations, next listed typical personality class labels and the primary psychic functions of alcohol use, and finally offered my best estimate of the percent of alcoholics who may be at a given developmental level.

At the *first level* of development achieved at about 12 months of age, the infant has a stable internalized part-object representation of mother. This level of personality organization is reflected in what we call inadequate personalities or primitive passive-dependent personalities. In severe psychotic regression we observe this level of personality organization.

TABLE 10

Development Personality Structure Correlations with Alcoholism Syndromes

AGE LEVEL	OBJECT RELATIONS	PERSONALITY ORGANIZATION	PRIMARY PSYCHIC FUNCTION OF ALCOHOL USE	ESTIMATED % OF ALCOHOLICS
12 mos.	G | B / S-O | S-O	Inadequate Passive-dependent	Alcohol = part-object 1° psychic incorporation and pleasure	5%
15-24 mos.	G | B / S | S / O | O	Borderline	Alcohol = transitional object 1° psychic whole object representation	10%
2-3 yrs.	S | O / G | G / B | B	Sociopath Narcissist	Alcohol = 1° pleasure object due to pharmacologic effect	15%
3-5 yrs.	S | O / G | G / B | B	"Neurotic Character" Paranoid Histrionic Obsessional Schizoid	Alcohol = "internal" coping device	15%
Adult	Mature	"Normal personality variation"	Alcohol = "external" coping device normless drinking (culture crisis) reactive drinking (crisis, aged) normed alcoholismic drinking	55%

Here we observe the use of alcohol as a primary psychological symbol. Bottle equals breast. Drinking provides both a pleasurable pharmacologic effect and a pleasurable psychological effect.

At this level we see little adverse behavior as a consequence of drinking and drinking is pursued only if alcohol is readily available. Many skid-row alcoholics present with this personality organization. They drink cheap wine or beer, but usually do not get drunk. They may go to sleep cradling an empty bottle in their arms, like a baby falling asleep sated at the breast. Usually their life history is one of aimless drifting with no social/vocational accomplishment.

Example: A 50-year-old single male had been arrested 200 times for public intoxication. He had dropped out of grade school, worked sporadically at manual labor for a few years, and had lived for 30 years on skid-row. He drank when he had money. He never misbehaved unless drinking.

Example: A 40-year-old single male lived with his mother. He had dropped out of high school and lived at home since. He occasionally did odd jobs, but mostly watched television. He drank several quarts of milk daily and ate cookies baked daily by his mother. When he had money he drank beer instead of milk. He weighed 300 pounds. He was seen for 200 hours of psychotherapy in an alcoholism clinic and discharged unimproved. He never misbehaved when drinking.

The *second level* of development is the rapprochement phase of individuation-separation from the mother. Here we have the primary good-object, bad-object split. The child learns to tolerate the absence of mother with a stabilized internal whole object representation of mother fused with self. Absence of mother triggers rage at abandonment. These are the familiar dynamics of the borderline personality. In this case, alcohol can clearly be used as a transitional object, representing the mother object. Alcohol is both loved and hated. In turn this type of alcoholic both loves and hates his alcoholismic lifestyle.

Example: A 60-year-old male school principal had been alcoholic since age 15. He grew up the youngest of seven sons of a prominent teetotal Baptist family. His father expected high achievement, as attained by all males in the family line. His mother kept him at home all the time and babied him. He entered college at age 15, the first time alone and away from home. At the first school dance he was derided by the girls as a baby-face child. He was offered a drink of vodka, which, he reported, immediately changed his whole experience of himself. He instantly became alcoholic. He graduated from college at age 18, summa cum laude, and consuming a fifth of vodka per day. He married and divorced five times. He did not drink at all early in each marriage, but when his external ambivalence with women disrupted each marriage, he would return to drinking. He became sober during treatment at an alcoholism clinic the day after he started a new flirtation. Alcohol was clearly a lifelong transitional object. He loved drinking and hated himself for drinking.

The *third level* of development I shall assign to the second and third years. Here there is primary self-object differentiation. Other persons and objects are used and manipulated for one's own self-satisfaction. I shall assign the narcissistic and sociopathic personalities to this level. Here alcohol is typically used because the pharmacologic effect provides a primary pleasurable experience. But the use of alcohol often triggers socially adverse behavior, with increased self-aggrandizement, increased manipulation, aggression, and control of others, etc., resulting in narcissistic rage behavior and/or criminal acts. These persons feel *entitled* to drink so that they can experience themselves with more *entitlement*.

Example: A 55-year-old salesman had completed college and embarked on a successful sales career. He found that he enjoyed luncheon cocktail drinking with clients because he could get clients drunk and sell his product, while at the same time he drank and felt more powerful and able to manipulate his clients. His drinking escalated to the point that he lost control over his luncheon drinking behavior and lost sales, status, and power in his company. He then entered AA and remained abstinent for 10 years. He still presented as an intensely narcissistic character who charmingly manipulated everyone. Clinicians thought he had just stopped drinking because of his pervasive use of denial, projection, and rationalization about his life. He stopped drinking because it posed more of a threat than an asset to his self-image. He is now president of his company.

Example: A 30-year-old male college professor was referred for treatment of drinking in the classroom. He had published four books and was already internationally renowned. He presented as vain, egocentric, preoccupied with his self-important reputation. He drank to reduce his anxiety over maintenance of his brilliant performance. He refused treatment because he had looked up my publication record, which was not as brilliant as his. He concluded he would not waste his time with an inferior and inept therapist like me!

Example: A 30-year-old single male was referred for treatment of alcoholism by a Baptist minister who was pastor for the patient's God-fearing parents. He was on probation for drunken driving. He had started driving at age 14, engaged in petty truancy, and eventually burglary. He had spent five years in prison. He was an only child born in late life to a working-class couple. They had tried to "give him everything we could." They always paid for his truant acts and had never chastised him. On evaluation he was a charming, smooth-talking man who averred that he felt good when he drank. He rationalized away his lifelong criminal career. His crimes always occurred when drinking. He showed no remorse over his life and no concern for the penurious plight of his parents. He promised to enter treatment only if his parents and pastor would provide a set of new clothes and spending money right away. That same evening he came home drunk, stole his parents' welfare check, and drove off in the stolen car of the minister. My diagnosis was sociopathic character disorder.

The *fourth* developmental stage I wish to discuss is the period of roughly four to five years of age. During this period the child begins to deal with other persons not just as objects of personal gain, but as person-objects of value in their own right. At this level, the child develops the capacity for neurotic ego mechanisms to cope with conflict with others and self. Now we are past primary good/bad object splitting. But the child can and does split the conscious good/bad representations of self and other. This neurotic splitting and repression, to follow Fairbairn (68), gives rise to what I shall term the neurotic character disorders: histrionic, paranoid, obsessive, and schizoid. To follow Fairbairn, the histrionic represses the bad self and bad other; the paranoid represses the bad self and good other; the obsessional ruminates over the perceived good/bad in self and other. The schizoid represses awareness of the good/bad in both self and other. I suggest that in these personality types we can observe the use of alcohol as a neurotic adaptive coping device to maintain these self-other splits and repressions. This is *internal* adaptive drinking.

Example—Histrionic: A 42-year-old married mother of three children presented with mysterious, complex psychosomatic facial pain. She loved everyone and denied any problems in her life. She recounted a happy family life and childhood development. She appeared as a "Pollyanna" of normality. Six months of intensive psychotherapy revealed that both parents were alcoholic and an older sister had died of alcoholism. Her intense anger at all three alcoholic family members had been repressed, since she always "feared I would become alcoholic like them." When conflict arose she would drink herself into a stupor to "forget about all the bad things" and "make me and everyone else nice." She was drinking heavily each night. During therapy, with the resolution of the "hysterical splitting," she stopped drinking except for an occasional glass of wine with dinner.

Example—Paranoid: A 32-year-old married black male was a security guard at an atomic bomb plant. He had always been suspicious, mistrustful, jealous, and socially aloof. He would allow no visitors to his home and kept several loaded rifles by the door. He always drank beer at night to "relieve my worries about intruders." His drinking increased over a 10-year period to public bouts of drunkenness in taverns and several fights. He became afraid he might kill someone when drunk and "then they would kill me." Therefore, he sought treatment and requested Antabuse to help him not drink. He refused to participate in any social or therapeutic activities on the alcoholism ward and refused marital therapy. He faithfully took his Antabuse and maintained sobriety. He remained paranoid and returned to work successfully as a security guard.

Example—Obsessional: A 35-year-old surgeon entered treatment because of marital conflict. His third unsuccessful marriage was about to break up. He loved his wife but felt furious about her. He could express neither emotion directly to her. At social gatherings he was frozen by a desire to approach people and fearful of reproach. He drank constantly to reduce his acknowledged internal anxiety and ambivalence. When drinking he could express small amounts of emotion to others. His obsessional approach-avoidance behavior was clearly linked to early conflictual relations with both mother and father. After a year of intensive psychoanalytic psychotherapy he had achieved major resolution of his obsessional ambivalence and had stopped drinking, except for one drink on special occasions.

Example—Schizoid: A 52-year-old single female was admitted for her fourth hospitalization in four years for acute alcoholic blackouts. She was an only child. Her father was alcoholic, her mother a nurse. During high school she helped nurse her father until he died. She never dated and was a social isolate. She became a well-paid computer programmer, but work was her whole life. She rarely attended any social functions. She started drinking at home alone after work to "reduce my anxiety about doing my job right." As her job demands grew, she socialized even less, worked longer hours, and drank more steadily. Five years previously she quit her job to move to her hometown, where her mother was retired. They lived next door to each other, said hello each day, but otherwise avoided each other, because "she and I just don't mix well together." She felt alone in this town and was alone. She felt depressed and drank more, which made her more depressed. In five years her life and physical status had deteriorated dramatically. Her lifelong social isolation left her with no one to turn to, except her mother whom she loved but could not tolerate.

Finally, I have listed at the bottom of my chart a large and significant group of persons who have no demonstrable major character disorder, although they may have high-risk personality traits and/or vulnerable ego operations of some degree. Here we can posit different personality typologies within the range of "normal personality variation." They engage in "*external* adaptive drinking."

Such persons may well drink alcohol sporadically or intermittently throughout their life without difficulty, unless or until environmental interactions make it feasible or quasi-adaptive to use alcohol to cope with intercurrent exigencies. Rather than alcohol use being an "internal coping device," it is used as an "external coping device." In these cases, the social reinforcement of alcoholismic drinking becomes important, while the direct pharmacologic effects of drinking create adverse social consequences and adverse degradation of psychic operations.

Examples of these types of alcoholism syndromes would include:

a) Normless drinking in small societies undergoing cultural disorganization;
b) Alcoholismic situational drinking in response to life crises, such as war, disasters, massive life stress, etc.;
c) Alcoholismic drinking in response to psychosocial loss and social isolation, as is commonly seen among the aged;
d) Alcoholismic drinking as a small group norm.

Overall, I would like to call attention to the last column in Table 10, where I have projected my best estimate of the distribution of alcoholism syndromes along a developmental continuum. The most primitive fixated character disorders found on skid-row account for no more than five percent of all alcoholics, while the distribution of all other definable "character disorders" is a rough guess of order of magnitude. The majority of alcoholics would appear to lie in our last category of relatively normal personalities.

CONCLUSIONS AND SUMMÁRY

My analysis of the relationship between alcoholism and personality disorders fails to sustain a simple or single relationship. Current theoretical positions are incompatible with the empirical data. Yet each theoretical formulation reflects some clinical reality.

Distinctive alcoholism syndromes are clinically correlated with different developmental personality disorders, but we do not have a precise correlational distribution.

Personality development may increase the vulnerability and risk for the development of an alcoholism syndrome, but personality structure or ego process alone cannot be judged as primary or sole etiologic factors.

The alcoholic personality may demonstrate fixation or regression. The pharmacologic effects of alcohol can produce personality deterioration and maladaptive reactive ego defenses, as can the person's responses and adaptation to an alcoholismic lifestyle.

Alcoholic persons demonstrate many different psychodynamic patterns, substantially different psychic uses of alcohol, and variable psychic responses to the pharmacologic effects of alcohol. In summary, I do find that there is a relationship between alcoholism and personality, but it is a complex combination of multiple variables.

REFERENCES

1. SUTHERLAND, F.H., SCHROEDER, H.G., and TORDELLA, C.L.: Personality traits and the alcoholic. *Quart. J. Stud. Alc.*, 11: 547-561, 1950.
2. SYME, L.: Personality characteristics and the alcoholic. *Quart. J. Stud. Alc.*, 18: 288-302, 1957.
3. FENICHEL, O.: *The Psychoanalytic Theory of Neurosis.* New York: W.W. Norton, 1945.
4. RADO, S.: The psychoanalysis of pharmacothymia. *Psychoanal. Quart.*, 2: 1-23, 1933.
5. CHEIN, I., GERARD, D.L., LEE, R.S., and ROSENFELD, E.: *The Road to H: Narcotics, Delinquency, and Social Policy.* New York: Basic Books, 1964.
6. MARSHALL, M. (Ed.): *Beliefs, Behaviors, and Alcoholic Beverages: A Cross-Cultural Survey.* Ann Arbor: University of Michigan Press, 1979.
7. KNIGHT, R.P.: The psychodynamics of chronic alcoholism. *J. Nerv. Ment. Dis.*, 86: 538-548, 1937.
8. BALINT, M.: *The Basic Fault.* London: Tavistock, 1968.
9. KERNBERG, O.: *Borderline Conditions and Pathological Narcissism.* New York: Jason Aronson, 1975.
10. KOHUT, H.: *The Analysis of the Self.* New York: International Universities Press, 1971.
11. KRYSTAL, H.: Character disorders: Characterological specificity and the alcoholic. In: E.M. Pattison, and E. Kaufman (Eds.), *Encyclopedic Handbook of Alcoholism.* New York: Gardner, 1982.
12. HARTOCOLLIS, P.: Borderline syndrome and alcoholism. In: E.M. Pattison, and E. Kaufman (Eds.), *Encyclopedic Handbook of Alcoholism.* New York: Gardner, 1982.
13. WURMSER, L.: *The Hidden Dimension: Psychodynamics in Compulsive Drug Use.* New York: Jason Aronson, 1978.
14. MACK, J.C.: Alcoholism, A.A., and the governance of the self. In: M.H. Bean, and N.E. Zinberg (Eds.), *Dynamic Approaches to the Understanding and Treatment of Alcoholism.* New York: Free Press, 1981.
15. KHANTZIAN, E.J.: Psychopathology, psychodynamics, and alcoholism. In: E.M. Pattison, and E. Kaufman (Eds.), *Encyclopedic Handbook of Alcoholism.* New York: Gardner, 1982.
16. BEAN, M.H.: Denial and the psychological complications of alcoholism. In: M.H. Bean, and N.E. Zinberg (Eds.), *Dynamic Approaches to the Understanding and Treatment of Alcoholism.* New York: Free Press, 1981.
7. VAILLANT, G.E.: Dangers of psychotherapy in the treatment of alcoholism. In: M.H. Bean, and N.E. Zinberg (Eds.), *Dynamic Approaches to the Understanding and Treatment of Alcoholism.* New York: Free Press, 1981.
18. ZIMBERG, S.: Psychotherapy in the treatment of alcoholism. In: E.M. Pattison, and

114   *Character Pathology: Theory and Treatment*

E. Kaufman (Eds.), *Encyclopedic Handbook of Alcoholism*. New York: Gardner, 1982.

19. NATHAN, P.E., MARLATT, G.A., and LOBERT, T.: *Alcoholism: New Directions in Behavioral Research and Treatment*. New York: Plenum, 1978.

20. VOGEL, W.H.: Chemical and pharmacological correlates of alcohol-seeking behavior. In: E. Gottheil, A.T. McLellan, and K.A. Druley (Eds.), *Matching Patient Needs and Treatment Methods in Alcoholism and Drug Abuse*. Springfield, IL: Charles C Thomas, 1981.

21. BACON, M.K.: Alcohol use in tribal societies. In: B. Kissin, and H. Begleiter (Eds.), *Social Aspects of Alcoholism*. New York: Plenum, 1976.

22. KLAUSNER, S.Z., FOULKES, E.F., and MOORE, M.H.: *Social Change and the Alcohol Problem on the Alaskan North Slope*. Philadelphia: Center for Research on Acts of Man, 1980.

23. GREELEY, A.M., McCREADY, W.C., and THEISEN, G.: *Ethnic Drinking Subcultures*. New York: Praeger, 1980.

24. MARLATT, G.A. and DONOVAN, D.M.: Behavioral psychology approaches to alcoholism. In: E.M. Pattison, and E. Kaufman (Eds.), *Encyclopedic Handbook of Alcoholism*. New York: Gardner, 1982.

25. POMERLEAU, O.: Current behavioral therapies in the treatment of alcoholism. In: E. M. Pattison, and E. Kaufman (Eds.), *Encyclopedic Handbook of Alcoholism*. New York: Gardner, 1982.

26. CADDY, G.R.: Evaluation of behavioral methods in the study of alcoholism. In: E.M. Pattison, and E. Kaufman (Eds.), *Encyclopedic Handbook of Alcoholism*. New York: Gardner, 1982.

27. CAHALAN, D., and CISIN, I.H.: Drinking behavior and drinking problems in the United States. In: B. Kissin, and H. Begleiter (Eds.), *Social Aspects of Alcoholism*. New York: Plenum, 1976.

28. SKINNER, H.A.: Profiles in treatment-seeking populations. In: G. Edwards, and M. Grant (Eds.), *Alcoholism Treatment in Transition*. Baltimore: University Park Press, 1980.

29. OGBORNE, A.C.: Patient characteristics as predictors of treatment outcomes for alcohol and drug abusers. In: Y. Israel, et al. (Eds.), *Research Advances in Alcohol and Drug Problems, Vol. 4*. New York: Plenum, 1978.

30. WILLIAMS, A.F.: The alcoholic personality. In: B. Kissin, and H. Begleiter (Eds.), *Social Aspects of Alcoholism*. New York: Plenum, 1976.

31. BARRY, H., III: A psychological perspective on development of alcoholism. In: E.M. Pattison, and E. Kaufman (Eds.), *Encyclopedic Handbook of Alcoholism*. New York: Gardner, 1982.

32. COSTELLO, R.M.: Alcoholism and the "alcoholic" personality. In: R.E. Meyer, et al. (Eds.), *Evaluation of the Alcoholic*. Research Monograph No. 5. Washington, D.C.: NIAAA, 1980.

33. KAMMEIER, M.L., HOFFMAN, H., and LOPER, R.G.: Personality characteristics of alcoholics as college freshmen and at time of treatment. *Quart. J. Stud. Alc.*, 34: 390-399, 1973.

34. McCORD, W., and McCORD, J.: *Origins of Alcoholism*. Stanford: Stanford University Press, 1960.

35. ROBINS, L.N.: *Deviant Children Grown Up*. Baltimore: Williams & Wilkins, 1966.

36. VAILLANT, G.E.: Natural history of male psychological health: VIII. Antecedents of alcoholism and "orality." *Am. J. Psychiat.*, 137: 181-186, 1980.

37. PATTISON, E.M. (Ed.): *Selection of Treatment for Alcoholics*. NIAAA-RUCAS Monograph No. 1. New Brunswick: Rutgers, 1982.
38. PATTISON, E.M., COE, R., and DOERR, H.O.: Population variation among alcoholism treatment facilities. *Int. J. Addict.* 8: 199-229, 1973.
39. THORNTON, C.C., GOTTHEIL, E., GELLENS, H.K., and ALTERMAN, A.I.: Developmental level and treatment response in male alcoholics. In: E. Gottheil, A.T. McLellan, and K.A. Druley (Eds.), *Matching Patient Needs and Treatment Methods in Alcoholism and Drug Abuse*. Springfield, IL: Charles C Thomas, 1981.
40. ZUCKER, R.A.: Developmental aspects of drinking through the young adult years. In: H.T. Blane, and M.L. Chafetz (Eds.), *Youth, Alcohol, and Social Policy*. New York: Plenum, 1979.
41. MELLO, N.K.: The role of aversive consequences in the control of alcohol and drug self-administration. In: R.E. Meyer, et al. (Eds.), *Evaluation of the Alcoholic*. Research Monograph No. 5, Washington, D.C.: NIAAA, 1980.
42. GOLDSTEIN, G., and NEURINGER, C. (Eds.): *Empirical Studies of Alcoholism*. Cambridge, MA.: Ballinger, 1976.
43. MAKELA, K.: Levels of consumption and social consequences of drinking. In: Y. Israel, et al. (Eds.), *Research Advances in Alcohol and Drug Problems, Vol. 4*. New York: Plenum, 1978.
44. SULKUNEN, P.: Drinking patterns and the level of alcohol consumption: An international overview. In: R.J. Gibbin, et al. (Eds.), *Research Advances in Alcohol and Drug Problems, Vol. 3*. New York: Wiley, 1976.
45. ROYAL COLLEGE OF PSYCHIATRISTS: *Alcohol and Alcoholism*. New York: Free Press, 1979.
46. CUMMINGS, N.W.: Turning bread into stone: A modern anti-miracle. *Am. Psychol.*, 34: 1119-1129, 1979.
47. ROBINS, L.N.: The diagnosis of alcoholism after DSM-III. In: R.E. Meyer, et al. (Eds.), *Evaluation of the Alcoholic*. Research Monograph No. 5, Washington, D.C.: NIAAA, 1980.
48. SOLOMON, J. (Ed.): *Alcoholism and Clinical Psychiatry*. New York: Plenum, 1982.
49. VAILLANT, G.E., and MILOFSKY, E.S.: The etiology of alcoholism: A prospective viewpoint. *Am. Psychol.*, 37: 494-503, 1982.
50. COSTELLO, R.M.: Evaluation of post-hospital adjustment: Path analysis of causal chains. *Eval. Health Prof.*, 1: 83-93, 1978.
51. MOOS, R.H., CRONKITE, R.C., and FINNEY, J.W.: A conceptual framework for alcoholism treatment evaluation. In: E.M. Pattison, and E. Kaufman (Eds.), *Encyclopedic Handbook of Alcoholism*. New York: Gardner, 1982.
52. CAMPBELL, D.T., and O'CONNELL, E.J.: Method factors in multitrait multimethod matrices: Multiplicative rather than additive? *Multivar. Behav. Res.*, 2: 409-426, 1967.
53. CAMPBELL, D.T., and STANLEY, J.C.: *Experimental and Quasiexperimental Designs for Research*. Chicago: Rand McNally, 1966.
54. ANGLIN, M.D.: Alcohol and criminality. In: E.M. Pattison, and E. Kaufman (Eds.), *Encyclopedic Handbook of Alcoholism*. New York: Gardner, 1982.
55. BRANDSMA, J.M., and PATTISON, E.M.: Homosexuality and alcoholism. In: E.M. Pattison, and E. Kaufman (Eds.), *Encyclopedic Handbook of Alcoholism*. New York: Gardner, 1982.
56. PATTISON, E.M.: Alcohol use: Social policy. In: E.M. Pattison, and E. Kaufman (Eds.), *Encyclopedic Handbook of Alcoholism*. New York: Gardner, 1982.

116 *Character Pathology: Theory and Treatment*

57. JELLINEK, E.M.: Phases of alcohol addiction. *Quart. J. Stud. Alco.*, 13: 673-684, 1952.
58. DAVIES, D.L.: Defining alcoholism. In: M. Grant (Ed.), *Alcoholism in Perspective.* Baltimore: University Park Press, 1977.
59. EDWARDS, G.: The alcohol dependence syndrome: Usefulness of an idea. In: G. Edwards, and M. Grant (Eds.), *Alcoholism: New Knowledge and New Responses.* Baltimore: University Park Press, 1977.
60. KISSIN, B.: Theory and practice in the treatment of alcoholism. In: B. Kissin, and H. Begleiter (Eds.), *Treatment and Rehabilitation of the Chronic Alcoholic.* New York: Plenum, 1977.
61. HORN, J.L.: Comments on the many faces of alcoholism. In: P.E. Nathan, G.A. Marlatt, and T. Lorbert (Eds.), *Alcoholism: New Directions in Behavioral Research and Treatment.* New York: Plenum, 1978.
62. PATTISON, E.M., SOBELL, M.B., and SOBELL, L.C.: *Emerging Concepts of Alcohol Dependence.* New York: Springer, 1977.
63. PATTISON, E.M., and KAUFMAN, E.: The alcoholism syndrome: Definitions and models. In: E.M. Pattison, and E. Kaufman (Eds.), *Encyclopedic Handbook of Alcoholism.* New York: Gardner, 1982.
64. MILLER, W.R.: Alcoholism scales and objective assessment methods: A review. *Psychol. Bull.*, 83: 649-674, 1976.
65. HALL, C.S., and LINDZEY, G.: *Theories of Personality.* New York: J. Wiley, 1957.
66. MILLON, T.: *Disorders of Personality: DSM-III: Axis II.* New York: J. Wiley, 1981.
67. RINSLEY, D.B.: *Borderline and Other Self Disorders.* New York: Jason Aronson, 1982.
68. FAIRBAIRN, W.R.D.: *An Object-Relations Theory of Personality.* New York: Basic Books, 1954.

Part III

TREATMENT APPROACHES

7

Assessing the Suitability of Patients With Character Disorders for Insight Psychotherapy

Peter E. Sifneos, M.D.
and John C. Nemiah, M.D.

INTRODUCTION

The widespread interest in narcissistic phenomena has led clinicians in recent years to view the term "character disorder" as synonymous with "narcissistic" or "borderline character disorder." It should be remembered, however, that in a larger sense the term "character disorder" (as Sarwer-Foner points out in Chapter 1) refers to a wide spectrum of characterological disturbances ranging from the psychotic to the neurotic. The focus of most of the authors represented in these pages is on individuals who, if not frankly psychotic, are afflicted with serious distortions of their character structure characterized by developmentally primitive defenses, problems with identity, and defective object relations that significantly disrupt their ability to love and live with their fellow human beings.

In this chapter we shall shift our attention to the neurotic end of the spectrum. Here we shall be dealing with individuals whose basic capacity for satisfying human relationships is intact. Their pathological character traits and disturbed relationships are the result not primarily of defects in their ego structure, but of neurotic inhibitions and defenses that prevent them from achieving their underlying potential for mature relationships. Such patients are able to reach a successful resolution of their psychological conflicts through insight psychotherapy, often in a short period of time. Our aim here is to examine the nature of these neurotic character disorders and to define those psychological features of the patients who suffer from them that constitute the criteria for their selection for insight psychotherapy. In so doing, we shall at the same time throw into relief the features of the more serious narcissistic and borderline character disorders; the contrast will help to sharpen our perception and definition of the major personality distortions in this latter group of patients.

THE NATURE OF INSIGHT PSYCHOTHERAPY

The techniques of insight psychotherapy are derived from the psychodynamic theory of psychopathology. In this theoretical model, symptoms and character traits are viewed as being the products of a psychological conflict between the drives (and their derivative emotions and fantasies) and the ego defenses that contain and modify them. A central feature of psychodynamic theory is the postulate that many of the conflicting psychological processes are unconscious—that is, they occur outside of the individual's conscious awareness and beyond his voluntary control. The aim of insight psychotherapy is to help the individual to become consciously aware of the previously unconscious elements of the conflict. Through the emotional insight thus gained, he is enabled to achieve a new and more adaptive psychological equilibrium, with a consequent disappearance of symptoms and neurotic behavior patterns and an improvement in his human relationships.

In the early phase of its development, psychoanalysis, the prototype and most intensive form of the insight psychotherapies, was applied only to the transference neuroses—that is, to patients suffering from hysteria, phobias, and obsessive-compulsive disorders. This was the group of patients whose illnesses had given rise to the discovery of psychodynamic processes in the first place, and in view of the rich network of conscious and unconscious associations that underlay their symptoms, it is not surprising that they were particularly fitted to conform to the requirements of psychoanalytic techniques.

The enthusiasm engendered in early analytic clinicians by the therapeutic effectiveness of psychoanalysis with this more restricted set of neuroses eventually led to its application to a wider range of emotional disorders. Patients with a variety of severe character disorders and even with frank psychotic illness came with increasing frequency to the analyst's couch. Although these clinical encounters were often unsuccessful, the opportunity to observe sicker patients in an analytic setting directed attention to the psychopathology of the ego as manifested in the developmental defects in ego functions, primitive defense mechanisms, and narcissistic disturbances in identity and object relations that are the focus of modern psychoanalytic investigation (1-5) and are extensively described elsewhere in this volume.

It was early recognized that modifications, or "parameters," in classical analytic techniques were required to meet the therapeutic needs of such patients (6-8). Two important developments in theory and practice have resulted from that recognition. The current widespread interest in the treatment of patients with narcissistic and borderline disorders has led to an increased understanding of the nature of the therapeutic parameters that either replace or form a necessary prelude to the application of more classical psychoanalytic procedures. At the same time, it has been possible to define more clearly the specific psychological capacities that enable an individual to make effective use of classical psychoanalysis, as well as of the insight psychotherapies that derive from psychoanalysis itself. These capacities constitute the criteria for the selection of patients for insight therapy.

GENERAL CRITERIA FOR INSIGHT PSYCHOTHERAPY

It is now generally agreed that the following attributes are prerequisites for anyone undergoing insight psychotherapy:

1) *Psychological-mindedness:* The patient must have the capacity for an introspective awareness of his inner psychological life. He must be able to see the relation of psychological conflict to symptom formation and to disturbances in his relationship patterns, to associate freely, to see the connections among his associations, and to reflect with curiosity and objectivity on the processes that self-observation reveals to him. In particular, he must have the capacity to create fantasies and to experience emotions and must be able to verbalize both fantasy and feelings to his therapist.

2) *Toleration of affects:* Since insight therapy requires the patient to recognize and resolve psychological conflicts, he will unavoidably be forced to experience painful affects (especially anxiety and depression) during the course of therapy. He must, therefore, be able not only to tolerate these affects but also to deal with them in such a way as to prevent their causing serious disruption of his daily work, behavior, and relationships.

3) *Ability to relate:* The patient must demonstrate the capacity for forming human relationships that go beyond a purely narcissistic attachment. In particular, he must be able to develop and analyze a transference relationship with his therapist, and to view it with psychological distance in alliance with his therapist.

4) *Motivation:* The patient must be motivated to aim in therapy for psychological change and growth rather than limiting his sights merely to relief of symptoms and psychic pain or to borrowing strength and comfort from a supportive relationship.

It should be evident from these criteria that there has been a shift from the earlier emphasis on symptoms (i.e., the presence of a transference neurosis) as the indications for insight therapy to a consideration of character structure in assessing the suitability of individuals for treatment. As a consequence, a central task of the initial evaluation interview is not so much to arrive at a symptom diagnosis as to delineate the nature of the patient's conflicts and ego functions (including his defenses) and the quality of his relationships.

It should be noted, furthermore, that the criteria listed here refer to the suitability of patients for the general category of insight psychotherapy. There are, of course, a number of different kinds of insight psychotherapies, each of which has special, often more restricted indications for its use. During the past two decades considerable clinical effort has been expended in the development of a variety of brief dynamic psychotherapies (9-16). These are distinguished from classical psychoanalysis not only in being far less time-consuming, but also in requiring greater activity on the part of the therapist as he focuses the patient's attention on the central conflict and directly confronts the patient with his pathogenic drives and the defenses with which they are warded off. Clearly, such a therapeutic process subjects the patient to the possibility of experiencing considerable anxiety and is limited in its use to a restricted group of individuals who fulfill special criteria for selection.

In what follows, we shall focus on one form of modern brief dynamic psychotherapy known as short-term anxiety-provoking psychotherapy or STAPP (13). We shall briefly describe the procedures that characterize this treatment, discuss the particular criteria for the selection of suitable patients, and demonstrate with quotations from a videotaped initial interview the manner in which patients are assessed for their suitability for therapy.

SHORT-TERM ANXIETY-PROVOKING PSYCHOTHERAPY

The Techniques of STAPP

Like the other brief therapies, STAPP is more focused and far shorter than classical psychoanalysis, though it rests squarely on the analytic goal of conflict resolution through emotional insight. Generally, the therapeutic task can be accomplished within 10 to 20 treatment sessions, and the patient is informed at the beginning that the number of hours will be limited, without, however, being given an exact figure. Initially, through encouraging the predominantly positive transference feelings the patient brings to treatment, the therapist establishes a strong working alliance as a secure base for the subsequent course of the therapy.

Throughout the treatment the therapist is continuously active in a variety of ways. He maintains a consistent focus on the specified central psychodynamic problem (either an unresolved Oedipal conflict or a pathological grief reaction) and studiously avoids dealing with pregenital characterological issues in order to prevent severe regressive transference reactions. Through anxiety-provoking confrontations, clarifications, and interpretations, the therapist helps the patient to achieve insight into his drives and the defenses employed to contain them. At the same time he repeatedly directs the patient's attention to the associative links and similarities of the patient's feelings for and his patterns of relationships with significant persons in his past and present, including the therapist as the transference develops.

As the therapy progresses, the patient learns new methods of problem-solving, which are manifested in the emergence of freer and more flexible patterns of behavior, more mature and gratifying human relationships, and healthier, more realistic attitudes. These changes are systematically documented by the therapist as indications of a resolution of the focal conflict leading to the termination of treatment.

Special Criteria for the Selection of Patients for STAPP

In addition to the general criteria listed above that determine a patient's suitability for insight psychotherapy, STAPP has several additional prerequisites.

1) *Circumscribed chief complaint:* First and foremost, the patient must be able to select one specific area of conflict as a focus for therapy. This is not to imply that the patient does not have other problems. These, however, will not be dealt with in the treatment, and the patient must, therefore, have sufficient ego strength to choose and assign priority to the primary conflict, and, because of time constraints, to forego attention to the secondary problems. The target problem, furthermore, must be the result of conflicts deriving from the Oedipal or genital phases of development.

2) *Documentation of a meaningful childhood relationship:* The patient must give evidence of at least one meaningful relationship during his childhood. This will usually have been with a parent, but may occasionally have centered on a grandparent or other person in a significant caretaking role. In the initial diagnostic interview, the therapist must actively search for a history of such a relationship, and must elicit documentation that at this early stage of life the patient was capable of forming an altruistic, give-and-take, loving tie to another person. The history of such a relationship provides assurance that the patient will form a relatively mature transference with the therapist unencumbered by serious narcissistic elements that pose a threat of unmanageable regressions during the course of therapy.

3) *Motivation:* Motivation is, of course, a vital ingredient for the success of

any form of insight psychotherapy. For the briefer types of therapy particularly, it has been convincingly shown in clinical studies that motivation for psychological change, not just symptom relief, correlates strongly with a favorable therapeutic outcome (11, 12). It is, therefore, of special importance to assess the nature and degree of such motivation in evaluating potential candidates for brief therapy. The following criteria are specifically aimed at making such an assessment:

a) The patient must be able to recognize that his difficulties are psychological in nature.
b) He must have a capacity for introspection and for truthful reporting of his self-observations.
c) He must have a curiosity about his inner psychological functioning and a desire for self-understanding.
d) He must have a willingness to change, to explore his conflicts, and to experiment with new ways of thinking, feeling, and behaving.
e) He must have the ability to participate actively in the treatment process.
f) He must have realistic expectations about the outcome of therapy.
g) He must be willing to make the tangible sacrifices, financial and otherwise, that are required by the treatment.

Having finished his assessment and having decided that his patient meets the criteria for brief psychotherapy, the psychiatrist has two final tasks to complete before bringing the evaluation interview to a close. He must first arrive at a psychodynamic formulation of the patient's clinical problem. Based on an understanding of the central conflict underlying the patient's symptomatic and characterological disorder, the formulation delineates the focus of the therapeutic process to follow. Secondly, the psychiatrist communicates the formulation to the patient and engages him in reaching an agreement to work together on the central conflict.

To summarize, if the patient reveals the features briefly described above, he will in all likelihood respond favorably to short-term insight psychotherapy. If, however, the patient fails to meet these criteria, the therapist should be alerted to the fact that he is confronted with a more serious character disorder that requires a longer psychotherapeutic intervention employing parameters determined by the disturbances in ego structure. It should, however, be noted that recent clinical experience suggests that some patients with severe narcissistic character problems may improve with insight psychotherapy if 1) they show motivation for psychological change and 2) demonstrate that they are functioning well in one area of their lives, especially in their work performance. This preliminary finding, which remains to be confirmed by more extensive clinical investigation, underscores the central importance of motivation as a factor in predisposing to a favorable outcome in psychotherapy.

The Case of the French Woman

We shall now turn our attention to several lengthy excerpts from a videotaped evaluation interview with a young woman. Although her character disorder fell in the neurotic range of the spectrum (being predominantly Oedipal in nature), it had greatly interfered with her overall functioning and relationships and was currently threatening her marriage. The material presented here provides a concrete, more denotative definition of the various criteria enumerated above, and demonstrates how the psychiatrist elicits and documents the evidence regarding them. The interview began as follows:

DR: I know nothing about what brings you here, and I would like to hear from you what your problems are so that we can try to evaluate them together and see what recommendations can be given. Is that OK?

PT: All right. I think my basic problem is my relationship with my father, and all the other problems derive from this one. Then, again, I am not sure if I have other ones. This is basically why I want to have psychotherapy to know what the problems are, to know myself better. Basically, I think the origin is that I really didn't have a good father. He has always treated me very poorly since my childhood. His behavior has always been pretty tough during the last ten years of my life. And I know the problem. I rationalize it, but I don't know how to deal with it emotionally. I get very sick. I don't write to him. I suffer a great deal, and I feel that all my relationships with men reflect somewhat the disappointment that I felt in my father. I'd like to analyze the whole thing.

DR: Well, I think that you present your problem in a very sophisticated way. You must have done, obviously, a great deal of thinking about it.

PT: I did. I did analysis for eight months.

DR: Oh, you did? Analysis?

PT: I went, yes, to a doctor. But I was a little bit disappointed. The doctor was an analyst. The therapy lasted about six or seven months, and then I gave up, because, number one, he had a tremendous problem about money, and he refused to talk about money. We agreed on a price, and after a month he sent me a bigger bill, without discussing it with me. And then he talked about sex. He was giving me little hints; maybe it was part of my transference, and I was afraid, but I had the feeling that he was sort of getting involved with me in some ways, and it scared me to death.

DR: I sympathize with that, and these are of course quite realistic problems. But let me ask you this—is it also possible because, as you pointed out, your relationships with men are affected by this early difficulty with your father that it also was displaced on your doctor?

PT: Yes.

DR: So it is possible?

PT: It is possible. I think so.

DR: OK. Could you then tell me, what is your present difficulty with men?

PT: My difficulty is with men and with my husband. I think about divorcing him. I have a little son, five years old, very sweet, and I have a good husband. I love him very much. He wants to be with me, yet I want to divorce him. Sometimes I fear that I don't get a divorce because I am scared to be left alone.

DR: This wish for divorce is also associated with your difficulty with your father?

PT: I think so. Somehow, all men disappoint me.

DR: All men disappoint you?

PT: Yes, my father included.

DR: I see. OK. Well, maybe we can come back to your current problem later.

In her opening remarks the patient presents succinctly and spontaneously a well-circumscribed focus. "My basic problem," she says, "is my relationship with my father, and all the other problems derive from this one." She clearly admirably fulfills a fundamental criterion for suitability for STAPP, that is, a circumscribed conflict. At the same time she gives evidence of having many of the other attributes required for insight psychotherapy of any kind. She associates easily, recognizes the connection between her psychological difficulties and "getting sick," and is strongly motivated "to analyze the whole thing." Although some of her psychological-mindedness may reflect her prior experience in therapy, the vivacity and facility with which she talks about herself are genuinely her own and enable her in a very short time to reveal the ubiquity of her problem with men as she moves in her associations from her disturbed relationship with her father, to a hint of a sexualized transference with her previous therapist, to her current serious difficulties with her husband, to her generalized disappointment in men. At the conclusion of this early interchange the therapist actively directs the interview to an exploration of the nature and qualities of her past relationships. "Now," he says, "we can start taking a brief history of your background. How old are you?" "Thirty-five," replies the patient, and then in response to guiding questions reveals that she is the oldest of three children, with a sister seven years and a brother twelve years her junior. She had been born in a small village outside of Toulouse. When she was one, her parents moved to Marseilles so that her father might attend medical school. The patient was left behind to live with her maternal grandmother, with whom she remained until she was six.

PT: My grandmother took care of me like a mother. Then, when I was six, I went to Marseilles with my parents, and they sent me to a nuns' school.
DR: So you lost your grandmother?
PT: No. She is alive. I lost my mother . . .
DR: Oh, you lost your mother? What I meant was that you lost this very good relationship that you had with your grandmother for those six years. Your life was interrupted.
PT: Yes. Certainly.
DR: Now can you tell me something about your grandmother?
PT: Yes. My grandmother has been very important to me because she was like my mother. I always loved her very, very much. She was devoted to me. She is clever and very hardworking.
DR: Were you devoted to her?
PT: I was devoted to her.
DR: Would you make any sacrifice for your grandmother?
PT: All the necessary sacrifices. I thought of bringing her to this country now that my mother has died.
DR: So your relationship with your grandmother was a good one?
PT: Good.
DR: OK. This is important because it is one of our criteria for this kind of short-term work.
PT. Oh, I see.
DR: So it must have been a big loss to have to go to the nuns' school and be away from her.
PT: Yes, it was.
DR: And whom did you blame for that? Whose fault was it that you were separated from your grandmother?
PT: You see, Dr. Sifneos, I don't remember my childhood. I do remember big, traumatic experiences at home. My father and mother had a terrible marriage, and there was violence at home. But other things I don't remember.
DR: So you do remember a few things?
PT: They were very unhappy—very unhappy. My father is highly neurotic, very violent, very unhappy, making everybody unhappy around him. My mother suffered a lot, sort of like a victim of his, because she was a good-natured, happy, optimistic person. And then I don't remember much love around, except screaming, violence.
DR: Now what was your relationship with your father like at that time?

PT: I was very well behaved and extremely polite, giving kisses to everybody. My father was tough with me all the time. He was like a dictator. "Did you do your homework?" I would come from the nuns' school after eight hours; I would have a little homework. "Can I see TV, Papa?" "No, you have to study; you have to work."

DR: But wasn't there ever any affection between yourself and your father?

PT: I don't remember that. If there was—see, the other day I saw a cute picture. I was looking at old pictures, and I was walking with my father. I think I was six. I was holding his—ah—he was holding me, my hand. I looked at the picture, and we looked so happy. You know, he looked very proud walking down the street with me, and I looked like a happy little girl. But . . .

DR: And you were holding his hand? You started saying that, and then you said *he* held *your* hand. So that means that there was something in you enjoying being with your father. Is it possible, then, that maybe there was some love between the two of you?

PT: You mean that we had a good relationship? Maybe.

DR: That picture tells us that there was something special.

PT: Yes. There was something. You see, sometimes I say I hate him. When my mother died, I couldn't bear that. I wish he had died and not my mother. But then, again, I must love him. It is just the ambivalence of feelings, you know.

DR: All right. What we know, then, is that at that time you were a very docile little girl. We have established that maybe there was something very special there between yourself and your father, in terms of the picture. You were very close to your grandmother, and you were also close to your mother? Or not? What was your relationship to your mother at that time?

PT: It always was a good relationship. In the later years when I grew up, my mother was always there. And she really loved me very much, and I loved her very much, and we became good friends.

DR: OK. Let's stick just for the minute to the age of five, six, seven. At that time your mother was also pregnant with your sister. Now do you remember that?

PT: Yes. She was very sweet, and she looked very sick; she got very, very fat. She had swollen legs, and I suffered a lot I remember. I was telling everybody my mother was so sick. She blew up, she is so sick, and then she got the baby. I remember my father coming to our village. I was with my grandmother. He came running, and I remember he said, "We have a girl! We have a girl!"

DR: You mean he was happy?

PT: Yes.

DR: Well, if he was happy to have another girl, then it means that he was happy with you.
PT: Oh, he was happy with me!
DR: Ah.
PT: He has been very happy with me. Sometimes I think he is in love with me. He loves me so much. But then he treats me terribly. He's been my worst enemy. He threw me out of the house three times.
DR: Wait a minute, now. You said some very important things just now. Is it possible that your father was so strict with you because he loved you so much that he had to put a stop to his own love for you?
PT: Well, right. But this is *his* problem. This is doing nothing but hurting me.
DR: I agree with you, but have you thought of it that way? Have you thought that he had such a desire for you that he had to stop himself?
PT: Yes. He is the one who controls his sentiments, and he does not want to give love because he is scared to give love. He needs you, or somebody else, badly.

Two important facts emerge from this portion of the interview. Under questioning by the doctor, the patient describes her relationships with both her grandmother and her mother. These, it turns out, had been close, loving and giving on her part as well as on the part of her elders, and the information thus obtained enables the interviewer to judge that the patient fulfills the criterion for meaningful past relationships. Of equal interest, however, is the patient's elaboration of her troubled relationship with her father. Initially she pictures him as being violent, harsh, demanding, tough, and difficult. When asked by the doctor if there was any affection between them, she disclaims any memory of such feelings, but immediately describes a photograph of herself as a little girl holding hands with her father in a happy, affectionate pose. Confronted with this information, the patient admits momentarily to having loved her father, but rapidly reverts to an emphasis on the distance and hatred in their relationship, and insists that the difficulty between them was *his* problem, not hers. Although it has now become evident that the patient's love for her father is a source of considerable anxiety and conflict, and that she defends herself against these feelings by repression, by projection and by emphasis of the negative side of her ambivalence, the doctor chooses, for the moment, not to confront her further in this regard. Instead he directs her attention to a more general discussion of the relationship among the members of her family.

DR: Your relationships with women were very good?
PT: Very good.
DR: How did you get along with your sister?

PT: Oh, very well. But seven years makes a lot of difference.

DR: But did you ever think of your father and your mother making love?

PT (barely audible): No.

DR: Why not?

PT: No. I never thought of my father and mother making love until very late in my life. Maybe I was 18.

DR: Why not?

PT: I don't know. Maybe I had this repressed. I don't know.

DR: Ah, that is interesting. Why do you say that? Is it possible that maybe you didn't like the idea?

PT: Maybe.

DR: After all, we know that your father was very fond of you, and he was trying to hold back. Did you ever think of the fact that maybe he preferred you to your mother?

PT: No. I thought that he always . . .ah. . . he always, not hated me, but that he was too tough with me. That he wanted a boy, and I was a girl. He wanted to have a son.

DR: But no, no, no! I am not at all sure about that, because why would your father be so delighted when your sister was born? He was happy to have another girl as you told me.

PT: Yes.

DR: So my assumption that maybe your father was tough with you to possibly protect himself . . .

PT (interrupting): Why does he have to protect himself from the love for his daugher?

DR: Well, maybe because he preferred his daughter (particularly when his daughter was 12, 13, 14, with her period) to his own wife.

PT: Oh, I see. Gee, it is complicated. I know what you mean.

DR: It is complicated! You mean to say there might be a possibility it is true?

PT: Maybe. There is certainly the thought that I feel that my father loves me deeply, if you put it that way. I don't want to say that too loud, because he doesn't deserve it, and I prefer to say that my father hates me and I hate him.

DR: All right.

PT: Now that you make me think about all that, I realize, yes, it could be that he loves me, and that I love him; or maybe he loves me more than I love him. It could be. All right. But the fact is that he always treated me so poorly, and the things he did—I can't tell you what he did to me, because we don't have the time. It is really unbelievable. He is my worst enemy, my father.

Again, in this section of the interview, one can see the patient's conflict over sexuality, especially in connection with her relationship with her father. At the same time, one notes that under the doctor's gentle but repeated confrontations, she is able to face more directly the possibility that she does after all have loving feelings and wishes for her father. One discovers that her defenses have a certain flexibility and that she can tolerate, if only momentarily, the emergence of anxiety-provoking thoughts and emotions. She has, in other words, the capabilities needed for self-exploration and for the analysis of her conflicts. At this point in the interview and as the doctor becomes aware of these strengths in his patient, he focuses more directly on the central Oedipal conflict through an interpretation aimed both at her defenses and her unconscious impulses—with surprising results:

DR: I have to add something now about your father in reference to you. Is it also possible that you have exaggerated—I am not saying that all these things that you said about your father were not so, far from it—but did you exaggerate the nastiness of your father to protect yourself from your feelings of attachment for him?

PT: Yes.

DR: And also from the guilt that you felt for your mother, who was a victim and who was being attacked constantly, and who was sick?

PT: Yes, yes.

DR: And finally, you had to run away from Marseilles to be far away because of your own wishes for your father.

PT: Because of my own wishes for my father.

DR: What does your father look like?

PT: Handsome, very handsome. They say he looks like me. I think I am mixed up in my mind. He's got gray hair, like you now. And he has a handsome face. He is 57, 56. A doctor.

DR: Do you know anything about your father's activity with other women? Does he have any?

PT: Ah . . . I don't think he is interested in women basically. He hates women.

DR: There we go again! There is no evidence that . . .

PT: See. I am a little bit—well, I want to be angry now. I think we are doing psychotherapy for my father. We are talking about my father for 45 minutes. I didn't come here for that.

DR: Well, I appreciate the fact that you are very straightforward and open in your feelings. But don't forget, also, that you may be angry with me now because I also have gray hair like your father.

PT: Phew! My god! (laughs)

DR: So already you are having some feelings for me, as we saw that you may have had for that other doctor.

PT: Right.

DR: For other men also?

PT: Yes, I do have feelings for my husband, and for all the men with whom I am angry. Right.

DR: OK. If this is so, you see then this could be part of your psychotherapy. But we are not doing psychotherapy here. What we are doing here is trying to evaluate your problem.

Following the doctor's Oedipal interpretations, the patient begins to talk more openly and warmly about her father. Then suddenly, in this context, she makes a direct association to the doctor's similarity to her father, and immediately becomes defensively angry at him. The sudden emergence of the transference does not escape the doctor, who calls it explicitly to the patient's attention. The patient responds with an exclamation of surprise and a brief laugh. The tension is broken, the patient's anxiety is relieved, and she proceeds to talk more freely and openly about her relationships with men (father, husband, previous therapist and others), with a full recognition now both of her attachment for them and her defensive warding off of her feelings by keeping an angry distance from them. With his properly-timed interpretation, the doctor has helped the patient through to a new plane of awareness of her neurotic patterns of heterosexual relationships in the past, in the present, and in the transference. The doctor now feels free to focus the patient's attention on the more specifically sexual nature of her feelings and leads her to a discussion of this by asking about her life at the university, where, in a state of rebelliousness, she had first indulged in openly sexual behavior.

DR: So let's go back to the university. What happened at the university?

PT: Then, at the university, I loved my freedom. I went to live with a lady. He wanted to put me with the nuns again at school, but I refused, and my mother helped me.

DR: Your father did?

PT: Yes. My father didn't want me to stay in a normal—in a house, you know, with a key. He wanted me with the nuns.

DR: Why?

PT: Because he . . .

DR: Because he was jealous?

PT: Yes. And my sexual life—my God! Should I ever go to bed with a man!

DR: Well, hold it, hold it now. If your father was so uninterested in you, if your father hated you, why would he give a damn about your sexual life?

PT: OK, OK. Let's say, let's say that my father doesn't hate me—and I thank you for letting me see that I am overreacting and exaggerating the whole thing. Let's say he loves me somewhat. I accept that he loves me somewhat. But he didn't act well. He mistreated me, and I am very hurt by him. This is my point. That's all.

DR: Yes, yes. I understand. I understand that completely. But he wanted, really, to keep you a virgin . . .

PT: Forever.

DR: Yes, forever, and going with the nuns was a way of keeping you a virgin forever.

PT: But that is wrong. He is sick.

DR: Of course it is wrong, but at the same time, could it be that his motivation was that he was jealous?

PT: Listen, I don't really care . . .

DR: When did you start going out with young men?

PT: Very early.

DR: Very early?

PT: I had boyfriends always, being a virgin of course. But I went out when I was 11.

DR: So you started quite early.

(At this point the patient describes a series of relationships with men and her first sexual experience at the age of 22. She was always attracted to men much older than herself, one of whom was a psychiatrist with whom she fell in love.)

DR: So you have a tendency to be attracted to older men?

PT: Yes, but I am married to a younger man. One year younger than I am.

DR: What about that discrepancy?

PT: I don't know. It's funny.

DR: Ah, but this is what we have to figure out.

PT (laughing): We won't have the time, I don't think.

DR: Ah, we have a few more minutes, and I think we can figure it out. Now tell me, when did you meet your husband?

PT: When I was 25.

DR: I see. And what was it about him that you liked?

PT: I like him physically.

DR: Now, you came to this country when?

PT: Three years ago. I was married already three years, with my husband, and with my son. And I felt very depressed. That is why I went to see an analyst.

DR: Are you here to stay, or are you going back to France?

PT: I want to think I am going to go back to France, but I am here to stay.
DR: Now tell me just briefly, your mother died . . .
PT: A month and a half ago, suddenly.
DR: Suddenly?
PT: Yes. She was here with me the month of June. She was asthmatic, and I took her to the Mt. Sinai Hospital, and they checked her up. They say there is nothing wrong. She has chronic asthma and bronchitis, and they are going to fix her up. When she went back to France, she had a heart attack and died.
DR: I am sorry to hear that.
PT: Thank you. And I feel very depressed.
DR: Yes. Well I understand, because obviously the two of you had a good relationship. But you have your grandmother.
PT: I have my grandmother. I went back to France to bury my mother, and I spent two weeks with my grandmother. I stayed there with her.

The emergence here of the history of the recent death of the patient's mother raises the questions as to whether this, rather than the patient's conflict over men, might be a potential focus of the therapy. The doctor, although recognizing that the loss is still a painful issue for the patient, judges that she is grieving in a normal way without evidence of neurotic distortions. Furthermore, the problem with men, which the patient herself had presented as her focal problem, long antedated her mother's death and clearly rests on her Oedipal conflicts. The therapist, therefore, elects to return the focus of the interview to the subject of her father.

DR: Did you see your father?
PT: I had to, yes.
DR: You did?
PT: I had fights daily with him. He didn't go to my mother's funeral. He didn't show up. And I didn't want to go to see him, but they sent me. Once again, everybody sends me, you know, "Your father, you have to go. He loves you. He is your father." And I went to see him, and it was hell for seven days. And I didn't want to fight because I was so depressed at that point.

(The patient then associated to the period before her marriage. She was spending the weekends with her fiancé in his apartment. Her father, upon discovering this, called her on the phone, accused her of being a "whore," disowned her as a daughter and withdrew his financial support for her schooling. Thenceforth the patient began to feel "very uneasy" and to have frightening dreams.)

PT: I had dreams about his screaming and me yelling.

DR: About him?

PT: Yes. Then they operated on him—no, forgive me—then I got married. And I called him, and I invited him to come to the U.S. for my wedding. He said. "Forget it. I am not coming. I am not your father." After I got married, I went back to France with the marriage certificate, and my mother sent me to see him. I didn't want to. She said, "You go and ask his forgiveness because he was very depressed since he knew what you did." So I went to ask forgiveness in case he felt depressed. And he threw me out of the house again. He said, "Go!" He started saying all kinds of nasty things to me. And then the third time, when they operated on him—they took a kidney out. And then they sent me back to him—my mother did. She was already seperated from him. . . . Then I went back to him, and he received me like if I was . . . ah . . . a fiancée. He gave me a Rolex. He bought me a raccoon coat. He opened his arms to me, you know. "I love you so much"—what am I going to do? And the relationship is going to be so beautiful—like a sexual relationship with a woman. I knew that he always liked my sister. I thought that he loved my sister more than me. He brainwashed my sister. My sister never rebelled against him, and therefore they became friends, and he threw me out of the house again.

DR: So it is quite clear that what I was saying before is true, namely that your father had some very strong and sexualized feelings for you. And that creates havoc with you.

PT: It is so sickening.

DR: Of course. Now what is the problem with your husband who is younger than you? Are you saying that you are thinking of divorcing him?

PT: Why did I marry my husband if I always liked bright, mature men? And I married a very immature Jewish boy, very sweet and loving, but . . . ah . . .

DR: Maybe because marrying a younger, immature Jewish boy was as different from your father as it could be—from your father, who was older with his gray hair.

PT: Absolutely.

DR: I assume your father is a Catholic?

PT: Yes.

DR: So you see two very different attitudes. But you keep on telling me that you are attracted to older men. One is seven years older, and one who is very special to you is ten years older. And you are constantly being sent by your mother to your father, and he is throwing you out and behaving in a very nasty way. And then suddenly he behaves as if you were his . . .

PT: Lover.

DR: Lover. What did you think at that time? Were you pleased?

PT: No, it makes me sick.

DT: It makes you sick because obviously the ups and downs are terrible. But does it make you sick also because of your guilt feelings for your mother?

PT: Maybe, maybe.

DR: So you see we are not that far away from understanding the whole problem. Why you were angry with me before was not so much because I seemed to be trying to understand your father, but because I was focusing on the interaction between the two of you. We have to see things in a different way.

PT: Absolutely.

DR: But now, tell me, how motivated are you, really to get down to understanding these things and changing these patterns? And to freeing yourself from these problems that have been with you for a long time?

PT: I want it very much.

DR: What do you think? You are here because we are interested in short-term therapy. I think we have covered a lot over a short period of time.

PT: Right, it has been marvelous, marvelous, yes.

DR: Why do you say it's been marvelous?

PT: Because I was afraid that if I go to psychotherapy, I would need a long psychotherapy, like four or five years.

In this penultimate phase of the interview, although the patient's defenses are still evident, she nonetheless talks much more directly and freely than before about her relationships, using terms and images that are increasingly sexualized. When the patient at last suddenly interjects the word "lover," the therapist has the final bit of evidence he needs to convince him that her Oedipal conflict should be the main focus of her short-term psychotherapy. And in the course and evolution of the interview to that point he has had ample proof of her suitability for such treatment and her strong motivation to pursue it actively and vigorously. There remains only, in the concluding moments, the task of summarizing for the patient the formulation of her problem and the way to its solution. This the doctor proceeds to do, and the interview ends on a warm and hopeful note.

DR: Well, I can summarize. You had some very good relationships as a child—with your grandmother and with your mother. I think you had a good relationship with your father, up to a certain point. And then all hell broke loose, and you had a terrible problem. I think you have a circumscribed problem. You put it in a nutshell. You want to understand your

relationship with your father because if affects your relationships with men and your husband. You have a good interaction with me. You spoke very openly, you expressed your feelings when you were annoyed, which was appropriate. You feel, however, that this interview was helpful?
PT: Yes.
DR: You seem to have a very strong psychological sophistication. Now, you told me that you are motivated to change. We have a specific problem in your relationship with your father, and how it affects your relationship with men. Well, I certainly think that this can become the focus of your therapy and can be worked on very intensely. And why should that take four or five years?
PT: Good.
DR: If you are motivated you can overcome it very quickly. Particularly if you can bring everything into the open.
PT: I am very much motivated. Let me tell you how motivated I am. I am thinking of studying psychology.
DR: I am very pleased about that. But tell me one last thing. You told me that this interview was helpful. In what way was it helpful?
PT: I think that you clarified many things to me in such a short time.
DR: It wasn't I. It was you.
PT: Thanks to you.
DR: It was my help.
PT: I couldn't do it alone.
DR: All right, you couldn't do it alone. But it wasn't what I did. I didn't pull a pigeon out of a hat or something like that. It was really putting some of the things that you told me in a different way. Sometimes you didn't like what I said, and you felt some anxiety. Of course, this is the role of the evaluator. We hope to sometimes put things in a different light.
PT: Not everybody can do that, let me tell you. Not all therapists are good. There are some good, some bad. I think you are first-rate.
DR: OK, thank you. I enjoyed this very much, and thank you for coming to be interviewed. I think it looks very positive.
PT: Thank you very much.

We need not recapitulate here all the criteria for brief insight psychotherapy, which have been listed and amply described earlier and are clearly demonstrated in the extended fragments from the interview with the French Woman. Suffice it to say that apart from her strong motivation for change and her ability to single out a central conflict for therapeutic exploration, the patient shows a remarkable degree of psychological-mindedness. She brings in many significantly related associations and memories from her past and current life. Though made anxious by them, she is able to tolerate and examine emerging elements of her unconscious drives and feelings, and she relates well to her doctor. In particular, she shows a capacity for psychological change and growth within the course of a single evaluation interview, as evidenced by her ability stage by stage to reveal more of herself, so that by the end of the interview she is talking openly about material that at the start had been hidden from view by her defenses. Perhaps most striking of all is the patient's very warm, positive response to the doctor and to the process of the interview itself. She clearly feels not only that she has been understood, but that even in the space of an hour she has learned something new about herself. She appreciates the active, guiding, searching help of the doctor and approaches the completion of the task of self-exploration in the therapy ahead with confidence and enthusiasm. The doctor too is gratified by the results of the interview and, fully satisfied that this patient demonstrates all the prerequisite criteria for brief psychotherapy, can recommend her with assurance for treatment.

EPILOGUE

It is not our purpose here to discuss the effectiveness of the brief psychotherapies in general or STAPP in particular. The growing body of literature on outcome may be consulted by the reader interested in the details of outcome studies and their favorable conclusions (17-19). It is perhaps not inappropriate, however, to conclude with a few words about the fate of this particular patient.

Having been adjudged eminently suitable for short-term anxiety-provoking psychotherapy after the interview presented above, the patient underwent STAPP with a therapist other than the physician who evaluated her. She was, however, seen a year later for a follow-up assessment by the initial evaluator. At that time she showed considerable insight into the emotional conflicts that had brought her to the clinic for help. She had learned a great deal about her relationship with her father. She saw him in a much more realistic light, no longer manifested the neurotic attitudes toward him that had emerged in the evaluation interview, and lost her anxious preoccupations about him, and could look at her earlier conflicts with mature, reflective distance. She spoke warmly and gratefully of her therapist for having helped her to explore and unravel her problems with her father in particular, and with men in general. Of special importance, her relationship with her husband, which had been on the verge of collapse when she was first seen, was now markedly improved. In sum, the patient's psychological difficulties had been resolved, she had learned new ways of living and loving, and was now a stronger, happier, and more mature woman.

REFERENCES

1. KOHUT, H.: *The Analysis of the Self*. New York: International Universities Press, 1971.
2. GUNDERSON, J., and SINGER, M.: Defining borderline patients: An overview. *Am. J. Psychiat.*, 132: 1-10, 1975.
3. KERNBERG, O.: *Borderline Conditions and Pathological Narcissism*. New York: Jason Aronson, 1975.
4. KERNBERG, O: Technical considerations in the treatment of borderline personality organization. *J. Am. Psychoanal. Assoc.*, 24: 795-829, 1976.
5. KOHUT, H.: *The Restoration of the Self*. New York: International Universities Press, 1977.
6. FREUD, S.: From the history of an infantile neurosis. *Standard Edition*, 17: 7-122. London: Hogarth Press, 1955.
7. FREUD, S.: Lines of advance in psycho-analytic therapy. *Standard Edition*, 17: 159-168. London: Hogarth Press, 1955.
8. EISSLER, K.: The effect of the structure of the ego on psychoanalytic technique. *J. Am. Psychoanal. Assoc.*, 1: 104-143, 1953.
9. ALEXANDER, F., and FRENCH, T.: *Psychoanalytic Therapy*. New York: Ronald Press, 1946.
10. MANN, J.: *Time-limited Psychotherapy*. Cambridge, MA: Harvard University Press, 1973.
11. SIFNEOS, P.: *Short-term Psychotherapy and Emotional Crisis*. Cambridge, MA: Harvard University Press, 1972.
12. MALAN, D.: *The Frontiers of Brief Psychotherapy*. New York: Plenum, 1976.
13. SIFNEOS, P.: *Short-term Dynamic Psychotherapy: Evaluation and Techinique*. New York: Plenum, 1979.
14. DAVANLOO, H. (Ed.): *Basic Principles and Techniques in Short-term Dynamic Psychotherapy*. New York: Spectrum Publications, 1978.
15. BURKE, J., WHITE, H., and HAVENS, L.: Which short-term therapy? *Arch. Gen. Psychiat.*, 36: 177-186, 1979.
16. MARMOR, J.: Short-term dynamic psychotherapy. *Am. J. Psychiat.*, 136: 149-155, 1979.
17. SIFNEOS, P.: Criteria for psychotherapeutic outcome. *Psychother. and Psychosom.*, 26: 49-58, 1975.
18. MALAN, D.: *Toward the Validation of Dynamic Psychotherapy*. New York: Plenum, 1976.
19. SIFNEOS, P., et al.: Ongoing outcome research on short-term dynamic psychotherapy. *Psychother. and Psychosom.*, 33: 233-242, 1980.

8

Severe Character Problems: Borderline and Related Disorders

Gerald Adler, M.D.

The introduction of DSM-III (1) in 1980 has given formal recognition to several diagnostic categories that clinicians have been using to describe primitive patients. For example, borderline personality disorders and narcissistic personality disorders are diagnoses that are now accepted, although the distinctions between these two groups are not always so obvious. Although we can find many patients who fit these DSM-III descriptions, a number of questions arise when we try to examine specific characteristics of these patients. Is the diagnostic category "borderline personality disorder" valid and useful? Or is it a wastebasket which is overused, perhaps even an iatrogenic myth (2)? Is narcissistic personality disorder a valid separate category or a subgroup of borderline personality disorder? Is there any relationship between borderline and narcissistic personality disorder? If so, how can we conceptualize this relationship? Finally, can we relate these two diagnostic categories to others, such as schizotypal, antisocial, paranoid, and schizoid personality disorders? In this chapter I shall attempt to clarify these questions and present a theoretical framework to help define the relationship between these disorders in a clinically useful way.

DSM-III DESCRIPTIONS

It is useful to review the DSM-III descriptions of borderline and narcissistic personality disorders in order to define the areas of our discussion. Since these categories refer to personality disorders, the long-term stable features of the person are being described, rather than transient fluctuations which can be defined as "states."

Borderline Personality Disorder

The DSM-III criteria of borderline personality disorder in adults require at least five of the following eight features:

1) Impulsivity or unpredictability in at least two areas that are potentially self-damaging, e.g., spending, sex, gambling, substance use, shoplifting, overeating, physically self-damaging acts.
2) A pattern of unstable and intense interpersonal relationships, e.g., marked shifts of attitude, idealization, devaluation, manipulation (consistently using others for one's own ends).
3) Inappropriate intense anger or lack of control of anger, e.g., frequent displays of temper, constant anger.
4) Identity disturbance manifested by uncertainty about several issues relating to identity, such as self-image, gender identity, long-term goals or career choice, friendship patterns, values, and loyalties, e.g., "Who am I?", "I feel like I am my sister when I am good."
5) Affective instability, e.g., marked shifts from normal mood to depression, irritability, or anxiety, usually lasting a few hours and only rarely more than a few days with a return to normal mood.
6) Intolerance of being alone, e.g., frantic efforts to avoid being alone, depressed when alone.
7) Physically self-damaging acts, e.g., suicidal gestures, self-mutilation, recurrent accidents or physical fights.
8) Chronic feelings of emptiness or boredom (1, pp. 322-323).

Thus, DSM-III emphasizes the affective, interpersonal, and identity instability of these patients, their problems with anger and action orientation, seen in their tendency to hurt themselves, often impulsively, as well as their feelings of emptiness and difficulties in being alone.

Narcissistic Personality Disorder

In contrast, let us examine the diagnostic criteria for narcissistic personality disorder:

a) Grandiose sense of self-importance or uniqueness, e.g., exaggeration of achievements and talents, focus on the special nature of one's problems.

b) Preoccupation with fantasies of unlimited success, power, brilliance, beauty, or ideal love.
c) Exhibitionism: the person requires constant attention and admiration.
d) Cool indifference or marked feelings of rage, inferiority, shame, humiliation, or emptiness in response to criticism, indifference of others, or defeat.
e) At least two of the following characteristics of disturbances in interpersonal relationships:
  1) Entitlement: expectation of special favors without assuming reciprocal responsibilities, e.g., surprise and anger that people will not do what is wanted.
  2) Interpersonal exploitativeness: taking advantage of others to indulge own desires, or for self-aggrandizement; disregard for the personal integrity and rights of others.
  3) Relationships that characteristically alternate between the extremes of overidealization and devaluation.
  4) Lack of empathy: inability to recognize how others feel, e.g., unable to appreciate the distress of someone who is seriously ill (1, p. 317).

The DMS-III description seems to emphasize the greater sense of stability in narcissistic personality disorder patients. Although both groups need people, the narcissistic personality disorder can use his own fantasies (acknowledged by DSM-III as a piece of behavioral data) to maintain himself. In fact, the fantasies of narcissistic personality disorder patients are elaborated in greater detail in these descriptions compared to the borderline personality disorder patient. The borderline patient's obvious neediness is contrasted with the narcissistic personality disorder's more frequent indifference and aloofness. The latter's sensitivity to slights and criticism is defined; however, possible interpersonal precipitants of the borderline's behavior are not noted. Both groups are seen as manipulative people who alternate between idealization and devaluation.

The clinician who attempts to use the descriptions of these two diagnostic categories may have difficulty in deciding whether his patient belongs in one or the other, or both, or neither. In addition, since choices of a certain number of items from different categories are required, the details may be hard to remember. The descriptions lack a central organizing coherence that make sense of the various features. Is it possible to define these data in a way that relates to our clinical experience which can be useful in the diagnosis and treatment of these patients?

Some consistent observations in the treatment of patients who fit the borderline personality disorder diagnosis can provide a possible link. In experiences with the psychotherapy of borderline patients, both as a therapist and as a supervisor, I have been impressed that borderline patients in successful treatment will look increasingly like narcissistic personality disorders over time. They will gradually become more stable in their relationship to their therapist and to other important people in their lives. When that stability finally occurs, their long-standing sensitivity to slights by these important people can become the focus of the therapeutic work, including the examination of their aloofness, arrogance, and ready feelings of shame and humiliation that accompany disappointments. As their lives become more coherent, they are more readily able to discuss their fantasies, rather than their neediness and out-of-control feelings. Thus, borderline patients ultimately become narcissistic personality disorder patients. Viewing these primitive patients along a continuum from borderline to narcissistic personality disorder can help define differences, similarities, and the process of change in psychotherapy (3).

The Borderline Patient in Treatment

The borderline patient may appear much more stable early in therapy than the DSM-III descriptions imply. The clue to the disorder may come largely from the detailed history of the patient's tumultuous object relationships, his characteristic ways of handling affect, and his defenses. However, in treatment, the borderline patient, over time, gradually or rapidly develops a familiar pattern (3-6). A common manifestation of this pattern is an increasing sense of dissatisfaction and emptiness which begins to appear over weekends or between appointments. Sometimes the dissatisfaction centers around feelings of being misunderstood by the therapist, or of not receiving the support or emotional holding the patient feels he needs. The escalation of these feelings can lead to the emergence of anger, which is rarely well contained. It can be intensely felt and rapidly become part of destructive and/or self-destructive acts. Sometimes the patient can be totally unaware of the anger, feeling only a sense of total badness, worthlessness, or need to be hurt and punished. For many of these patients, the experience of anger is totally unacceptable; instead, the theme of the patient's own feelings of his badness assumes the central position.

As these intense feelings appear in psychotherapy, many borderline patients begin to describe feelings of abandonment that precede or accompany the anger. Increasingly, they may speak of feeling empty, dropped, unsupported, and alone. The aloneness experiences not only include feelings of isolation and detachment in the presence of others, but also consist of difficulties in remembering important people in their lives, both past and present, including their therapist. Not only are they unable to summon up positive images of their therapist at those times when their anger is intense, but they may also fantasize about hurting or injuring their therapist or may have only frightening negative images of him. Such experiences often are accompanied by a feeling of panic and sometimes by serious suicidal preoccupations. Unless the therapist can find ways to understand and respond to these intense feelings and events, the treatment may be disrupted by a serious suicide attempt or an escalation of these feelings to such an extent that hospitalization may be required.

The Narcissistic Personality Disorder Patient in Treatment

In contrast, the narcissistic personality disorder patient remains in a more stable position throughout his treatment. He may protect himself from involvement with his therapist by an aloofness or sense of grandiosity, but communicates his neediness, which is often low keyed, through his often exquisite sensitivity to misunderstandings and slights in the therapeutic relationship. However, these experiences do not escalate to the progressive rage and aloneness issues described above. In addition, when these patients feel understood, they often idealize the therapist in an increasingly stable way and utilize his responses to help with their tenuous sense of feeling understood, appreciated, and validated.

Fear of Closeness and Guilt in Borderline Patients

Two important factors, implied in the DSM-III descriptions of borderline and narcissistic personality disorders, play an important role in the less stable capacity that borderline personality disorder patients have in maintaining a relationship with their therapist. The borderline patient, as a manifestation of his identity or self-disturbance, experiences terror because of his neediness and longings for closeness. Although he feels at times that he cannot live without the presence of the other person, he fears that he will totally lose his sense of separateness, i.e., merge or fuse with that person in a psychotic decompensation. These feelings are akin to those described by Burnham et al. (7) in their work with schizophrenics: the need-fear dilemma. However, schizophrenics actually experience these merger feelings and lose their separateness; borderlines *fear* it, and if they do become psychotic, it is a short-lived experience.

Since Kohut (8, 9) and Kernberg (10), two of the major contributors of our understanding of primitive patients, both use the terms "merger" and yet mean very different things, it is important to clarify the distinctions. Kernberg utilizes an object-relations framework derived from Fairbairn (11) and Jacobson (12) in which merger means a breakdown of the separation of self-representations and object representations. When that breakdown occurs, the person is psychotic by definition—he loses the inner distinction between himself and the other person. This state is also described as a breakdown in ego boundaries. Kernberg distinguishes this psychotic situation from the one with borderlines. He states that borderline patients largely maintain the separateness of self- and object representations; their difficulty is in their inability to bring together self- and object representations of negative valence with self- and object representations of positive valence. By definition, this ''splitting'' phenomenon becomes the essence of borderline personality organization in Kernberg's schema.

Kohut uses merger to mean areas of incompleteness in the self of a person; a sense of completeness is established when that person makes use of the other person in the area of incompleteness. In Kohut's definition of merger, the person is separate except for the area of the missing function which requires the other person. This description does not imply psychosis, for most aspects of the person are separate, except for the required functions of the other person. However, conceptually, if the areas of incompleteness are too great, the merging with the other could become a psychotic experience.

The borderline patient's fear of closeness, with the accompanying fears of psychosis, makes it much harder for him to use the therapist. In contrast, narcissistic personality disorder patients can more safely merge in areas of incompleteness. However, narcissistic personality disorders may have to defend against merger for other reasons, for example, in order to avoid dependency, shame, and humiliation. Yet, these fears pose less danger than those of the borderline patient.

Guilt, with its accompanying need for self-punishment, is present and pervasive in the borderline patients. The borderline patient may physically hurt himself for a variety of reasons. These include a need to feel alive or to keep himself from feeling that he is totally disintegrating. However, more commonly there is a feeling of overwhelming badness and worthlessness, with an active need to punish oneself. The borderline patient often feels that he is bad because of his murderous wishes, impulses and feelings, and deserves the most intense punishment for them. He will thus put himself into situations where the punishment will occur, destroy opportunities for success by his decisions or behavior in such situations, or physically hurt himself to mete out his inevitable punishment. The self-punishment is so intense, in part, because the guilt is very primitive, deriving from superego elements that are unmodified by the loving, more mature aspects that become part of a normal conscience. In addition, the intensity of the rage the patient experiences is interpreted by him as horrible enough to deserve such punishment. These patients are often the ones who have to destroy their therapy as a manifestation of their self-punishment; such therapeutic failures are often described as a negative therapeutic reaction (13).

Narcissistic personality disorder patients are also frequently guilt-ridden people. However, their guilt is often not so overtly visible in active self-punishing feelings and acts. It is more likely to be subtly manifested in the repeated failures to pursue plans, careers, and relationships. Often it is intertwined with feelings of low self-esteem, inferiority, and shame. But, at the same time, an element of guilt and a need for punishment because of the patient's perceived badness can be teased out of these other feelings.

A Theoretical Framework

How can we understand the differences between borderline and narcissistic personality disorder patients, their overlapping areas, and the changes that occur in borderline patients as they progress toward narcissistic personality disorder in therapy? It is possible to develop a framework which clarifies some of these issues, utilizing some of the recent clinical and theoretical literature about primitive patients and early child development observations. I have found the work of Kohut (8, 9) and of Winnicott (14) particularly useful. The contributions of Mahler et al. (15), Kernberg (10), Guntrip (16), Balint (17), and Fairbairn (11) are also important.

Winnicott and Kohut

Winnicott's description of the holding environment, transitional objects, and good-enough mothering, and Kohut's discussions of selfobject transferences and the cohesiveness of the self are related. They offer cornerstones in conceptualizing these two groups of patients. When Winnicott discussed the holding environment, he was describing a mother-child interaction in which the mother was sufficiently attuned to the child's needs to provide relatively optimal support as different maturational aspects of the child emerged over time. Since these mothers could be expected to fail the child from time to time, Winnicott described good-enough mothering as the adequate response of the parent which allowed sufficient support for the child in spite of the parent's intermittent failures to respond to the shifting needs of that child. This holding environment concept of the mother-child dyad was then utilized by Winnicott and others (4, 18) to define the holding qualities of a therapeutic relationship. Such a holding environment allows the patient to feel understood, contained, and supported, to settle down into treatment and gradually to develop an optimal working therapeutic relationship. Here, too, the therapist's occasional failures are not significant, if, over time, he is "good enough."

Narcissistic Personality Disorder and Selfobject Transferences

Winnicott's concepts have some relationship to those of Kohut. Kohut's description of selfobject transferences, in essence, defines the relatively stable situation that emerges in the treatment of a narcissistic personality disorder and, by definition, delineates that disorder. In order to understand Kohut's use of selfobject transferences, the concept of the selfobject must first be elaborated. Kohut describes the selfobject as someone outside the individual who performs a function that is missing and needed by that individual but is experienced as part of that person. This description implies a certain degree of fusion or merger, specifically in the area involving the missing functions for that individual. As defined by Kohut, patients with a narcissistic personality disorder are people who have areas of incompleteness; within these areas they require another person to provide the functions, and, therefore, the sense of completeness that they themselves lack. These selfobject experiences comprise the relatively stable transferences in the treatment of narcissistic personality disorder patients.

Kohut defined two varieties of selfobject transferences: mirror and idealizing. The mirror selfobject transferences relate to the child's/patient's needs to be understood, appropriately appreciated, and ultimately validated throughout his development. The idealizing selfobject transferences refer to needs of the child/patient to have an admired person with whom he can merge; ultimately he will acquire aspects of that person that he needs for completeness. The parents' and therapist's appropriate phase-specific response is required for the evolution of the child's/patient's grandiosity to be channeled into mature ambitions; the child's/patient's merger with the idealized selfobject ultimately leads to a process in which the functions provided by that selfobject are taken in as part of the child/patient. This latter process is called "transmuting internalization" by Kohut.

As stated, Kohut utilized his concept of selfobject transferences to define narcissistic personality disorder, i.e., patients who primarily formed selfobject transferences in psychotherapy or psychoanalysis. Such patients have a vulnerable sense of self-cohesiveness, manifested by their "fragmentation" when these selfobject bonds are transiently severed. The patient's perception of the therapist's failures when he falls short of the patient's longing for perfect responses can lead to a momentary feeling of disorganization, hypochondriacal concerns, or aloof, arrogant responses, all of which are aspects of fragmentation.

Selfobject Transferences in Borderline Personality Disorder

It is possible to apply Kohut's selfobject transference concept to disorders other than those of the narcissistic personality disorder patient. For example, borderline patients, as implied earlier, do form selfobject transferences at the beginning of treatment; however, their vulnerability to issues of abandonment, rage, and aloneness leads to a regression in which these selfobject transferences disintegrate in a more prolonged and profound fashion. One may therefore state that borderline patients have a much less cohesive sense of self and a less stable capacity to maintain selfobject transferences in the face of their emerging anger.

It is only when the issues of aloneness are resolved that borderline patients develop the capacity to establish stable selfobject transferences similar to or identical with narcissistic personality disorder patients. As will be described, these borderline patients then face the therapeutic issues, which are the same as those of narcissistic personality disorders, specifically, issues of their incompleteness and low self-worth.

These observations are in part at variance with those of Kernberg (10), who defines narcissistic personality disorder patients as a subgroup of borderline personality organization. Kernberg uses this latter designation as a broader concept that includes descriptive, genetic, defensive, and dynamic features. Although Kernberg and Kohut agree relatively closely in their clinical descriptions of narcissistic personality disorder patients, Kernberg stresses the pathological self-formation in these patients. The pathological amalgam he describes consists of a fusion of the real self, ideal self, and ideal object within the patient, which supports the latter's grandiose fantasies of self-sufficiency. It is this pathological self-formation which distinguishes narcissistic personality disorder patients from the broader category of borderline personality organization. Within this framework, these patients utilize defenses that Kernberg has described in detail: splitting, projective identification, primitive idealization, devaluation, and denial. Thus, both borderline and narcissistic personality disorder patients use similar defensive operations. Kernberg's observations about defenses are consistent with descriptions in DSM-III which imply that borderline and narcissistic personality disorder patients cannot be readily distinguished by their defenses.

Aloneness and Borderline Pathology

Buie and I have described in detail the borderline patient's problems with aloneness (6, 19). These observations were based upon direct clinical experience with borderline patients and the supervision of psychiatric residents and other clinicians working with them. We were impressed by feelings of abandonment in all borderline patients, the frequent appearance of an escalating anger in many in spite of very good therapists treating them, and the appearance of obvious aloneness phenomena in the more severe borderlines. These latter patients help us clarify a major aspect of borderline psychopathology—borderline patients specifically have difficulties tolerating separation anxiety through the use of their own internal resources. As described earlier, in the face of their mounting anger, they lose the capacity to maintain positive memories of sustaining, holding, and soothing people, both past and present. We define these primitive memories as holding introjects, i.e., felt presences of important people who help soothe, hold, and contain the person. The borderlines' vulnerability is related to their tenuous capacity to maintain these holding introjects when faced with disappointment in the significant people in their lives, usually experienced as abandonment. At such times, the loss of holding introjects leads to an experience of separation anxiety, which gives way to annihilation anxiety, with the panic and desperation that accompanies the latter state.

Child Development Literature and Object Permanence

The study of the child development literature has given us hints about certain developmental issues that seem related to these adult experiences. We are aware that the direct correspondence from childhood to adult experience is an oversimplification which ignores the many transformations and developmental stages that follow these earlier experiences. Yet, the cautious examination of this literature seems to enrich our understanding and helps provide an aspect of a useful framework for the treatment of these adult patients. Piaget (20) has described the stages in development of the infant, in which the concept of object permanence is gradually developed. At four to eight months of age, in Stage IV of sensorimotor development, the child can follow an object when it is hidden behind a screen. However, he does not pursue or follow it when it is moved from one screen to another until he is about 18 months of age. At that time, Stage VI of sensorimotor development, it can be postulated that the child has the concept of object permanence. He has an internal image of the object which persists even when the object is hidden from him. Fraiberg (21) has emphasized the child's capacity to evoke the memory of the object at that time and called this phenomenon "evocative memory." In contrast, she has called the Stage IV capacity to remember the object only when in its presence "recognition memory."

These observations by Piaget and Fraiberg relate to some of Winnicott's (22) descriptions of the transitional object. Winnicott said that transitional objects are utilized by the child as an illusion to help him recreate, for example, his mother, when the mother is not present at the time of need. Tolpin (23) elaborated that the transitional object is not mourned when it is relinquished because the figures and functions it represented become a permanent part of the child. (In contrast, Winnicott stressed that transitional object phenomena become part of the shared cultural experience when they are given up.) This internalization process, described by Tolpin, coincides with the development of solid evocative memory capacity. As Winnicott noted, transitional objects are first used by the child at four to eight months of age and are no longer required as an object of intense need at 18-24 months of age. Thus, the origins of the transitional object occur at the time of recognition memory, and its urgent need ends at the time of evocative memory capacity.

The issues of evocative memory formation and its relationship to object permanence resonate with the adult borderline patient's difficulties. As stated earlier, under the stress of his emerging anger, he undergoes a regressive experience in which he may ultimately lose the capacity to remember the positive aspects of important sustaining past and present people. At his most intense feelings of rage, the borderline patient experiences total aloneness, often feeling that his rage has annihilated the important person. The empty aloneness he feels at those moments can be frightening and may be accompanied by serious suicidal risk. Although the experience that no one is there and the inability to have an image of the absent person occur at moments of intense anger, the borderline patient does not have difficulty with evocative memory for areas of his life which are not invested with his intense neediness.

I emphasize the holding quality of introjects as particularly important in the fantasies of borderline patients. Borderline patients are specifically vulnerable to the loss of these holding introjects when enraged and require the presence of the person in order to remember him at these times. Thus, they regress from having evocative memory capacity (Piaget's Stage VI of sensorimotor development) to a state in which only recognition memory exists (Piaget's Stage IV of sensorimotor development). This borderline experience, thus, can be conceptualized in a way that is very similar to the child development schema described by Piaget and Fraiberg.

Winnicott's description of transitional object phenomena is relevant to the way both the child and the borderline patient attempt to compensate for a tenuous evocative memory capacity. They use the transitional object until evocative memory and object permanence is solidly established. The child is developing the capacity for object permanence, while the borderline patient lacks that solid capacity as a manifestation of borderline vulnerability.

These child development concepts and their relationship to the borderline patient are summarized in Figure 1.

TREATMENT ISSUES

The discussion of aloneness difficulties in the borderline patient helps define the issues of treatment in both the early and later phases. The aloneness vulnerability must be addressed first, before the patient can develop the stability that places him into the narcissistic disorder level of development. In this formulation, I conceptualize that the borderline patient moves toward the narcissistic personality part of the continuum, from borderline at one end to narcissistic personality disorder at the other (3), as he gradually develops the capacity to maintain holding introjects.

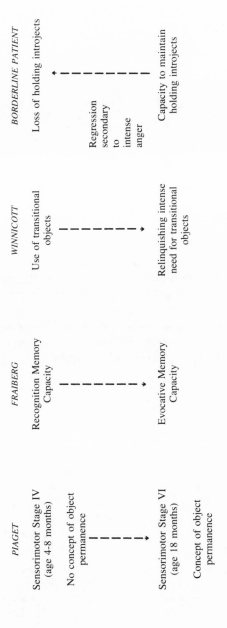

F<small>IGURE</small> 1

Aloneness Issues in Treatment

Since the borderline patient may often be enraged and feel that his anger destroys the person at whom he is angry, the initial crucial experiences of the first phase of therapy often involve feeling some of this anger. The patient must ultimately find that his anger does not destroy the therapist; at the same time he must test whether or not the therapist retaliates or withdraws. These repeated experiences, often in small doses, ultimately lead to the increasing capacity of the patient to remember the therapist between sessions even while he is angry.

The therapist is faced with the problem of helping a patient who is transiently enraged, often demanding, and sometimes panicked that he cannot remember his therapist between appointments. How much to encourage the use of brief phone calls at these times when holding introjects are lost, as well as diaries and postcards during the therapist's vacations to help reestablish the tenuous evocative memory, is an important and delicate therapist decision. If the therapist respects his own limits, individuality, and privacy as he cares about his patient, he can be empathic, firm, adequately limit-setting, and allow the patient to feel that the therapist holds, contains, and protects. At the same time, he does not become engulfed or engulf, rescue or retaliate. Such a careful balance defines the holding environment of the good-enough therapist (4). The experience of anger is not the primary event that leads to change in the patient. Instead, it is the therapist's willingness to bear his own distress as he tries to understand and contain the patient without acting on his countertransference impulses and feelings. An experience can then occur which is different from the one in the patient's childhood that was partly responsible for his vulnerability.

Self-worth and Incompleteness Issues

Once solid evocative memory has been established, the borderline patient is no longer borderline. The transition from borderline to narcissistic personality disorder includes transient regressions back to the borderline aloneness phenomena, but these experiences are briefer, less intense, and less frightening. The patient now also has the capacity for more solid maintenance of selfobject transferences, both mirror and idealizing, in contrast to their ready breakdown when the aloneness issues were paramount. However, the focus of therapy often becomes the more manageable disappointment in the therapist when he inevitably fails as the idealized selfobject. These disappointments are now more likely to be viewed as experiences which are also related to disappointments in important people, usually parents, in the patient's past. The exquisite sensitivity to disappointments, often arousing feelings of not being understood, relates to the therapist's inevitably imperfect empathic capacities. In addition, separations over weekends and vacations may become the focus of the work as these separations recreate losses and failures of important people in the patient's past.

Gradually the patient develops the capacities within himself that were provided by the selfobject therapist. His sense of self-worth increases as his sense of incompleteness diminishes. As part of this process, he gradually requires fewer fantasies of his own grandiosity, as he works toward his more realistic ambitions with increasing satisfaction and does not have to defend himself against the disappointment of involvement with another person by becoming aloof and utilizing the illusion of his self-sufficiency.

Validation

In the final phase of treatment for these patients, the experience of having their new functions and achievements validated by their therapist becomes a major aspect of the therapy (19). An emerging ego function or new aspect of the self cannot be integrated into that person satisfactorily until the person has the experience of seeing that function mirrored, appreciated, and validated by someone else. Thus, a crucial part of the last phase of treatment is the repeated acknowledgment by the therapist that the patient does possess new skills and capacities to feel and to relate to other persons and is, indeed, demonstrating these achievements in his therapy and daily life.

For some patients, therapy is completed at this point; they feel that they have what they need to live their lives in the way they want. For others, classical Oedipal issues emerge and are worked with in ways similar to those of neurotic patients.

OTHER PERSONALITY DISORDER DIAGNOSES

This framework of viewing primitive character disorders along a continuum from borderline to narcissistic personality disorder allows us to fit other primitive patients into this schema. For example, schizoid patients have some of the same issues as borderline patients but protect themselves from the intensity of their neediness by non-involvement and the illusion of self-sufficiency. They utilize the latter defense in much the same way as severe narcissistic personality disorders. Paranoid personality disorders have much in common with borderline and schizoid patients, but use projection as a more prominent defense. Antisocial personality disorders often have many borderline and narcissistic personality disorder features; however, they use action and antisocial activity as a way of expressing their anger and needs for holding and containing. Many inmates in the prison system are borderline patients who turn to society for the holding and control they cannot get from interpersonal relationships because of the intensity of their needs and the inadequacy of their ego capacities to contain them (24). Finally, schizotypal personality disorders seem to be variants of borderline personality disorder, but with a greater propensity for primitive thought disorder content.

COUNTERTRANSFERENCE

Borderline patients present such a challenge to therapists in part because of the intensity of the responses they arouse (25, 26). The therapist's feelings about the demands, engulfment, inconsiderateness, anger, and idealization alternating with devaluation by these patients can be overwhelming. The therapist may view these patients as all bad, manipulative, entirely hostile, hateful people. It is as if one part of them has become their entire personality in the therapist's eyes. The therapist himself may alternate among rescuing, rejecting, and attacking them. He may confront them (27) in a sadistic manner, while feeling that he is only helping to clarify some important piece of reality or setting the limits they need. Such intense therapist feelings have played an important role in the evolution of the term "borderline" from a descriptive diagnostic statement to one that has a pejorative, rejecting flavor.

Once the patient achieves the narcissistic personality disorder level of functioning and relating, countertransference issues more frequently involve the boredom that the therapist experiences when he feel unrelated to the patient as a separate person. This countertransference experience is common during the partial merger in a mirror or idealizing selfobject transference. In addition, therapists may have difficulty being comfortable with the idealization of these patients during phases of the selfobject transferences. These countertransference difficulties can seriously impair the optimal psychotherapeutic work with these narcissistic personality disorder issues. However, the distress of the therapist is usually mild when compared with the overt intensity of feeling that he experiences when treating borderline patients.

These countertranference issues can provide the challenge to the therapist to develop as a clinician who is able to work with intense feelings, occasionally of life and death import. The framework described in this chapter can provide the structure that allows the therapist sufficient distance and an opportunity to use his intellect when he is affectively overwhelmed. Such theoretical frameworks, as well as the use of trusted colleagues for consultation and support, can be the transitional objects to help therapists with their own feelings of being alone in the middle of a storm. Useful theory and colleagues can become the inner companions who help provide the links when such patients challenge us momentarily beyond our capacity. Yet, we have enough clinical evidence to encourage us to continue working with such patients, not only because they can move along the borderline-narcissistic personality disorder continuum as they improve, but also because we have so much more to learn from our work with them.

REFERENCES

1. *Diagnostic and Statistical Manual of Mental Disorders,* Third Edition. Washington, D.C.: American Psychiatric Association, 1980.
2. BRANDCHAFT, B., and STOLOROW, R.D.: The borderline concept: Pathological character or iatrogenic myth? In: J. Lichtenberg, et al. (Eds.), *Empathy.* (in press).
3. ADLER, G.: The borderline-narcissistic personality disorder continuum. *Am. J. Psychiat.,* 138: 46-50, 1981.
4. ADLER, G.: The usefulness of the "borderline" concept in psychotherapy. In: J. E. Mack (Ed.), *Borderline States in Psychiatry.* New York: Grune & Stratton, 1975.
5. ADLER, G.: Transference, real relationship, and alliance. *Int. J. Psychoanal.,* 61: 547-548, 1980.
6. ADLER, G., and BUIE, D.H.: Aloneness and borderline psychopathology: The possible relevance of child development issues. *Int. J. Psychoanal.,* 60: 83-96, 1979.
7. BURNHAM, D.G., GLADSTONE, A.I., and GIBSON, R.W.: *Schizophrenia and the Need-Fear Dilemma.* New York: International Universities Press., 1969.
8. KOHUT, H.: *The Analysis of the Self.* New York: International Universities Press., 1971.
9. KOHUT, H.: *The Restoration of the Self.* New York: International Universities Press., 1977.
10. KERNBERG, O.: *Borderline Conditions and Pathological Narcissism.* New York: Jason Aronson, 1975.
11. FAIRBAIRN, W.R.D.: *An Object-relations Theory of Personality.* New York: Basic Books, 1952.
12. JACOBSON, E.: *The Self and the Object World.* New York: International Universities Press., 1964.
13. FREUD, S.: The ego and the id. *Standard Edition,* 19: 19-39. London: Hogarth Press, 1961.
14. WINNICOTT, D.W.: *The Maturational Process and the Facilitating Environment.* New York: International Universities Press, 1965.
15. MAHLER, M.S., PINE, F., and BERGMAN, A.: *The Psychological Birth of the Human Infant.* New York: Basic Books, 1975.
16. GUNTRIP, H.: *Psychoanalytic Theory, Therapy, and the Self.* New York: Basic Books, 1971.
17. BALINT, M.: *The Basic Fault: Therapeutic Aspects of Regression.* London: Tavistock Publications, 1968.
18. MODELL, A.H.: The holding environment and the therapeutic action of psychoanalysis. *J. Am. Psychother.,* 24: 285-308, 1976.
19. BUIE, D.H., and ADLER, G.: Definitive treatment of the borderline patient. *Inter. J. Psychoanal. Psychother.,* 9: 51-87, 1982.
20. PIAGET, J.: *The Construction of Reality of the Child (1937).* New York: Basic Books, 1954.
21. FRAIBERG, S.: Libidinal object constancy and mental representation. *Psychoanal. Study Child.,* 24: 9-47, 1969.

22. WINNICOTT, D.W.: Transitional object and transitional phenomena (1953). In: *Collected Papers*. London: Tavistock, 1958.
23. TOLPIN, M.: On the beginnings of a cohesive self: An application of the concept of transmuting internalization to the study of the transitional object and anxiety. *Psychoanal. Study Child.*, 26: 316-352, 1971.
24. ADLER, G.: Correctional (prison) psychiatry In: H. Kaplan, A.M. Freedman, and B. Sadock (Eds.), *Comprehensive Textbook of Psychiatry*, 3rd ed. Baltimore: Williams & Wilkins, 1980.
25. ADLER, G.: Valuing and devaluing in the psychotherapeutic process. *Arch. Gen. Psychiat.*, 22: 454-461, 1970.
26. ADLER, G.: Helplessness in the helpers. *Br. J. Med. Psychol.*, 45: 315-326, 1972.
27. ADLER, G., and BUIE, D.H.: Misuses of confrontation with the borderline patient. *Int. J. Psychoanal. Psychother.*, 1: 109-120, 1972.

Part IV

RELATED
MANAGEMENT ISSUES

9

Doctors in Trouble:
The Caretaker's Character
and Its Flaws

Douglas A. Sargent, M.D., J.D.

INTRODUCTION

Recently, organized medicine has begun to scrutinize the physician's own personality for elements that adversely affect medical practice (1). In this chapter, I will focus on how the reciprocal interaction between the imposing demands of practice and flaws in the physician's character may harm the physician's practice and even shorten the physician's life. To paraphrase Clemenceau,* character is to personality as climate is to geography. Both character and climate refer to recurrent, stable, and roughly predictable tendencies that give a region or a personality its unique "flavor." Just as climate cannot forecast the weather on any particular day, so character does not predict behavior from moment to moment, but only roughly outlines the range within which behavior may be expected to vary.

Character and the environment which evokes characteristic behavior interact complexly. But we must try to separate these elements if we are to understand their relative contributions to the resultant balance. Since the ideal "medical character" is presumed to suit the normal demands of medical practice, one may fairly consider these character types that appear to be incompatible with tranquility and effectiveness in the "average expectable medical environment."

_____

*"Military justice is to justice as military music is to music."

159

Since charater is the focus, I will omit practice failures that result from accidents or from circumstances clearly unrelated to the caretaker's character.

After briefly reviewing some concepts of character, characterologies and character disorder, I will illustrate with case vignettes how character traits thought characteristic of the "ideal physician" may be incompatible with successful practice if they grow out of proportion. Where the facts permit, I will suggest how some of these traits originated, why they became exaggerated, and how this led to the physician's downfall. Attributes of the medical system which conspire in this process will be identified and remedies suggested. Before launching into the clinical material, I will summarize some fundamentals.

Why Characterize?

Character is, among other things, a diagnosis that tries to predict future behavior in unpredictable circumstances. Characterizations vary in complexity and specificity according to their intended use. At one end of a spectrum lie supposedly simple and clear divisions, such as male and female, which are useful in deciding which washroom to enter. Nearer the middle lie categories used in selecting candidates for medical school and other situations resembling battlefield triage. At the other end lie exhaustive catalogues of personality traits exquisitely attuned to nuances of personality explicated by diligent research embracing and accounting for manifold data, such as those generated by the need to impress one's colleagues. Each of the resulting categories are labeled by traits common to the group or by names that convey something characteristic of each group, that is, that which gives the group its *character*.

In what follows I will describe the practice behavior of some "characteristic" residents of the category "doctors who have gotten into trouble." My purpose is to sketch recognizable profiles of physicians who have survived the ordeal of medical education only to succumb to the rigors of postgraduate training or medical practice. Like those aircraft recognition silhouettes which enabled defenders to distinguish between reconnaissance planes, fighters, and bombers so as to neutralize the dangers peculiar to each, these profiles may help us to recognize traits that jeopardize medical practice, the practitioner, and the patient. Rather than fleshing out these sketches, I hope only to present vivid images that will impress the reader by their very excesses, raising questions about the absolute nature of the "medical virtues" they caricature.

What Is "Character"?

Although I intend to avoid the contradictory definitions, meanings, and purposes that dot the extensive literature on character and its disorders, I will briefly acknowledge its scope, if only to show respect for those who have labored diligently in that thorny thicket. In 513 B.C. Heraclitus (2) emphasized the role character plays in human affairs by declaring: "Character for man is destiny." Freud (3) paraphrased this historical opinion in his famous pronouncement, "*anatomy* is destiny," and proceeded to find the roots of character in instinctual development, " . . . unchanged prolongations of the original instincts, or sublimations of those instincts, or reactions against them." In so doing Freud also built on another ancient tradition, recorded by Aristotle:

> It is the universal belief that in some sense the moral qualities are each and all the *gift of Nature;* if we have a disposition to justice, to temperance, to courage, and the other virtues, we have it from birth (4, p. 190, emphasis supplied).

Most psychoanalytic definitions of character following Freud's emphasize the interplay between nature and nurture. To this dynamic view Reich added the tension between individual drives and the demands of society. As used in psychoanalysis today, character refers to ". . . the constellation of relatively fixed personality traits . . . that govern habitual modes of response," while character disorder refers to a ". . . personality pattern characterized by maladaptive, inflexible behavior" (5, p. 3315). But some clinicians say that "character," used merely as an epitaph to mark a process that is finished, loses some of its interest for them.

Character Types

Characterologies are as numerous and varied as the purposes giving rise to them. Whether they emphasize constitutional "givens" or environmental "experience," all characterologies have trouble with the question: Does character *describe* a range of relatively fixed and predictable behaviors unique to an individual, or groups of similarly behaving individuals, or does character *determine* behavior according to the demands life places upon individuals with unique, though varying, predispositions to respond? Samuel Butler, an older exponent of the determinative school, emphasized the determinative power of constitution: "Every man's work, whether it be literature or music or pictures or architecture or anything else, is always a portrait of himself, and the more he tries to conceal himself the more clearly will his character appear in spite of him" (6, p. 70).

Ovid, on the other hand, expounded the view that, whatever its roots, character is molded by experience: "Note too that a faithful study of the liberal arts humanizes character and permits it not to be cruel" (7, p. 363).

Shakespeare's (8) characterology ("All the world's a stage . . .") employed a developmental schema in which constitutional predispositions interact with the "average expectable environment" at each of life's seven stages. Thus, his character types (the mewling and puking infant, the whining schoolboy, the lover sighing like a furnace, the soldier jealous in honor, the justice in fair round belly, the lean and sipper'd pantaloon) have a dynamic compass and a fidelity to life unmatched until the present era. Those who treat character as the immutable result of a developmental process completed in childhood ignore at their peril Shakespeare's recognition that, among other influences, character is affected by the life cycle.

E.L. Pincoffs, a contemporary philosopher, supplies a brief definition that I find especially useful:

> A personality trait . . . is a relatively stable and permanent disposition by means of which one individual may be distinguished from another . . . character traits are a subclass of personality traits. Character traits include moral character traits—those which we have a moral right to demand of one another. . . . Character traits are personality traits which are generally approved or disapproved (9).

THE IDEAL PHYSICIAN

Pincoffs' definition best captures the sense in which the term "character" is used when delineating the "ideal medical character." Medical authors often use these traits as if they were moral imperatives. A partial list of character traits that various authors have claimed to be *essential* to the ideal physician includes the following: altruism, idealism, selflessness, dedication, self-denial, humility, wisdom, cultural breadth, expertise, effectiveness, health, stability, energy, self-control, equanimity, empathy, concern, humaneness, benevolence, sensitivity, social responsibility, conservation, propriety, honesty, righteousness, success, and public respect. Of course, these traits supplement the routine requirements: omniscience, omnipotence, and omnipresence.

"Medical Character" in the Context of Practice

Marmor (10) has shown how the stresses of medical practice, especially role strain, can predispose physicians to feelings of inadequacy and depression. Vaillant, Sobowale, and McArthur (11) have recorded the attrition of biologically and educationally superior college graduates from disorders popularly attributed to weak character or constitutional inadequacy. Elsewhere (12) I have pointed to features of the medical system that may cause vulnerable physicians to exit medicine prematurely from suicide or "lethal lifestyle."

The vignettes that follow highlight character traits ordinarily regarded as desirable but which, when overgrown, accelerate the process of professional failure. Vaillant et al. also have identified four character traits perceived by physicians themselves to be of paramount importance to the medical character: belief in one's own judgment, independence, altruism, and emotional self-control (11). I will use these traits as benchmarks, adding a sixth suggested by Crawshaw:* success, which easily deteriorates into greed. Using case vignettes, I will show how these desirable traits can be grotesquely amplified when the stresses of medical practice catalyze vulnerabilities carried over from earlier life stages. Each vignette** describes a physician whose practice caricatures an element of the medical character generally believed to be a virtue.

CASE VIGNETTES

Belief in One's Own Judgment

Jack was a typical surgical resident in a metropolitan hospital. He was under continual stress. Since becoming Chief Resident, his 100-hour week had grown to 110 hours, and there was no end in sight. Jack's new duties exhilarated him. A super-responsible caretaker all his life, Jack gloried in his ability to carry any load, to take pains to do the job right. As a medical student he always checked his work twice; as intern he repeated the other medical students' work "to make sure"; as a resident he pushed himself to check the work of the medical students and interns.

Now that he was Chief Resident there was not enough time to check up on everyone. At night he came home too drained to eat or talk. Jack had always been proud of his superior rational capacities. He had always striven to outdo an older brother, who had become "only" a dentist. During adolescence, with his brother away in dental school, Jack had to referee his parents' arguments, bringing his rationality to bear upon their emotional excesses. Later, in medical school, he diagnosed his mother's coma, which had baffled her physicians, and participated in the neurosurgery that cured her and confirmed his astute diagnosis. Jack believed that he could reason his way out of any difficulty. In emergencies he remained coolly competent and aloof from emotions that sidelined others.

But recently Jack's cool veneer had been wearing thin. Jack had a new daughter. Even more burdened by the additional expense and responsibility of fatherhood, Jack tried, vainly, to meet these new demands, but could see no solution beyond working even harder, a patent impossibility. As his vaunted self-con-

---

*In an address to the 5th National AMA Conference on the Impaired Physician, Portland, Oregon, September, 1982.
**The identity of each physician has been disguised for obvious reasons.

fidence began to falter, he could not allow anyone, especially his wife, to see his "weakness." He drew even farther away from her. Always self-sufficient, Jack could not ask for help. Instead, pleading preoccupation with his demanding work, he grew remote.

As pressures mounted, Jack sought hurried relief in what he thought of as "compressed vacations." Alone in a motel room (though available by beeper even when not on call) Jack banished the pressures with up to 800 mgm of Meperidrine. Refreshed by an interlude of euphoria, Jack could return to the grind and continue the race to keep ahead.

His wife knew about his "vacations" but, though she disapproved, she did not know how to stop him. Until she learned that she was pregnant, Jack's wife joined him in what they considered recreational drug use, common to their social group. They began using marijuana and other "soft" drugs in undergraduate school and continued throughout medical school and residency. Typically, Jack had reassured her that *they* could take drugs or leave them alone. But when his wife became pregnant, she refused to join Jack in his increasing use of drugs. Unknown to his wife, Jack's secret "vacations" came more frequently and lasted longer. Occasionally the hospital couldn't find Jack. He was falling farther behind. One day he got his Meperidrine by forging perscriptions for a fictitious patient. He was caught, arrested and arraigned for drug violations. Jack's highly vaunted judgment had become unreliable.

Early the next morning, still reeling under the shame of the public spectacle the newspapers had made of his arrest and arraignment, Jack could not rid himself of the conviction that his life was over. He remembered the image of the somber-faced members of the licensure board who had impressed the newly-licensed physicians with their medical obligations when he had been admitted to practice three years earlier. Their words echoed in his head, intoning the high ethical principles of medicine. He believed that he had degraded this oath and had ended his promising surgical career. The images of his wife and daughter, whose lives he felt he had ruined, haunted him. Jack was filled with self-revulsion. Atonement seemed possible only through death. Since he felt that he did not deserve to live, this was no sacrifice.

With his head filled with these thoughts, Jack found himself on a lonely mountain road high above a deep gorge. He stopped the car at a notoriously dangerous curve. Walking to the edge of the precipice, Jack peered over the guardrail. It seemed a sheer drop. Returning to the car, Jack made a U-turn. When he had gone far enough, he turned again and drove through the guardrail at 60 mph. Jack had done all he could to assure his death. He left no suicide note. Miraculously, his car had struck the top of a forked pine and wedged there on a small promontory 400 feet below the road. Jack's right arm was paralyzed and his back hurt from crushed vertebrae, but the wish to die was gone. Thus Jack lived to tell this tale.

Independence I

Butch, a first year resident, bolstered his uncertainties with grandiose fantasies of ostentatious achievement in a surgical specialty he associated with *machismo*. Yet his ambivalence created anxieties that he could assuage only by jeopardizing his success in surgical training.

Butch's hope for a political career, fueled by success in running for class office in high school, faded in college when he confronted the "lack of connections" with which his parents' poverty, lack of education, and immigrant status supposedly burdened him. Robbed of this goal by the accident of birth, Butch feared that he would lapse into the morass of passivity and helplessness he associated with his chronically depressed mother. Butch had grown up in his mother's sticky embrace, pushed into academic achievement by her ambitions, and dependent upon her advice for most decisions. He learned from her to view his father as rough, ignorant, and weak. His mother warned that the alternative to success was a life as an "underpaid failure" like his father, dependent upon the whim of his boss or the approval of his wife. In addition, Butch's own secret fear that he might too closely resemble his mother crippled his virility. He approached women with ambivalence. Still a virgin at 30, Butch's rigid moral stance against premarital sex sheltered him from confronting his fear of impotence or ineptitude. He could dare nothing that his mother did not permit. Yet Butch yearned to be independent.

In medical school Butch had a superficially successful but inwardly turbulent time. Dubbed "Mr. Clean" by his classmates, he strove to achieve recognition yet sabotaged his own efforts. He was attracted to the surgical specialities, especially orthopedics, which he viewed as satisfyingly virile and which promised the kind of self-confidence that had eluded him since his "failure" in politics. Through alternately under- and overstudying, Butch had managed to fail in his first attempts at National Boards and entered a competitive surgical specialty in a state of great ambivalence and high anxiety. He realized that, despite his hope for spectacular success as a surgeon, in medical school he had felt relaxed and comfortable only during a rotation under the tutelage of a warm and friendly rural family practitioner whom Butch secretly disparaged as inept and bumbling like his father. Thus he feared that his decision to become a surgeon might have been a mistake.

Butch sought treatment for his anxiety several weeks before he began surgical residency, fearing quite realistically that anxiety would overwhelm him once his residency began. He was urged to cancel a planned Board cram course that was clearly incompatible with his surgical duties. Yet he still approached each new rotation fearing failure and success equally. Butch could not choose between the swashbuckling surgical life whose audacity and independence he admired and the safe obscurity of a lower profile life in medicine. Here we leave him, his future still in doubt.

Altruism

Doris was equipped by nature to be a good businesswoman. But throughout her medical life she strove vainly to become, instead, the good caretaker her parents had programmed her to be. Misplaced "kindness" sabotaged both her parents' hopes and her own aspirations.

Doris knew after her first month in private practice that she was not cut out to be a practitioner. She had done well in the basic sciences and had found the intellectual rivalry of medical school stimulating. She also had enjoyed the challenge of internship. But once all of these structured experiences were behind her, Doris was adrift on a sea of uncertainty. She soon learned that this sea was full of sharks in the form of patients with inscrutable ailments only vaguely resembling the "classical" cases of medical school. When she could not readily diagnose these parents she felt assailed by their demands for help. Though disillusioned, Doris was not a quitter; she continued to practice medicine for 25 years.

Overcoming her disappointment that medical practice did not live up to her expectations, Doris tried to relieve the anxiety practice caused by devoting herself to the *business* of medicine, where her talent for organization and head for figures brought her satisfaction and recognition. She organized a medical group which prospered under her direction. Yet she also felt impelled to carry on the busiest practice of the group, since she believed that a "real doctor" healed the sick and comforted the dying. Until a patient told Doris' husband that she had been having sexual relations with Doris, she had managed this dual burden with an outward appearance of benign calm.

The investigation (and treatment) that followed this astonishing news disclosed that, over the years, Doris had gathered about her a group of clinging, waif-like women whose elusive complaints defied her best therapeutic efforts. Although she could not cure them, neither could she bring herself to refer them elsewhere or to say that she could not help them. Each alternative seemed to admit medical ineptitude. When she could not quiet their demands with traditional medical skills, Doris brought them sexual comfort; she relieved their distress by giving them herself. Perhaps she recognized that an inability to assuage loneliness lay at the root of her waif-patients' distress. Doris' husband, an orphan whose personality strikingly resembled her importunate patients, readily understood that Doris' "therapy" was a grotesque parody of the ideal "caring physician" she had wanted to be but somehow never could become. Doris' rebellion against her family-imposed duty to be a "good physician" traduced the principles she had sworn to uphold. Needless to say, this sabotage also catapulted her out of medicine.

$uccess

Victor exploited the esteem and financial reward that a grateful society accords successful physicians in order to counteract chronic depression and a legacy of parental pessimism about his ever achieving success in life. Since outstanding financial success could not evoke from his long-dead parents the acknowledgment he craved, he turned vainly to drugs and the praise of his patients for a relief which he finally achieved only in death.

Victor's pessimistic parents had disparaged his youthful success in athletics and repeatedly predicted that he would "end up a bum," since his diligence and scholarship did not meet their expectations. A younger sister obtained the praise that they withheld from Victor, even though he was as bright as she. He entered medical school determined to best his sister and prove his parents wrong. His talent and intelligence carried him through a good residency and into a thriving suburban practice. He soon acquired a veneer of elegance that, for a time, concealed the rawer evidence of his drive for success measured by wealth. He also acquired a country club practice and prided himself in being the doctor of the moneyed set. To outsiders he appeared to enjoy a satisfying lifestyle. Yet each evening, to the annoyance of his wife and children, he ostentatiously tallied his net worth on a calculator. By the time he killed himself, Victor boasted to his family he had become a millionaire.

Victor had also become a drug addict. His social esteem and affluence could not assuage constant, gnawing feelings of inadequacy and chronic depression. His black moods and drug-driven instability thwarted the efforts of several therapists. His wife and children became estranged. At the end of his life this rich waif was practicing incompetently and making confessors, confidants, and "therapists" out of his patients, who grew bored with listening to his problems and left. Colleagues to whom Victor's desperate wife reported his drug abuse and the dangers this posed for his patients ignored her pleas that they stop him. Victor's suicide note catalogued his reasons for despair: loneliness, estrangement from his family, and the fear of becoming incompetent. These reasons seemed persuasive.

Emotional Self-control

All his life Dan's icy exterior concealed inner turmoil held rigidly in check. Early one Sunday morning he awoke in an empty house, needlessly mowed his neat lawn, tidied up a spotless kitchen, and wrote a farewell note to his absent family. On the kitchen table he made a cairn of his important papers, topped with a wristwatch inscribed "To the Doctor of the Year." Then he drove to a remote spot and washed down a fatal dose of Seconal with a martini he had brought with him to commemorate a ritual he often had shared with his wife in happier times.

Dan was the youngest of four children born to an indulgent mother and a harsh, driving father. A sickly infant who "should have died," Dan was special to his mother, who expected great things of her son. Dan exceeded her expectations, but could never please his dour, inaccessible father, whose approval Dan nevertheless continued to seek. No one ever heard his father acknowledge Dan's achievements.

Dan graduated near the top of his medical class and went on to success in a demanding specialty. After marrying his childhood sweetheart, Dan settled into a busy hospital practice where his drive and intelligence soon brought him the respect, but not the warm friendship, of colleagues. As his reputation grew, he worked a 12-hour day which left no time for giving his sons the fatherly attention he often complained that he had missed in his own childhood. Social life, too, was skimped. The marriage withered.

Dan was 40 when his colleagues named him "Doctor of the Year." Soon after, he fell ill and was ordered to reduce his work load. With typical efficiency, Dan found a half-time job in a small town and left with his family for semi-retirement. But his new colleagues recognized Dan's talent for organization and "rewarded" him with duties he could not resist. Soon he was again working a 12-hour day and taking work home. Retirement was shelved.

Dan's austerity and perfectionism rubbed his colleagues the wrong way, though they reluctantly admitted that usually he was right. Not without an astringent sense of humor, Dan once jokingly remarked, after correcting a colleague; "But then, I'm never wrong." Dan also carried his drive for perfection home with him. His lawn and garden beds were weedless. His garden tools hung in precise rows. His family, too, was pressured by his insatiable demands for perfection. Interference with his efficient routines drew Dan's cool, irrefutable correction.

A year-long campaign to improve the hospital's classification was accomplished under Dan's driving leadership, but this success did not satisfy him. Instead, he continued to press for even higher standards of performance, sometimes citing nonexistent "regulations." Failure to meet his increasingly irrational demands brought Dan's contemptuous outburst, usually followed by a graceful apology, which temporarily disarmed his wounded colleagues. Often Dan seemed distracted. Sometimes he came to work unshaven, his wrinkled clothes contrasting sharply with his customary immaculateness.

At home Dan's irritability and criticism further repelled his sons and exhausted his wife. Yet he rejected her attempts to break through his infuriating reserve. Finally, defeated by Dan's intransigence, she consulted a lawyer. Summoned to the administrator's office by the telepage, Dan was handed divorce papers. Three days later he was dead. His wife and children were sick with grief and guilt, feeling that they should have been able to save him, yet reluctantly acknowledging that they could not penetrate Dan's controlled isolation.

A driven overachiever, Dan never ceased to strive for his father's unattainable approval. Later he adopted his father's unrelenting nature as his own. While he set himself high goals, their attainment never brought him satisfaction. Instead, each success triggered a new demand.

When a debilitating disease threatened Dan's belief in his invincible self-control, he tried to deny his impairment by redoubling his achievements. But with the resilience of youth gone, Dan slid inexorably into his final depression, whose signs were masked by his characteristic aloof, prickly manner. Those perceptive enough to approach him about his growing signs of distress were rebuffed. Only a small group of foreign physicians reported, to everyone's surprise, that with them Dan was warm, friendly, and fatherly. As Dan's defense crumbled, he thwarted all attempts to help him. His desultory efforts to evoke sympathy alternated with a stiffening of his defensive façade, so that no rescuer was bold enough to save Dan from his self-destructive course. When the end came, he was alone. Dan's final medical act was also typically controlled: He prescribed death and filled the prescription himself.

Independence II

Joshua made his own decisions. He had to—he could trust no one. In a high risk specialty, he prided himself on having never lost a patient through his own fault. He was acknowledged as a leader in his field and in the community. His probity and decisiveness had earned him the respect of colleagues and patients. His practice flourished. At home, too, all was well with him. His wife and children affirmed his effective fatherhood.

But Joshua had a secret—for over 20 years he had successfully concealed his bisexuality from his wife and from the medical community. Though a few members of the gay community knew of his secret, they held their tongues. He confined his homosexual exploits to out-of-town trips. He managed to preserve his medical life (which, to him, embraced not only his practice but also his social and family life) free from the "taint" of his secret sexual life. He had walked this tightrope with growing confidence until it seemed that his medical life had a magical invulnerability akin to sanctity. He managed this by keeping his own counsel in all things.

The spell was shattered by his first "mistake." A patient died inexplicably during a simple procedure. While brooding over the possibility that he might have made an error, he got an anonymous call threatening to disclose his sexual secret. Stunned by these twin disasters which jeopardized his precarious "independence," Joshua opened his radial artery, inserted a cannula, and prepared to die. Saved by his alert wife and an efficient emergency service crew whom he had trained himself, he lived and, with psychiatric help, grudgingly learned to accept a degree of dependency.

CHARACTER AND THE MEDICAL MISSION

Medicine is not only a discipline, a science, and an art, but also a system, part of the health care delivery system with which it is sometimes confused. Although physicians are not cut from the same cloth, they are molded to a degree by the medical system in rough conformity to an ideal personality type with many of the stereotypical character attributes Vaillant et al. found.

Medicine both attracts and selects a range of character types. What is known about those who drop out of medical school suggests that many do so because of a variety of character flaws (13). Those who complete medical training tend to resemble one another in many ways. The medical system further shapes these survivors to its needs by pressing them through the die of daily patient care conducted according to an inflexible, demanding standard. This formative process is supposed to weed out physicians who lack enduring, or, at least, self-renewing character traits approximating the ideal. Those who remain have, in theory, a rugged character expected to sustain them throughout the stresses of a long life in medicine. Of course, it often seems to work out as planned. But exceptions like those I have described never achieve a tolerable harmony between their capacities and the demands practice places upon them. Many fail in spectacular ways. These exceptions may slip through the filters intended to intercept them because they ostentatiously exemplify one or more "ideal" character trait(s) so that they project a deceptive image of suitability.

In addition to these acknowledged failures, there are likely to be many more distressed physicians for whom medicine proves excessively demanding and oppressive, but whose discomfort never reaches disastrous proportions. Sometimes the failure results from a clash between impossible medical demands and an equally unsatisfied compulsion to try to meet them. More often the conflict is between stereotyped, transgenerational expectations imposed upon "bound delegates'' (14) who blindly or unconsciously try to fulfill traditional family goals in a medical context that cannot be made to yield satisfaction.

SUGGESTIONS FOR RISK MANAGEMENT

Against the dangers exemplified by these tragic cases, Warton has recommended that something like a Surgeon General's warning, "This occupation may be dangerous to your health," may be appropriate (15). But, if it is to be effective, full disclosure of the risks must stand, like Dante's famous warning, at the threshold of the medical career. Even such a warning is not likely to deter those "bound delegates" sent into the medical world with knapsacks full of potent family instructions.

The abandonment of John Wayne as a role model also might reduce the carnage on both sides of the operating table. While Dr. Christian might be a more attainable model, he did ooze homilies a bit too freely for the fastidious.

Another approach might be for medical educators to openly acknowledge the legitimacy of the solution chosen by such physicians as James Boswell, Somerset Maugham, Michael Crichton, Jonathan Miller or even Julius Caesar Stein (speaking of family instructions!), an ophthalmologist who never practiced, but who founded Music Corporation of America, and, with a small part of the profits, later endowed the Stein Eye Institute at UCLA. An early decision to leave medicine might save many doctors of this world a lot of grief.

Many have suggested that a public, frontal assault on excessive self-sufficiency and the other malfunctional traits Rogers Smith (16) has called the "M.D.iety complex," might diminish the attraction medicine holds for those medical aspirants already deeply imbued with the need for omniscience and omnipotence. Yet one must ruefully acknowledge that these attributes spring eternal from the projections of patients hoping for magical cures from god-like doctors. If we do not come to medicine with the trappings of deity, our patients soon supply them. Still, medicine might do a better job of weeding out those candidates already anointed and of immunizing the rest of us against this danger through education and conscious role-modeling by medical educators. Scheiber has catalogued constructive suggestions rooted in medical education (17). Unfortunately, profiles like those above are not specific enough to help admissions committees with their difficult work.

SYSTEMIC FAULTS

I have, however, focused on character distortions without paying sufficient attention to the medical system in which they find expression. This system contributes to these startling departures from customary medical deportment that I have presented. Often medical education seems to foster in students an austerity beyond the temperamental disposition of normally gregarious individuals. The rigors of residency training often seem to exceed those absolutely needed for effective learning; excessive Spartanism seems to be associated with needless mistakes (18). By setting standards of medical achievement beyond the reasonable expectations of enlightened patients, we court astronomical malpractice awards when results fall below this impractical standard. When we modestly acknowledge responsibility for "medical miracles" without sharing the credit with chance or divine intervention, we call down upon ourselves reactions like the Tarasoff decision or lawsuits for "wrongful life." Perhaps if we did not hold ourselves out to be so wonderful, we would avoid the boomerang of inflated expectations.

In a positive vein, if physicians were to more clearly warn neophytes of the many opportunities for disappointment awaiting them in medicine, a more productive dialogue about the realities of practice might be initiated *before* they are inundated. By admitting that physicians are *expected* to feel pain and to need help, we might abandon the apprenticeship in malfunctional Spartanism. Medical training too often seems to leave us unable to feel our own pain until it is beyond remedy. The following case poignantly illustrates a relevant, and, unfortunately, common systemic failure.

Independence III

This sad story told by the widow of a young resident physician presents a third subcategory of hypertrophied "independence": overcompensation for a handicap that its possessor fears will bar him or her from medicine. Jason, the Chief Resident in a large city hospital, tried to ignore the limitations of the heart defect that finally killed him. Until he died, he drove himself furiously to excel in all areas of his life and did not ask for favor when his medical duties called for physical exertion that was life-threatening. His widow bitterly complained that his superiors did not modify his work load despite their knowledge of his handicap and the risk to his life that his defensive hyperactivity represented. Instead, she complained, the medical system conspired with Jason to work him to death.

Gargantuan but "admirable" character traits also can lead physicians into dangers outside of medicine from which no amount of skill or daring can extricate them. One last vignette will serve to illustrate the point that many doctors appear to die prematurely from the consequences of these character flaws even without the cooperation of the medical system.

Belief in One's Own Judgement II

Harold, a respected surgeon, was driving East to join his family. His busy schedule had prevented him from leaving when they had, and he was hurrying to meet them so that he could enjoy a much-needed and delayed family vacation. He had been driving through a blizzard, alone, for 11 hours. When he stopped at dusk to ask directions, he also called his wife, who urged him to stay where he was for the night and continue the trip over the mountains in the morning. But he argued that he could be with her in only a few more hours and pressed on into the blinding snowstorm. At dawn the State Police found him in his car, dead, at the bottom of a ravine below an icy curve. According to the police, he had skidded on ice because he was going too fast for the road conditions and had ignored travelers' advisory warnings against driving in the storm. Further investigation suggested that he also may have fallen asleep at the wheel. Harold's failure to heed the dangers of the weather and his need for sleep could be termed less than prudent, but not inconsistent with his personal philosophy: never to be daunted by the obstacles of life.

CONCLUSION

In this work there are no "final solutions," although some draconian ones have been suggested. Perfectionists have urged that physicians such as I have described should be forever banned from medicine. This harsh view ignores the lesson that many impaired physicians have been restored to practice through treatment. We should not be reluctant to acknowledge that such rehabilitation usually benefits from psychiatry's help. Compassionate, effective treatment may be available nowhere else, since we recognize that the troubled physician, like many of our other patients, often requires firmness as well as understanding. For example, temporarily suspending the privilege to practice well before the late stages described in the vignettes often may be necessary, even though the recipient may only appreciate this form of helpfulness later on. Such restriction should serve safety, not conformity. Unfortunately, from some hands, "help" for impaired physicians may come as an amalgam of benevolence and spleen not easily recognizable as therapy. We should avoid such mixtures. As Pincoffs has observed:

> . . . we have a right to expect others to act in a certain way, but not to be a certain kind of person . . . to confuse the question what rules we should observe with the question what kind of people we should be is morally abhorrent. For then the purely administrative necessities of living in community would give us open license to set about shaping one another's characters in the name of social harmony or efficiency (9, p. 6).

REFERENCES

1. STEINDLER, E.M.: *The Impaired Physician*. Chicago: AMA Dept. of Mental Health Bulletin, 1975.
2. HERACLITUS: *Ancilla to the Pre-Socratic Philosophers: A Complete Translation of the Fragments in Diels, Fragmente du Vorsokratiker*, Freeman, K., Cambridge, MA: Harvard University Press, 1962.
3. FREUD, S.: Character and anal erotism. *Standard Edition*, 9:167-176. London: Hogarth Press, 1959.
4. ARISTOTLE: *The Ethics of Aristotle: The Nicomachean Ethics Translated*, Vol. 13. Thomson, J.A.K., Baltimore: Penguin Books, 1959.
5. KAPLAN, H.I., FREEDMAN, A.M., and SADOCK, B.J. (Eds.): *Comprehensive Textbook of Psychiatry*-III. Baltimore: Williams and Wilkins, 1980.
6. BUTLER, S.: *The Way of All Flesh*. New York: Dutton, 1952.
7. OVID: *Epistulae Ex Ponto*, 11:9:47. In: *Ovid: With an English Translation*, Wheeler, A.L. London: Heinemann, 1924.
8. SHAKESPEARE, W.: *As You Like It*, Act II, Scene 7, In: *The Complete Poems and Plays of William Shakespeare*. New York: Houghton Mifflin, 1942.
9. PINCOFFS, E.L.: Legal responsibility and moral character. *Wayne Law Review*, Detroit: Wayne State University Law School, 1973.
10. MARMOR, J.: Some factors in occupationally related depression, *Psychiat. Annals*, 12: 913-920, 1982.
11. VAILLANT, G.E., SOBOWALE, N.C., and MCARTHUR, C.: Some psychological vulnerabilities of physicians. *New Engl. J. Med.*, 287: 372-375, 1972.
12. SARGENT, D.A.: Work in progress: Preventing suicide among physicians and other members of the health care team, *Conn. Med.*, 54: 583-586, 1981.
13. THOMAS, C.B.: What becomes of medical students: The dark side. *Johns Hopkins Med. J.*, 138: 185-195, 1976.
14. STIERLIN, H.: *Separating Adolescents and Parents*, New York: Jason Aronson, 1982.
15. WARTON, R.: The problem of psychiatric treatment of physicians, or, being a doctor may be dangerous to your health, Draft, circa 1976.
16. SMITH, R.J., MODLIN, H.C., and SARGENT, D.A.: The impaired physician. *Am. Coll. Psychs. Psychiat. Update*, 2: 1982.
17. SCHEIBER, S.C.: The emotional problems of physicians II: Current approaches to the problem. *Ariz. Med.*, 35: 336-337, 1978; and III: A longitudinal approach to the problems. *Ariz. Med.*, 37: 568, 1980.
18. MCCUE, J.D.: The effects of stress on physicians and their medical practice. *New Engl. J. Med.*, 306: 458-463, 1982.

10

Legal/Psychiatric Interfaces in Treating Character Disorders

W. Walter Menninger, M.D.

THE PROBLEM

Influenced by a humanistic tradition which argues for the dignity and worth of each individual and finding increasing enlightenment as to the change-ability of man's nature, modern society does have some wish to provide better treatment for all its deviant citizens. Friendly attitudes toward law violators, however, do not come easily. The criminal has wronged us, and our concern for his rehabilitation is also accompanied by our urge to punish him. This ambivalent attitude has led to a number of compromises in our treatment of offenders. Among them is an increased willingness to call upon psychiatrists to find arbitrary linkages between mental illness and criminality.

—Seymour Halleck (1, p. 38)

It is well-known that a substantial number of persons with characterological problems behave in ways that offend others. This may include the violation of a law which brings the individual into the purview of the criminal justice system. This is particularly true for persons with antisocial personality disorders or with paraphilias which involve sexual offenses. In some cases, because the offensive behaviors may be considered unusual, particularly abnormal, or difficult to un-derstand, the individual is referred to a psychiatrist for diagnostic evaluation, prognostic opinion, and/or recommendations for disposition/management/

175

treatment. On occasion, the referral is more an effort on the part of the offender or his legal counsel to seek some amelioration of the consequences of the behavior, enlisting the psychiatrist to find the individual more "sick" than "bad."

In his discussion of mental health and the law, Stone observes that the criminal justice system and the mental health system deal with a relatively constant pool of deviants and have a functional reciprocity (2). The same observation is made by Miller in his discussion of the similarity of the people managed by the two systems:

> On occasion we invoke some rather elaborate diagnostic and sorting procedures—psychiatric exams, psychological tests, and the like—to determine who goes into which slot—the mental hospital, the prison, etc. But for the most part, this sorting process is crude, unreliable, arbitrary, and only partially related to the condition of the people being sorted . . . (3).

Miller calls attention to recent studies which reflect the interchangeability of the correctional and mental health institutions. In California, it was found that judges were not so much concerned with the treatment of sex offenders as they were concerned that the offender serve time in an institution. Even when the mental hospital staff might report that a patient had been cured or was no longer a problem, if the period spent in the institution was less than the "going rate" for that particular offense, the judge would remand the individual to prison to spend the remaining period of time there (4). Another California study found little difference in individuals referred to a mental hospital compared to those sent to jail. Interestingly enough, in that study, the more aggressive individuals were not sent to jail but to the hospital (5).

In fact, mental health practitioners in every type of practice may be called upon to work with persons with a character problem who have been apprehended for violating the law. Consider the following case examples.

Case #1

S is a 19-year-old, single, white male who was apprehended for interstate transportation of a stolen motor vehicle and referred for psychiatic evaluation in a federal prison setting. The pre-sentence report observed, "Due to the extremely complicated nature of this subject's interpretation of life, his lack of self-control, and his chronic involvement in delinquent behavior, it is recommended that he be committed for study. . . . Possibly through skilled analysis of S's case, sufficient insight might be gained to enable those concerned to work effectively with him."

S was the second of six siblings born and raised in a small, northern Minnesota community. His father had a grade school education, worked as a farmhand and laborer, had an alcohol problem, and was abusive toward his children. For a number of years, he was physically and emotionally ill, and he committed suicide when S was 13. His mother also had only a grade school education. She worked as a waitress and was described as irresponsible, promiscuous, and alcoholic. Reportedly, she had two of S's siblings by men other then her husband.

S's antisocial behavior was first noted at age seven, when he was involved with a number of other boys in shooting out $300 worth of Christmas light bulbs. At age ten, he broke into a gas station with two older adolescents and ran away from home to spend the money. He was removed from the parental home at age 11 and went through a succession of two foster homes, a boys industrial school, and the state reformatory. His offenses were repeated stealing, car theft, and possession of a dangerous weapon.

In the clinical examination, he presented as a self-centered, immature, and naive young man of average general intelligence, with less ability to express himself verbally than by action. Impulsive in his behavior, he thought primarily of his own needs and desires, with no regard for the rights and feelings of others. His relationships were largely superficial, keeping others at a distance. He denied ever feeling angry toward people. He did have the capacity to function well in a goal-directed manner when given adequate supervision and control. He felt unable to provide his own leadership, but was also angry about having to follow the leadership of others. He consistently had difficulty understanding the things that happened to him, but there was no evidence of gross emotional disorganization or severe emotional illness. Diagnostically, he satisfied the criteria for an antisocial personality disorder.

He acknowledged that he did need to change, but he felt he could only do that on his own. He saw change as coming about by a complete change in the environment which would give him "something to live for and base my life on." His pattern was to search for someone who would provide him with leadership and love, which he never got as a child; yet, he would consistently act in a way to be rejected in such a relationship.

Case #2

R is an 18-year-old, white youth who was referred to a public mental hospital by the juvenile court after persistent defiance of his parents, truancy, drinking, fighting, and traffic violations. R was born into a middle-class family; his parents were divorced when he was ten. His father was a prominent attorney who tended to be matter-of-fact and resentful of his son. He had not wanted to have a child so early. Mother, who had two years of a college education, felt close to the boy and protected him from his father. The marriage was tumultuous from the beginning, with a disorganized household and little consistency in the life pattern.

When he began school, R had difficulty learning to read and write. He was evaluated and treated with play therapy at a local guidance center. During his grammar school years, he presented behavior difficulty and performed poorly. He had to repeat the fifth grade. After the parents' divorce, he first stayed with his mother. Increasingly defiant, he moved to live with his father. He was continually truant, evasive with his parents, and more and more disruptive. He stayed out all night, got drunk, fought with his parents, drove without a license, ran red lights, and finally came to the attention of the juvenile court authorities.

Admitted to the psychiatric hospital, he continued to be disruptive. He left without authorization 17 times in eight months and was finally discharged as untreatable because of lack of motivation. He returned home, functioned well for a brief period, and then returned to a pattern of late hours, drinking, and carousing. One night, while riding around with some friends, he (and they) robbed a parked car on a country road and were subsequently apprehended, charged, and convicted of grand larceny.

He was again referred to the hospital, through the efforts of his attorney father. At that time, the clinical examination found him a somewhat anxious young man who was reluctantly cooperative with the process. He had difficulty looking at the examiner and responded to most of the inquiries with ''I don't know'' or ''I guess so.'' His thinking was rather concrete, and under stress he became arbitrary and less well organized. Overall, he was of generally average or slightly less intelligence. His mind was preoccupied with a constant, most often fruitless, search for sources of gratification; at the same time, it was clear that his search, in spite of being persistent, met mostly with failure. There was no evidence of any distortion of psychotic proportions in his perception, thinking, or feeling. The clinical diagnosis was of a character disorder.

He denied any significant attachments in his life, and his relationship with his parents was one of distance, extreme distrust, and intense feelings of being misunderstood and neglected. He was capable of little reflection on the nature of his difficulties. Although he professed an interest in receiving help for his ''emotional problems,'' he did not want to be in an institution, either hospital or prison. He felt strongly that only he could work out his problems, and he insisted he had learned his lesson and was ready to take full responsibility for himself.

Case #3

L is a 37-year-old, twice-married, white male who was referred by his attorney for an outpatient psychiatric evaluation after apprehension on several counts of rape. The second of three children, he was raised in a small, rural community with a fundamentalist religious orientation. His father was a heavy equipment operator and his mother a religious counselor.

L dates difficulty controlling his sexual desires back to early childhood. Caught by his mother in the act of undressing with two neighborhood girls when he was seven, he recalls that his mother immediately fell to her knees to pray with him so that he wouldn't go to hell and that it wouldn't happen again. Nevertheless, from age eight on, he exposed himself intermittently to young girls and women. The tempo increased in early adolescence although his first arrest for indecent exposure was not until age 16. Over the years since, he continued the behavior, with arrests at ages 22, 27, and 33. Each time he was apprehended, he was forced to seek psychological help, but, consistently, when the legal pressure passed, he discontinued seeking assistance. He relates being told he had a "personality problem" with which he "would just have to learn to live."

After he graduated from high school, he went to work in a building trade. He steadily improved his status, ultimately owning his own business, in which he was fairly successful. After one unsuccessful marriage of eight years and two daughters, he married his present wife. Both he and his wife report having a good relationship in every respect, including sexual. Over the years, however, L has had a wide range of extramarital affairs, as well as continuing to intermittently expose himself. When his second wife became pregnant with their now-infant son, L began a series of encounters in which he would coerce a woman to participate in masturbation, fellatio, cunnilingus and finally intercourse. Consistently, he went to one of two other cities to perform these acts, doing so 13 or 14 times. His apprehension came only after what appears to have been an unconscious wish to be caught led him to compulsively return to several sites of his previous offenses on the same day.

He appeared for examination as a well-dressed, good-looking, articulate, and engaging gentleman. (Victims had previously described him as "a man you would feel comfortable with.") He was well oriented to his situation and struggling with the prospect of the loss of his freedom, separation from his wife and young son, and the failure of his business. He presented several contrasting facets of himself: a nice guy, polite, gracious, personable, "hail fellow well met"; a private, narcissistically oriented, special person who felt he would be readily forgiven if people really understood him; and an uncaring, aggressive, and sexually obsessed monster. In coping, he used dissociation to compartmentalize his feelings and behavior. Thus, he could experience shame and remorse, and then put those feelings aside without further concern.

Intellectually, he was average. The psychological testing suggested a possible learning disability in childhood. He had some difficulty in articulating thoughts and feelings clearly, and there was concreteness in his thinking. Overall, it appeared he was operating on a borderline level of ego functioning, with narcissistic as well as borderline personality disorder features. Under the pressure of strong feelings, his capacity to judge himself and control his behavior was limited. Only six days prior to the examination, out on bail, in yet a different city, he compulsively exposed himself to "a hundred women" in a five-hour period before being beaten up, arrested, and released after one day in jail (because the authorities in that city had no awareness of his other pending charges).

In each of these case illustrations, there was an interaction of some facet of the criminal justice system—court, correctional authorities, defense counsel—with the psychiatrist who was operating in different areas of practice—in the prison, the mental hospital, and in an outpatient clinical setting. The efforts and concerns of both systems were directed toward an individual whose functioning reflected a significant personality disorder and who was identified to some degree both as an offender and as a patient. In the context of this interaction, there is a potential for more effective understanding of and response to the needs of both the offender/patient and society; there is also potential for misunderstanding and disillusionment. Which potential is achieved in the interaction of law and psychiatry is a function, in part, of how well each system understands the purposes and operations of the other and how realistic the expectations are of what psychiatry and psychology can and cannot provide to the process.

CRITICAL QUESTIONS

Certain questions arise from the hopes and expectations of those in the criminal justice system that psychiatry and psychology might help in the control and/or change of offenders. More specifically, critical questions are raised about the capacity of psychiatry:

1) To diagnose or understand persons with behavior disorders;
2) To make predictions about the future behavior of these persons, both with and without clinical intervention; and
3) To make recommendations and/or provide treatment for such persons, with particular concern for what may prompt these persons to change and no longer engage in antisocial behavior.

With regard to the first question of diagnosis, there has long been a concern in the minds of many in the criminal justice system that psychiatric diagnosis is imprecise, arbitrary, inconsistent, and might or might not contribute to an increased understanding of the offender/patient. This view is reinforced every time psychiatrists testify to differing and contrasting diagnostic formulations about the same patient. The introduction of the more carefully outlined and precisely defined diagnostic criteria of the American Psychiatric Association's Diagnostic and Statistical Manual of Mental Disorders (Third Edition) (6) should improve the performance of psychiatrists in this respect.

A continuing point of confusion is whether a "mental disorder" as included and defined in DSM-III is ipso facto a mental illness, insofar as it may be seen in the eyes of the law as reducing an individual's capacity for mens rea (criminal intent). Judge David Bazelon had high hopes that psychiatry could make a substantial contribution to the criminal justice process, and he articulated those hopes in his 1954 Durham opinion (7), which held that "if defendant's unlawful act was the product of mental disease or defect, he was not criminally responsible." Bazelon sought to permit the psychiatrist to inform the jury of the character of the accused's mental disease, so that the jury could then determine whether the unlawful act stemmed from and was the product of a mental disease or defect, hence "moral blame should not attach" (7, p. 876). Initially, as cases were evaluated at St. Elizabeth's Hospital, the diagnosis of sociopathic (antisocial) personality was not considered to be a mental illness. Precipitously, the staff reversed itself on that point, concluding that since that condition was included in the then official APA diagnostic manual, it must therefore be a mental disease. The sequence of events was cited in the later court decision which overturned Durham:

> . . . In the absence of a definition of "mental disease or defect," medical experts attach to them the meanings which would naturally occur to them . . . The problem was dramatically highlighted by the weekend flip flop case, In re Rosenfield, 157 F.Supp. 18 (D.D.C. 1957). The petitioner was described as a sociopath. A St. Elizabeth's psychiatrist testified that a person with a sociopathic personality was not suffering from a mental disease. That was on Friday afternoon. On Monday morning, through a policy change at St. Elizabeth's Hospital, it was determined as an administrative matter that the state of psychopathic or sociopathic personality did constitute a mental disease (8, p. 978).

Actually, that "flip flop" had prompted the court in an earlier decision to differentiate between the legal and medical definition of "mental illness":

> What psychiatrists may consider a "mental disease or defect" for clinical purposes, where their concern is treatment, may or may not be the same as mental disease or defect for the jury's purpose in determining criminal responsibility . . . For that purpose, the jury should be told that a mental disease or defect includes any abnormal condition of the mind which

substantially affects mental or emotional processes and substantially impairs behavior controls (9, p. 851).

Beyond the definitional problem is the question of just how helpful a diagnosis is to the legal system, beyond its prognostic implications. For the most part, the criminal justice system, particularly corrections, is not prepared to respond to a diagnostic formulation with a disposition which includes psychiatric treatment. In states where the department of corrections has a reception and diagnostic center to evaluate offenders, all too often the system has no capacity to follow through on any finding and recommendations for treatment. In the past three years, where nine states have followed the lead of Michigan to create statutorily a verdict of "guilty but mentally ill," there has not been a parallel commitment to provide treatment facilities and services for offenders so categorized.

IMPOSSIBLE TASK—PREDICTION

The second critical question concerns the capacity of psychiatrists to make reliable predictions about the future behavior of offenders/patients, with or without clinical intervention. In a wide range of situations, demands are made on the psychiatrist to make some prediction. For example, in Kansas, the criteria for release of persons found not guilty by reason of insanity requires psychiatric opinion that the individual is no longer dangerous to self, others, or property (10). In capital offense cases in Texas, psychiatric opinion is commonly utilized to influence juries to find the defendant incorrigible and invoke the death sentence. Over a four-year period, one psychiatrist consistently testified to that effect after determining in a one-hour examination that the defendant showed no remorse and had committed other antisocial behavior. So effective was this physician's testimony that he became known as "Dr. Death" (11).

In his definitive review of the clinical prediction of violent behavior, Monahan acknowledges that prediction has "always been a part of life and a part of the law." Yet, it has come under significant attack in recent years with three major criticisms:

1) That it is empirically impossible to predict violent behavior;
2) That, even if such activity could be forecast and averted, it would, as a matter of policy, violate the civil liberties of those being predicted; and
3) That, even if accurate prediction were possible without violating civil liberties, psychiatrists and psychologists should decline to do it, since it is a social control activity at variance with their professional helping role (12, p. 6).

Repeatedly, studies have questioned the validity of psychiatric predictions of dangerousness. Notes Monahan, "Rarely have research data been as quickly or nearly universally accepted by the academic and professional communities as those supporting the proposition that mental health professionals are highly inaccurate at predicting violent behavior." Task forces of the American Psychiatric Association (13) and American Psychological Association (14) have both found the professions not competent to make such judgments. In fact, the five major studies cited by Monahan show a fairly consistent overprediction of dangerousness, with the false positive prediction (i.e., dangerousness not demonstrated on three- to five-year follow-up) ranging from 59 to 86 percent; in other words, the accuracy of predicting dangerousness ranged from a low of 14 to a high of 41 percent. The record in the three applicable studies where non-dangerousness was also predicted was better. There, the accuracy of true negatives was as high as 92 percent, and the low was only 69 percent (12, pp. 44-48).

The dilemma underlying the psychiatric overprediction of dangerousness is a function of another legal/psychiatric interface. Namely, the psychiatrist is in greater jeopardy from a lawsuit claiming malpractice or malfeasance in the case of violence by an individual who is discharged after being predicted to be nonviolent, than one claiming excessive detention and violation of a patient's rights. In a Kansas case, Durflinger v. Artiles, et al. (15), a deceased's estate won a substantial jury verdict against four state hospital staff including a psychiatrist, psychologist, and two physicians. They were held liable for a wrongful death committed by a patient they discharged. The patient was initially hospitalized after he threatened his grandparents, acknowledging that at one point he planned to kill them. He had no history of any actual aggression directed toward either his grandparents or any others. In the hospital, there was no evidence of any psychotic thinking, and he was diagnosed as having a passive-aggressive personality with sociopathic features. His usual pattern of handling stress was running away or withdrawing into himself, and there was no expression over four months of hospitalization of threats toward others. Arrangements were made for him to be discharged to return to another state where his parents were going to help him get continued treatment. There was no indication during his hospitalization of the likelihood of his committing the acts of murder which he subsequently did, killing his mother and younger brother. Nevertheless, at the district court level, the jury felt the psychiatrist should have prevented it.

"Tort liability for the wrongful discharge of dangerous mental patients," observes Rein, "often assumes that dangerousness and further need for treatment are one and the same. But in point of fact, some risks must be borne by society itself. . . . It must be by some form of magic that psychiatrists are expected to cure both the mental impairment and the dangerousness of their referrals, an act which is not similarly expected from corrections" (16). Increasingly, to protect against tort liability, psychiatrists are reluctant to discharge questionable cases, preferring that the release decision be made by a judge. In that way, the ultimate responsibility for the decision is removed from the psychiatrist and assumed by an agency immune to liability, should there be subsequent damage by the released offender/patient.

Ethical Dilemma—Coercing Cure

Once an individual has been identified as being characterologically disturbed and also a law violator, what then? What is the role of treatment, especially when the offender may have no interest in or feel no need for treatment? There has been considerable discussion in legal and psychiatric circles over the propriety and feasibility of forced treatment of offenders. Concerns have been expressed about the ethics as well as the efficacy of enforced treatment of serious character disorders (3, 17-23).

"There is a continuously expanding tendency to medicalize all conflict and social problems and to turn to experts for solutions. The movement is well advanced, and the role of the state in providing coerced treatment progresses steadily." So observed Miller, who is skeptical of the therapeutic commitment toward mentally ill offenders:

> It seems that there is a dark side in most of us that fights against relin-
> quishing power and enjoys the exercise of power in the name of benev-
> olence. Lionel Trilling says it succinctly: "Some paradox of our nature
> leads us, when once we have made our fellow men the objects of our
> enlightened interest, to go on to make them the objects of our pity, then
> of our wisdom, ultimately of our coercion" (3, p. 96).

With reference to the sociopath, Szasz raises the question of whether treatment is for change or for social control. He believes that coercion or compulsion "to enforce rule-following behavior is far more rule-less than any other area of society. . . . Therapy for social control should be administered by a new profession, policemen, and not by doctors." He goes on, "How do we treat somebody who doesn't want to be treated? We don't. If we do, that's punishment" (17).

Halleck expresses his reservations in this way:

> In an age when the technologies for changing behavior are becoming more
> precise, we have come to appreciate that even those who have violated the
> law have certain basic rights. There are limits to the extent to which we
> can legally try to change an individual's behavior, if the individual does
> not welcome such change. . . . Even if we are convinced that we can

change criminal behavior in a manner which society desires, we must consider the ethical justification for implementing such change (18, p. 62).

Rappeport acknowledges that enforced treatment does present serious ethical considerations and requires constant surveillance "lest our efforts at treatment be abused for political purposes or used inconsiderately." Nonetheless, citing a range of studies, he demonstrates that if a genuine external force motivates the patient to receive and remain in treatment, enforced treatment for many repetitive, acting-out, antisocial offenders is effective. He concludes that "in our zeal to prevent unethical coercion, we must not forget that we cannot, with our present tools, treat so-called 'acting-out' patients unless they are forced to attend treatment sessions" (19, p. 152).

In a review of the legal aspects of enforced treatment, Schwitzgebel found that prisoners have no right to refuse treatment or rehabilitative efforts, but they do at least have a right to refuse unconstitutional interventions presented in the guise of treatment. Believing that procedures should be developed to help prisoners avoid such legal and personal harm, he suggests the development of a Human Rights Committee which would review cases of offenders who wish to refuse treatment. The committee, after study, would have to conclude:

1) There is a compelling State interest, e.g., the prisoner should present a substantial risk of harm to others.
2) The proposed treatment is reasonably related to the State interest, e.g., there would have to be substantial likelihood that the treatment would be effective.
3) The proposed treatment conforms to professionally accepted standards of practice.
4) Procedures for periodic and on-site review of the treatment have been arranged in light of the risk and intrusiveness of the proposed treatment.
5) As nearly as can be determined, the proposed treatment meets constitutional and other legal requirements (20, p. 67).

CLINICAL APPROACHES—TREATMENT

The issue of enforced treatment of personality disorders is but one area where law and psychiatry interface when it comes to the management of offenders. In fact, treatment and treatability are not included in most legal definitions of mentally ill offenders. Nonetheless, society has an interest in requiring some kind of change in the offender/patient (24), and, as Rappeport noted, treatment can produce changes which are desirable from the standpoint of both the individual and society (19). Such treatment, however, is subject to various legal and administrative constraints, depending on the setting and the technique. In the setting of a correctional institution, treatment procedures and goals may be quite limited; also, treatment techniques which utilize negative reinforcement have been subject to court review and in some instances ordered discontinued. Before addressing those aspects of the interface of law and psychiatry, it is well to consider certain general strategies and principles involved in the treatment of criminal personality disorders and review some of the psychotherapeutic approaches which have been proposed for the treatment of these individuals.

Halleck outlines four major strategies for changing criminal behavior:

1) Change an individual's biological state, through the use of psychoactive drugs, convulsive therapy, psychosurgery.
2) Change the individual's environment so as to provide him with new learning experiences, reinforcing certain behaviors and seeking to extinguish others; establishing an "artificial" environment in which the behavior can be carefully monitored and influenced, including specific therapeutically controlled relationships (individual, group, family psychotherapy) which may allow for new learning to take place.
3) Change the contingencies of reinforcement within the environment and the nature of environmental stimuli by an increase or decrease of stress, acknowledging that most maladaptive behavior is diminished when levels of environmental stress diminish.
4) Provide the individual with new information, about his own motivations (insight), about the impact of his actions on others, about the nature of the environment, about how to increase his coping skills through education and training (18, p. 63 ff.).

Drawing on experience in the Patuxent Institution in Maryland, Carney believes there are four essential elements in the treatment of severe personality disorders: acceptance, control, support, and learning. He believes treatment of these persons "requires some degree of authoritarianism. The problem generally is not how much control to impose initially . . . , but at what point and to what degree the controls should be relaxed" (25, pp. 277-278).

With particular reference to outpatient psychotherapy with the so-called psychopath, Lion suggests that clinicians be cognizant of the following:

First, the therapist must be continually vigilant with regard to manipulation on the part of the patient. Second, he must assume, until proved otherwise, that information given him by the patient contains distortions and fabrications. Third, he must recognize that a working alliance develops, if ever, exceedingly late in any therapeutic relationship with a psychopath.

The element of coercion and the presence of a third party (like the court or probation officer) are not conducive to developing trust, particularly when the clinician may be under some obligation to report to an outsider the progress of the treatment (26, p. 286).

To cope with the problem of trust, Lion believes the only recourse is to openly share with the patient all the impressions and communications generated and received concerning him. "Complete frankness and honesty are the only hope for these relationships and often lead to a fruitful dialogue in therapy." Other technical problems include dealing with the patient's anger—"often a problem in the early course of coercive therapies, since a patient whose lifestyle is psychopathic becomes frustrated when he or she cannot cope with situations in the usual manipulative manner"; absences—"patients will often come armed with all kinds of ammunition and alibis, as though they were about to appear before a magistrate"; acting-out; and payment of fees (26, pp. 286-294).

Several modified psychotherapeutic approaches have been developed to work with offending personality disorders. Glasser's reality therapy (27) contrasts the behavior of "responsible people" with the mentally ill criminal. The latter is viewed as irresponsible, denying the reality of the world, and failing to understand right and wrong. The reality therapist utilizes both individual and group techniques to engage and become involved with the offender/patient, accepting the individual, rejecting the irresponsible behavior. Another "relearning" process is outlined by Yochelson and Samenow (28) from their elaborate formulation of the "criminal personality," which is viewed as having 52 "errors in thinking." Assuming that "the criminal chooses the criminal path in his search for power, control and excitement, and the criminal can choose to eliminate these patterns and develop new ones," Yochelson and Samenow attempt to bring about change by an "unashamedly moral approach" which emphasizes "guilt rather than forgiveness" and spells out corrective thinking patterns. The therapist's role is as a conscience confronting the offending "criminal." Vorrath and Brendtro (29) put their emphasis on the peer group, seeking to establish a positively oriented gang or positive peer culture which has each participant assuming responsibility for helping the others. They assume that as the individual gives help, he becomes of value to others, increases his own feelings of worth, and builds a positive self-concept.

In an effort to prompt change, a wide range of behavior modification programs have also been developed in correctional settings, and these have provoked an additional interaction between law and psychiatry. This has developed particularly from programs with aversive or negative reinforcement techniques, which have been viewed more as punishment than treatment. Perlin summarizes the premise underlying the legal challenges: "All persons—including those who participate in behavior modification programs voluntarily and involuntarily—

have the constitutional right to be free from cruel and unusual punishment, a right often characterized as 'freedom from harm' '' (30). One significant court decision came out of a case of an inmate at the Iowa Security Medical Facility. The inmate/patient sought relief from a "therapy" program in which vomiting was induced by an intramuscular injection of apomorphine whenever the inmate refused to get up, swore, lied, traded cigarettes, or otherwise misbehaved (Knecht v. Gillman) (31). The court held that aversive procedures, especially of a medical nature, could be used only when three conditions were satisfied:

1) A written consent from the inmate specifying the nature of the treatment; a written description of the purpose, risks and effects of treatment; and advising the inmate of his right to terminate the consent at any time. The consent must include a certification by a physician that the patient has read and understands all of the terms of the consent and that the inmate is mentally competent to understand fully all of the provisions thereof and give his consent thereto.

2) The consent may be revoked at any time after it is given, and if an inmate orally expresses an intention to revoke it to any member of the staff, a revocation form shall be provided for his signature at once.

3) Each injection shall be individually authorized by a doctor and be administered by a doctor or by a nurse. It shall be authorized in each instance only upon information based on personal observation by a member of the professional staff. Information from inmates or inmate aides . . . of behavior in violation of an inmate's protocol shall not be sufficient to warrant such authorization (31, p. 1140).

Both the Knecht decision and a comparable decision in a case emanating from California (Mackey v. Procunier) (32) do not prohibit the use of recognized aversive behavior modification procedures when the offenders properly consent to the procedures. However, Perlin advises practitioners of behavior modification to be aware of the potentialities and dimensions of legal challenges to their treatment programs and keep in mind the observation of Justice Brandeis in his dissent in the case of Olmstead v. United States (33):

. . . Experience should teach us to be most on our guard to protect liberty when the Government's purposes are beneficient. Men born to freedom are naturally alert to repel invasion of their liberty by evil-minded rulers. The greatest danger to liberty lurks in insidious encroachments by men of zeal, well-meaning, but without understanding (33, p. 479).

Sex offenders represent another significant area of interaction between law and psychiatry. In the late 1930s, state after state—ultimately more than half of the states—enacted special "sexual psychopath" statutes in which treatment was an essential element, although treatability was rarely included as a necessary condition for identification of the sex offender. Characteristically, the laws imposed an indeterminate sentence and provided for treatment or rehabilitation of the offender either in a prison or a hospital. While such statutes have been repealed in many states, court rulings held that as long as an individual was detained by way of a sex psychopath statute, the state had a responsibility to provide treatment. Reviewing the evolution of the statutes, the Committee on Psychiatry and Law in the Group for the Advancement of Psychiatry noted, "There is uncertainty about the uniform need for treatment of the sexual psychopath, the likelihood of his satisfactory response to it, and the availability and effective application of accepted treatment modalities for the institutionalized offender" (34). Concluded the committee:

> Although we clearly recommend the abolition of sex psychopath statutes, nothing in this report should be interpreted as a rejection of voluntary treatment for sex psychopaths, or any criminal offenders for that matter. . . . What we reject in particular is stigmatization by way of special . . . statutes with an indeterminate nature and with generalizations about treatment, when the main goal is really to remove these people from society (34, p. 940).

Treatment efforts which have been formulated for the sex offender include traditional psychotherapy, behavior modification, aversive techniques, and organic treatment utilizing drugs and surgery. In the treatment programs for rapists, Abel and colleagues identify five major components:

1) Establishment of an empathic relationship between the patient and therapist;
2) Confrontation regarding the rapist's responsibility for his sexual behavior;
3) Heterosocial-heterosexual skills training as a means of facilitating appropriate interaction with adult females;
4) Increasing heterosexual arousal to adult women, exploring any fear of women; and
5) Decreasing sexual arousal to the urge to commit rape by methods of self-control, confrontation, catharsis, drug treatment and/or castration (35).

As with other instances of coerced treatment and behavior modification techniques, these treatments may be subject to court review over issues of harm and informed consent.

A review of psychiatric participation in the treatment and correction of criminal personality disorders would be deficient without mention of the Patuxent experience, what Lejins has called the "grand experiment" (36). In 1955, Maryland established Patuxent as a special, model institution to deal with "defective delinquents" who were sentenced to be detained indefinitely, until no longer dangerous. Treatment, as such, was a secondary goal. Utilizing psychiatric and psychological expertise, a treatment program was developed with four key elements: 1) a graded tier system of increasing privileges and responsibilities; 2) individual and group psychotherapy; 3) a complete educational program including vocational training; and 4) a unit treatment team system (37). Almost from the beginning, the institution was challenged; arguments centered on the staff's ability to accurately diagnose "defective delinquents" and predict dangerousness, on the efficacy of the treatment programs, and on the constitutionality of the indeterminate sentence (38). Early follow-up studies suggested the program was effective in reducing recidivism, but increasing criticism prompted the legislature to mandate an outside review of the institution and its operations. Completed in 1976-77, that study ended with a recommendation to abolish the indeterminate sentence as well as the classification of the "defective delinquent" (39). After his review of the recidivism data, Steadman concluded:

> Apparently some limited benefit for society has been produced by Patuxent in that it takes a very hard core offender population and reduces their rearrest rate to the level of other offender groups. Since to produce this result has been shown . . . to cost approximately twice as much per year as the conventional system, the taxpayer may ask whether it is worth it (40).

SPECIAL TREATMENT PROBLEMS

Inevitably, psychiatric work with personality disorder individuals who have committed offenses presents some special problems, not the least of which are transference and countertransference experiences between the therapist and offender/patient. The offender/patient may, with a repetition compulsion-like pattern, proceed to establish a relationship with the authoritarian therapist/parent in a manner which assures frustration and splits the staff when the treatment takes place in an institutional setting (41). Lion calls particular attention to the capacity of the psychopath to create dissension on a hospital ward and actively manipulate events so as to produce staff and patient distrust. He notes, "the psychopath is particularly skilled at generating conflicts over power and authority and may become an uncontrollably defiant member of the patient population" (26, p. 298). In working with such patients, therapist and staff respond with their own conscious and unconscious patterns. They must be constantly alert to and aware of their limitations and seek consultation to deal with their feelings of impotence and helplessness in treating the resistant offender/patient. Further, the wish for vengeance and the discomfort of having to accept and tolerate a person who has committed a serious offense can impair the capacity of the treaters to be consistently therapeutic with such a patient. One colleague's anger and repulsion forced him to give up treatment of an unremorseful, antisocial young kidnapper who repeatedly tortured and raped his female victim until finally murdering her (42). To again quote Lion on the qualities needed for the therapist to work effectively with a psychopath:

> Generally, these clinicians . . . have had experience in forensic matters and are more skilled at detecting manipulation than their more psychoanalytically oriented colleagues. . . . In addition, the therapists most skilled at treating psychopaths have some degree of entrepreneurial spirit which puts them in touch with the narcissism and grandiosity inherent in these patients (26, p. 299).

The institutional setting can present another special problem for the treatment of the offender/personality disorder. In the milieu of the hospital, the patient may be unable to utilize the caring and supporting role of the hospital, preferring to eschew the identity of being "sick" for the identity of being "bad." The inability of the antisocial personality to trust the caring intentions of the treatment personnel and his need to maintain an interpersonal distance may prompt him to act in a way that leads to his rejection or discharge from the hospital (much as happened in case #2 cited previously). In the prison setting, where the dominant theme is control and punishment, there is a reinforcement of the inability to trust others; the offender may find it easier to deny any need to change his internal sense of self.

An additional difficulty in the prison setting is the emphasis in that institution on control and custody, so that decisions are determined more on the basis of security than on therapeutic need. The institutional policies and procedures may well compromise the autonomy of the clinical practitioner. At the same time, the correctional staff may look to the psychiatrist as a "giving" or "caring" agent in the prison who will be less harsh and more understanding toward the offender/patient (43). While the correctional staff may be ambivalent about the psychiatrist, there is an expectation that he will be more permissive toward the inmate, and give the inmate some relief from the pressures and distress of the prison "compound." The psychiatrist practicing in that setting must respect the rationale for administrative decisions and operations. As observed by the Group for the Advancement of Psychiatry Committee on Mental Health Services:

It is difficult to work within any system which has a complex technical pattern of communication when this system is partially controlled on different occasions by another system. When two systems have a common area which may be viewed as belonging clearly to each side, then antagonisms can arise (44, p. 34).

Finally, in treating an offender/personality disorder in the prison setting, the psychiatrist must consider the appropriate goal of treatment. Is it to help the offender/patient more effectively adjust to the institutional setting, i.e., life in prison? Or is it to prepare the individual to function effectively in the outside world? While the goal will obviously be influenced by the expected duration of confinement, the reality of the inmate/patient's life situation must be reflected in the treatment goal.

INTERFACES—LAW AND PSYCHIATRY

Clearly, the evaluation and treatment of certain personality disorders—especially antisocial personalities—and sexual offenders brings the psychiatrist into contact with the legal system. In the process, the psychiatrist can experience a loss of clinical autonomy and feel co-opted by the criminal justice system. In seeking to function effectively under such circumstances, the psychiatrist must clarify his role both to the criminal justice system and to his patients who are beholden to that system. This requires a willingness on the part of the psychiatrist to become familiar with the rationale and operational principles of the criminal justice system—the laws, law enforcement, the discretion of prosecution, tactics of defense, the adversary process, the court, the correctional institution, parole decision-making and supervision. It also necessitates that the psychiatrist learn to communicate with the representatives of that system in language they can understand. Finally, the psychiatrist must educate those representatives about what he can and cannot provide for the criminal justice system. For example, he can offer some understanding of factors which contribute to character formation and behavior. He can, within limits, offer a prognosis. Further, he can help some character disorder persons change. He cannot, however, guarantee such change or cure, nor can he predict future behavior with any certainty.

In these litigious times, the psychiatrist must acknowledge that, increasingly, persons look to the courts for redress of grievances. He must accept that there will be occasions when he is unable to practice in the manner he might believe ideal because of the constraints related to a judicial determination that liberty is more important than health.

Most important is the challenge to find a mutuality of purpose in the larger society, so the psychiatrist can work in concert with the system of law, addressing shared concerns and achieving common goals. This requires effective communication and respect for what each profession has to offer toward the greater good. It also requires that each recognize and openly admit shortcomings and limits, and each acknowledge that some goals may be accomplished only by collaboration. One sobering aspect of the treatment of certain personality disorders is the fact that, working independently, both the psychiatrist and the criminal justice system may fail to bring about change. Successful therapeutic intervention in those cases is dependent upon a shared participation by both the system of law and the system of psychiatric care.

REFERENCES

1. HALLECK, S.L.: *Psychiatry and Dilemmas of Crime.* New York: Harper & Row, 1967.
2. STONE, A.A.: *Mental Health and Law: A System in Transition.* DHEW Pub. No. (ADM) 75-176. Washington, D.C.: U.S. Government Printing Office, 1975.
3. MILLER, K.S.: *The Criminal Justice and Mental Health Systems—Conflict and Collusion.* Cambridge, MA: Oelgeschlager, Gunn & Hain, 1980.
4. FORST, B., LUCIANOVIC, J., and COX, S.J.: *What Happens After Arrest?* Publication 4, PROMIS Research Project, Institute for Law and Social Research, 1977.
5. URMER, A.H.: *The Burden of the Mentally Disordered on Law Enforcement.* Chalsworth, CA: ENKI Research Institute, July, 1973.
6. *Diagnostic and Statistical Manual of Mental Disorders,* Third Edition. Washingon, D.C.: American Psychiatric Association, 1980.
7. DURHAM, V. UNITED STATES, 214 F.2d 862 (1954).
8. UNITED STATES V. BRAWNER, 471 F.2d 969 (1972).
9. McDONALD V. UNITED STATES, 312 F.2d 847 (1962).
10. KANSAS STATUTES ANNOTATED, 22-3428 (1977).
11. They Call Him Dr. Death. *Time,* 117:64, June 1, 1981.
12. MONAHAN, J.: *The Clinical Prediction of Violent Behavior.* DHHS Pub. No. (ADM) 81-921. Washington, D.C.: U.S. Government Printing Office, 1981.
13. AMERICAN PSYCHIATRIC ASSOCIATION: *Clinical Aspects of the Violent Individual.* Washington, D.C.: APA, 1974.
14. AMERICAN PSYCHOLOGICAL ASSOCIATION: Report of the task force on the role of psychology in the criminal justice system. *Am. Psychol.,* 33: 1099-1113, 1978.
15. IRVIN L. DURFLINGER, et al., v. Benjamin Artiles, et al. U.S. District Court: KS (Unpublished).
16. REIN, W.C.: Unpublished communication to the Kansas Governor's Advisory Commission on Mental Health, Retardation and Community Mental Health Services. December 16, 1981.
17. SZASZ, T.S.: Unpublished lecture, Eighth Annual Arthur P. Noyes Memorial Conference. Morristown, PA, October 9, 1971.
18. HALLECK, S.L.: Rehabilitation of criminal offenders—A reassessment of the concept. *Psychiat. Annals,* 4 (3): 61-85, 1974.
19. RAPPEPORT, J.R.: Enforced treatment—Is it treatment? *Bull. Am. Acad. Psychiat. & Law,* 2 (3): 148-158, 1974.

20. SCHWITZGEBEL, R.K.: *Legal Aspects of the Enforced Treatment of Offenders.* DHEW Pub. No. (ADM) 79-831. Washington, D.C.: U.S. Government Printing Office, 1979.

21. HALLECK, S.L.: Legal and ethical aspects of behavior control. *Am. J. Psychiat.*, 131: 381-385, 1974.

22. MORRIS, N.: *The Future of Imprisonment.* Chicago: University of Chicago Press, 1974.

23. NASSI, A.J.: Therapy of the absurd: A study of punishment and treatment in California prisons and the roles of psychiatrists and psychologists. *Corr. & Soc. Psychiat.*, 21 (4): 21-27, 1975.

24. MENNINGER, W.W.: Causes and management of criminals: Psychiatric aspects. In: R.H. Williams (Ed.), *To Live and To Die: When Why and How.* New York: Springer, 1973.

25. CARNEY, F.L.: Inpatient treatment programs. In: W.H. Reid (Ed.), *The Psychopath.* New York: Brunner/Mazel, 1978.

26. LION, J.R.: Outpatient treatment of psychopaths. In: W.H. Reid (Ed.), *The Psychopath.* New York: Brunner/Mazel, 1978.

27. GLASSER, W.: *Reality Therapy: A New Approach to Psychiatry.* New York: Harper & Row, 1965.

28. YOCHELSON, S., and SAMENOW, S.E.: *The Criminal Personality,* Vols I and II. New York: Jason Aronson, 1976 (I), 1977 (II).

29. VORRATH, H.H., and BRENDTRO, L.K.: *Positive Peer Culture.* Chicago: Aldine, 1974.

30. PERLIN, M.L.: Legal implications of behavior modification programs. *Bull. Am. Acad. Psychiat. & Law,* 4 (2): 175-183, 1976.

31. KNECHT V. GILLMAN, 488 F.2d 1136 (8th Cir. 1973).

32. MACKEY V. PROCUNIER, 477 F.2d 877 (9th Cir. 1973).

33. OLMSTEAD V. UNITED STATES, 277 U.S. 438 (1927).

34. GROUP FOR THE ADVANCEMENT OF PSYCHIATRY, Committee on Psychiatry and Law: *Psychiatry and Sex Psychopath Legislation: The 30s to the 80s.* New York: GAP, 1977.

35. ABEL, G.G., BLANCHARD, E.B., and BECKER, J.V.: An integrated treatment program for rapists. In: R.T. Rada (Ed.), *Clinical Aspects of the Rapist.* New York: Grune & Stratton, 1978.

36. LEJINS, P.P.: The Patuxent experiment. *Bull. Am. Acad. Psychiat. & Law,* 5 (2): 116-133, 1977.

37. HOFFMAN, P.B.: Patuxent Institution from a psychiatric perspective, Circa 1977. *Bull. Am. Acad. Psychiat. & Law,* 5 (2): 171-199, 1977.

38. RAPPEPORT, J.R.: Editor's commentary for symposium issue on the Patuxent Institution. *Bull. Am. Acad. Psychiat. & Law,* 5 (2): v-vii, 1977.

39. SHEAR, H.B.: An overview of the Contract Research Corporation evaluation of Patuxent Institution. *Bull. Am. Acad. Psychiat. & Law,* 5 (2): 134-143, 1977.

40. STEADMAN, H.J.: A new look at recidivism among Patuxent inmates. *Bull. Am. Acad. Psychiat. & Law,* 5 (2): 200-209, 1977.

41. MENNINGER, W.W.: Catching the conscience of the king, or the strange relationship of psychiatry and sociopathy. Unpublished lecture, Eighth Annual Arthur P. Noyes Memorial Conference, Norristown, PA, October 9, 1971.

42. ORDWAY, J.: Personal communication.

43. MENNINGER. W.W.: Role of the hospital in the prison. Unpublished paper, presented to Conference of Federal Prison System Wardens and Chief Medical Officers, Boulder, CO, June, 1962.
44. GROUP FOR THE ADVANCEMENT OF PSYCHIATRY, Committee on Mental Health Services: *Interfaces—A Communications Casebook for Mental Health Decision Makers.* San Francisco: Jossey-Bass, 1981.

11

Money and Character Disorders: Or How to Get the Recalcitrant Third Party and the Impossible Patient to Pay Your Bills

Steven S. Sharfstein, M.D.,
Thomas G. Gutheil, M.D.,
and Frederick J. Stoddard, M.D.

INTRODUCTION

Issues of reimbursement are in the forefront for individual psychiatrists and for psychiatry as a medical specialty in the 1980s. Third-party insurers have been most reluctant to foot the bill for even a portion of needed care (1). This historic truth, when combined with our current economic doldrums, has hit psychiatric benefits hard even in those plans which have had an outstanding record of generous benefits, predictable costs, and effective peer review.

Psychiatric benefits have been a recent addition to insurance coverage in the last 15 years and, with escalating medical care costs, are considered for reductions in a version of "last hired, first fired." These benefits compete poorly with other medical benefits when reductions are considered necessary. Psychiatrists, as contrasted to surgeons and internists, are at the periphery of the policy councils which govern insurance and have little input to the designers of benefit packages. It is now extremely difficult to find insurance carriers who will reimburse longer term outpatient and inpatient treatment, which aims at a more substantive characterological change, rather than short-term, more symptomatic improvement. The treatment goal of characterological change is questioned because of the reluctance or difficulty in financing the means to reach that goal. If the insurance carrier adds limits on visits, additional deductibles, and copayments to its psychiatric benefit, it is then up to the patient or his family to foot the bill.

The resistance, reluctance, and vicissitudes of getting the patient with a character disorder to pay his psychiatric bills are major clinical issues as well as a reimbursement question (2). This chapter is an effort to look at both sides of this issue: first, at the difficulty and reluctance of third parties to pay for care for individuals with lifetime or chronic histories and with at least a modicum of social and vocational functioning; and, second, at the clinical issue of money as it appears in the treatment situation. This chapter, therefore, focuses not only on the third party as a subject of intense current interest in psychiatry but also on the willingness of the patient and/or family to sacrifice in order to achieve a certain treatment objective. As such, this essay combines macroscopic economic questions and insurance marketing issues with microscopic clinical vignettes on the role of the financial contract in the therapeutic process. The macroanalysis in the first part, and microanalysis in the second part capture different aspects of the therapeutic and payment issues and are not as closely related as might be assumed. They are opposite sides of economic aspects of psychiatric therapies.

THIRD PARTY PAYERS: A MOST RELUCTANT BENEFACTOR FOR THE TREATMENT OF CHARACTEROLOGICAL PROBLEMS

Today, fewer plans include outpatient, as compared to inpatient, benefits for mental disorders; if these are included, there are greater "inside limits," such as higher deductibles and copayments for the treatment of mental disorders (3). These limitations make it extremely difficult for the individual to depend on his third-party insurance as a reliable means to pay for longer term, reconstructive, outpatient, character-changing therapy. In many instances such limits are increasing tensions between organized psychiatry and third parties (4). In some cases, third parties do not cover even short-term treatment, creating an economic barrier to early access for care.

The proportion of the general population under 65 with mental health outpatient coverage in 1979 was 57 percent of the non-Medicare eligible population. Those that have such coverage almost always have additional limits on dollars and extra co-insurance rates as well. A recent study of 455 major U.S. employees programs in 1980 found equivalent outpatient coverage for health and mental health in only 10 percent of the plans (5). Mental health coverage was subject to higher copayment in 87 percent of the plans, and 45 percent of the plans had visit and dollar limits in addition to the higher copayments. The result of this discriminatory coverage for mental disorders is that approximately 12 percent of the payment for the treatment of mental illness comes from the private third-party dollar, contrasted with 26 percent of the payment for general medical conditions. The trend today is to increase this disparity between health and mental health coverage. For example, the Federal Employees Health Benefits Program cut its psychiatric benefit in 1982 by limiting patients' visits to all physicians to 50 per year and inpatient days to 60 per year.

Third-party insurance coverage for illness ("health insurance" is a misnomer) is an effort on the part of a larger community of individuals to pool resources in order to afford timely access to needed care. It is also an effort on the part of the providers of care to create a predictable source of financial support and not to be put in the ethical and economic dilemma of denying access because an individual is unable to pay the bill. It is an effort on the part of a group to spread the financial risk for individuals so that the impact of the costs of care is not felt upon the receipt of such care by the sick person.

One can see from the above philosophic and economic perspective that in order for insurance coverage to be acceptable and effective, certain medical and economic objectives and assumptions must be approximated. At the core of an insurance system, and its feasibility as a means of payment for mental disorders, is the capacity of psychiatrists as physicians to represent their treatments for their patients as medically necessary and similar to treatments for other physical disorders. And, although this is possible to some extent, the medical model for mental illness works to some extent but breaks down at significant points. The economic interface with third-party insurance makes such coverage extremely problematic. The continuing questions from the third parties about the illnesses we treat, the treatments we utilize, the length and scope of our services have, in part, led to our current crisis in capturing a fair share of the insurance market.

Insurance coverage problems make the third party a most reluctant partner in the payment for extensive outpatient or inpatient treatment for character disorders. Understanding these problems is difficult when it concerns our patients and our pocketbooks, but essential if we are to try to deal with these issues in a straightforward way, recognizing that there will always be limits on third-party reimbursement.

How Does Outpatient Treatment for Character Disorders Violate Insurance Rules for Coverage?

At the core of the insurance system is the need for definition of risk and illness. The estimation of benefit expenditures (and premium rates) requires that the covered conditions be definable with some precision, both in the individual and in relation to an expected prevalence in the community to be insured. A definable onset and end of illness (the average episode) should also be specifiable, and the types and duration of treatment should be of limited number and scope. The cost per unit of care must also be defined.

It is clear, then, that predictable incidence and prevalence, as well as an understood course of illness, treated and untreated, are key in the ultimate definition of financial risk for the third-party insurance carrier. There are also basics of the medical model and of economic expectations which derive from the medical model and its assumptions. If we apply these assumptions to definitions of risk for individuals with Axis II character disorders, we can immediately see some of the problems that the third-party carriers encounter. Is there adequate consensus on characterological diagnoses among psychiatrists? If so, can psychiatrists make themselves understood to third-party administrators? In DSM-III (6) we define characterological disorders on a different axis from other mental illnesses. Can we document the "medical necessity" of available treatments for specific disorders? Can we say with any specificity the nature of the onset of these conditions and predict with any certainty the end of these conditions with or without treatment? Character disorders are, by definition, not acute illnesses. Perhaps they are more analogous to chronic medical illnessess such as diabetes, rheumatoid arthritis, and hypertension, which often have an insidious onset and a long-term, even lifelong, course. There are, however, more clearly defined epidemiologies, clincial courses, and pathophysiologies for these chronic medical illnesses than for character disorders. In one respect the analogy with chronic medical illness probably applies: Patients with characterological problems are "at risk" for a range of acute medical/mental illnesses from depression in the case of obsessive-compulsive characters to schizophrenia in the case of borderline characters.

Perhaps these conditions more precisely correspond to a "disability model" rather than a medical model—that is, lifelong handicap and not short-term disease? If, indeed, a person's problem represents a problem since early childhood, do not preexisting condition and prior illness exclusion clauses prevent the person with a character disorder from ever claiming insurance reimbursement? Are the types and duration of treatments for characterological disorders sufficiently clear, with a professional consensus on what might be expected during an episode of care? Can cost per unit of service also be spelled out in a clear and agreeable manner? What is the prevalence of these conditions in the community at large and in the subgroups to be insured?

Indeed, this last question may be the final straw for coverage for these conditions because, if characterological problems are of extremely high prevalence in a community, restrictions on coverage become an economic necessity. One example of this was the coverage provided by Actors Equity in the 1950s for psychoanalysis: Many actors with longstanding neurotic and/or characterological problems availed themselves of the opportunity of this treatment. Rapidly the treatment became economically unfeasible for the third-party payer and created a 10- to 15-year hiatus before any carrier would even touch the notion of unrestricted visits as part of an insurance benefit for psychiatric disorder.

The issue of which treatment is the most cost-effective is missing from this discussion of economic risk. It eventually comes into the picture, however, but only after these more fundamental questions are answered.

Moral Hazard

There is an additional issue which creates stress for the carrier in the coverage of disorders which are characterological in nature. This is summed up by an insurance term called ''moral hazard,'' in which the use of a service or treatment is encouraged by the insured status and not by the illness status (7).

A problem generic to all insurance, even with a definable economic risk, is the temptation for its enrollees to be careless in controlling their insured losses. If use of services is under the control of the insured, the insured may be tempted to use their insurance whether they need it or not. If illnesses are not clearly beyond the control of the insured and/or use of more extensive services is under the control of the insured, then the economic risks to a third-party carrier are again heightened. The extent of this danger is referred to by the insurance industry as ''moral hazard.'' Insurers attempt to combat this problem by adding co-insurance, deductibles, and other limits on their insurance policies. Moral hazard can destroy the marketability of insurance by forcing people to pay through premiums for services they would not have found worthwhile if payments were made just purely out of pocket.

If the demands for psychotherapy for people with character disorders were independent of the price of such care, there would be no ''moral hazard'' in providing insurance. The moral hazard problem describes the case in which the service demand depends in some part on the price of the services. Since insurance lowers the price for the consumer, more services are used.

This brings us to the issue of the goals of treatment. If the nature of treatment is in terms of growth and development or self-actualization, as contrasted to a medical model of relief of painful symptoms, then the moral hazard issue may indeed be quite pertinent. If many of the patients with character disorders in intensive treatment are not ''sick'' (indeed, the physical and psychological symptoms are less measurable than for DSM-III Axis I diagnoses), the use of psychotherapy for learning rather than for treatment creates a major problem in terms of the insurability of this care.

Empirical studies on psychotherapy in relation to this ''moral hazard'' issue are sparse. In one recent study by McGuire (7), data from a sample of 600 psychiatrists on their last 10 patients in psychotherapy were analyzed with an econometric model looking at the likelihood of patients opting for more extensive treatment with more extensive insurance coverage. Indeed, McGuire concludes that the moral hazard issue was real and that the patients with insurance coverage demanded 200 percent more treatment than people without insurance. It must be stressed that psychiatry is not alone with this issue. General medical care also has moral hazard problems. A recent study by Newhouse et al. (8) showed individuals with insurance demanded 50 percent more medical services than people with comparable conditions without insurance. Whether this utilization is of appropriate use, overuse, or underuse was not answered by these studies. It does, however, create additional issues of economic risk for the insurance carrier. If the moral hazard problem for psychotherapy is four times greater than for general medical care, we have another major problem on our hands in justifying third-party reimbursement for long-term treatment for individuals with character disorders.

The Consumer Demand Issue

If the above problems were not enough, insurance tradition also necessitates a public need and a clear demand for coverage on the part of the big buyers of care. These large buyers determine benefit packages. They consist of the labor unions or large private corporations. Unless they demand adequate to excellent psychotherapy coverage for individuals with character disorders, such coverage is likely to continue to be covered as optional, minimal, or not at all. The low priority for mental care coverage among the Federal Employee Labor Unions and the minimum benefits provided in the union-sponsored plans gave the strong impression to the Office of Personnel Management in 1981 that this coverage was not a desired option for the vast majority of Federal employees. Indeed, coverage such as dental or vision care has been introduced at the expense of mental care starting in 1981. Certainly, less stigma is attached by consumers to the advocacy of dental as compared to mental benefits.

Employers, however, might be quite responsive to the issues posed by people with character disorders because of related problems such as absenteeism, turnover, or low productivity in people with these conditions. If treatment of these disorders is an effective tool in combating these problems of industry, these big buyers of care might demand more extensive treatment coverage (and if premiums paid continue to be a non-taxable wage supplement).

Consumers of psychotherapy, i.e., patients and their families, are also reluctant to speak up and let their needs be known. There may be a latent demand for coverage for psychotherapy for individuals who are incapacitated by character-ological problems, but a more focused effort by these consumers directed to the benefit package policy-makers is needed as well.

Peer Review and Claims Review Issues

Further issues have been raised as to the accountability of benefits when provided. This, in part, gets into the issue of the lack of definition of appropriate treatment and of the most cost-effective treatments. Peer review committees are needed to monitor more extended and expensive services. In addition to the clinical peer review consensus, there is a need for peer review itself to correspond more adequately to a model of diminishing marginal returns which implies that, in any medical treatment, eventually a point is reached when an additional increment of this treatment will not provide an additional increment of health. Psychotherapy for individuals with character disorders probably does not correspond to this incremental curve. The phenomena of resistance, regression, and negative transference lead to a wavy curve of treatment progress. If there is some short-term improvement after the first 10 visits, there may be some regression during the next 20 visits, and then, only later, will progress toward health resume. How, then, is one to measure progress in characterological change during treatment and help it correspond to a model which can be reviewed by a group of peers? Available criteria on appropriateness of treatments do not resolve these issues.

An additional issue of relevance to both claims and peer review processes is the degree of information communicated from provider to carrier. This compromises the privacy of the therapist-patient relationship. Strict confidentiality is often critical for psychotherapy to proceed. If there are many questions about the medical necessity for treatment, its length, and its intensity, how much information should be provided to an insurance carrier and how often? If there is fear that characterological diagnoses stigmatize the individual, diagnoses submitted to the carriers may be inaccurate and masked by substituting less serious but reimbursable conditions. The Mental and Nervous Disorder Cost Survey (9), done in 1977 in Washington, D.C., confirmed the suspicions of the insurance carriers that information was being inaccurately reported to them on diagnoses. This creates an important credibility problem for psychiatry, for unless we can be held accountable for our treatments and the diagnoses of our patients, it is unlikely that a third party will be willing to continue to support our treatments. Indeed, the third party may feel that we as a profession suffer from an incurable character disorder!

Problems with Provider Credentials

Further, difficulties in defining illnesses and treatments are compounded by the current claim of expertise by a wide range of nonmedical professionals to perform extensive therapies. The psychologists, in particular, have been extremely effective in achieving independent practice status and winning court battles such as the recent Virginia suit against Blue Cross for restraint of trade. Social workers have also won independent practice capacity in seven states and are intensively lobbying state legislatures to allow themselves to provide services without referral or supervision from a physician. Psychiatric nurses, marriage and family counselors, and licensed counselors are not far behind.

On the one hand, it is argued that increasing the competitive pool of mental health professionals might reduce costs from a supply and demand perspective. On the other hand, increasing the supply of medical professionals and mental health professionals could increase the demand and the cost for care by expanding the patient pool from more serious to less serious disorders. "Talking treatments" are more difficult to justify as "medical," and those treatments that might be specifically oriented towards characterological change, never involving the use of medications or other somatic interventions, might be even more difficult to justify.

It is asserted that psychotherapy is a difficult, technical task, but there is no national certification for psychotherapists. Given our Federal system, the regulation of psychotherapy has assumed many forms. It is clear from the perspective of the fiscal third party that as you expand the provider pool, you expand the cost. The success of nonmedical mental health professionals in gaining third-party insurance is further evidence to the insurance company that psychiatric treatments are nonmedical. If you don't need a doctor to diagnose and treat, you don't qualify for the illness insurance coverage.

In summary, the difficulties of obtaining insurance to pay for anything more than short-term treatment of character disorders are as follows:

1) The lack of a definable illness for payment.
2) Moral hazard.
3) Lack of consumer demand.
4) Difficulties in accountability.
5) Problems with provider credentials.

The next part of this chapter will review the other vexing question of how to get the character disorder patient to pay for treatment and money as an important clinical issue in the treatment process.

MONEY AS A CLINICAL ISSUE IN PSYCHOTHERAPY OF CHARACTER DISORDERS

The economic contract between psychotherapist and patient can become quite complex if there is third-party insurance coverage. The clinical issues which emerge are fascinating "grist for the mill" but may also pose ethical dilemmas for the professional in practice (2). Below we provide a series of case examples and anecdotes as we have collected them over the years from our own practices or have heard them from our colleagues; these examples illustrate the subtlety and complexity of the meaning of coverage in therapy. While not all relate directly to character disorders per se, they shed light on the central issues.

The Interaction of Reimbursement and the Dynamics of Psychotherapy

Case #1: The Devaluing Woman

A single woman in her mid-thirties had been unable to get into stable relationships with men because of her characterological tendency to devalue them as inferior. She came from an aristocratic background where, after being brought up under conditions of relative wealth and status, the family became poor and had to move to a poorer part of town. The family was scorned by former peers because of their reduced circumstances. The patient's mother was extremely devaluing of the father as a failure and as a poor provider, and the mother would enlist the daughter as an ally in this devaluation.

In therapy the patient's arrangement was to pay by check and to receive reimbursement from the insurance policy; she was paying a reduced therapy fee based on her low income. The policy one day increased her allowance, but the patient kept this fact secret. In theory this increase, added to the fee, would have brought her close to full fee for the sessions.

The "secret holding" of this extra money created a good feeling in the patient, but she came to therapy beginning to devalue the treatment and the therapist, especially insofar as the therapist "wasn't doing enough" for her. During the exploration of this view, the patient commented almost parenthetically, "after all, you may not be that good a therapist; you charge such ridiculously low fees."

The therapist noted this particular turn of phrase and explored it. This investigation revealed the patient's fantasy that the low fee implied that the therapist needed *her* rather than the opposite. Furthermore, this "need" was believed based on how interesting the patient was in an almost quantitative way: The patient is receiving "X" dollars "credit" for her fascination as a patient, "X" being in effect the difference between her fee and what she felt she should pay. The patient then openly admitted the insurance increase.

In the exploration, the devaluation was linked to previous devaluation experiences; the patient experienced guilt at this devaluing but worked this through and experienced a recommitment to treatment. Since she had just had a raise at her job, she now wanted to pay even more than before.

Comment: This incident resonates in several ways with the clinical formulation. If unresolved, the incident might well have led to the patient's fleeing treatment out of guilt. The guilt was balanced by the good feeling that came from the sense of specialness to the therapist, "demonstrated" by the low fee, now effectively even further lowered by the reimbursement increase. The patient had been sensitized to this issue by the family-wide narcissistic injury of a major financial reverse during her childhood. The patient's conflicts around dependence and turning to someone for help were also countered defensively by her specialness. In addition, she repeated the mother's (and her own) tendency to devalue men; seeing a "cut-rate" therapist echoed mother's cry of "marrying beneath her."

Thus, the relatively small financial increase in reimbursement, kept as a secret, mobilized these dynamically important issues with the resulting possibility for exploration in the ongoing treatment.

Case #2: Deprivation and Entitlement

A single woman with a pronounced history of socioeconomic deprivation and low income agreed to see a therapist at a very reduced fee; she had insurance coverage, and the agreed upon plan was to bill the patient at the insurance profile* and then, when the coverage was exhausted, to bill the patient at a significantly discounted fee—a fairly common practice in private treatment.

Although the patient had, in fact, agreed to it, she remained absolutely enraged at this arrangement on the following basis: she felt that she had suffered all her life and incurred many educational debts. She now wanted to enjoy her life and saw the "extra" money (i.e., the differences between her discounted fee and the full fee determined by the profile) as the money she deserved with which to enjoy life. The therapist was then experienced as "soaking" the patient for this "extra" money, and thus depriving her of the pleasure that was her due. This view in treatment accorded with her general view of men depriving her of pleasure and having an advantage over her in all areas of her life. Although agreeing to the plan in an explicit contract, the patient remained angry and resistant to the procedure. When she received her first insurance check, which

---

*A formula based on a two-year profile of fees in a specific geographic area.

she was to sign over to her therapist, she was reluctant to do so, and instead, put a down payment on a refrigerator.

Comment: This patient experienced the insurance company's money as compensation for her longstanding deprivation. Her entitlement is similar to another type of patient we have seen who wishes to see the insurance check as a "return on their investment" made in the form of paying premiums and who fails to grasp the purpose of the coverage as payment for the provider. In either case, when the doctor insists on payment, this is experienced as therapist greed.

Case #3: Fraudulent Relationship

A woman going by the name of "Mrs. Jones" (not her real name) has been living for a long period of time with Mr. Jones but is not actually married to him. Mr. Jones has a Blue Cross-Blue Shield insurance policy. Mrs. Jones wishes to be billed through the clinic to Mr. Jones' insurance policy as though she were his spouse. Since the policy is based on an essentially fraudulent relationship, the clinic elects not to accept the insurance policy as a payment, and the patient thus pays "X" number of dollars out-of-pocket on a therapeutic basis.

Comment: One obvious dynamic in this element is the use of the clinic and the insurance policy to, in a sense, ratify a relationship in an indirect manner. If the clinic or physician were to conspire to charge the insurance company, it would place the company in a role of an externalized "patsy," which not only would provoke ethical concerns, but also would generate an externalized conflict, creating a burden for openness and honesty in therapy.

Case #4: Family Therapy

A family of six is being seen in family therapy. Each of the members of the family has various amounts of their Blue Cross-Blue Shield allowance used up in a variety of health provider settings. The mother in the family has a certain percentage of her policy used up; the children have some of theirs used up individually; the father's insurance policy is intact—none of his coverage has been used to date.

In this family the father plays an extremely dominant and controlling role. He tends to take over the entire family and to run the entire family's activities from an authoritarian position. The family takes the attitude in treatment, "Why should we not all use the father's insurance policy? The money is just sitting there; it's lying there, it's not being used. Should we not make use of it? Let's do that."

The role of this arrangement in feeding certain family patterns or pathological interactions as well as entitlement was recognized and—in the service of avoiding a resistance expressed in the claim that everyone gets the same amount of benefit in therapy—each person is billed individually and separately. As a result, each member pays his own way and, in practical terms, only the father's debt is thus, in fact, covered by the insurance. Needless to say, this arrangement mobilizes enormous amounts of discussion. The father wishes to take the position that mother is the one—and the only one—who is, in fact, "crazy." The children see everyone else as having a share in the pathology, and the mother is ambivalent about who has the real problem.

Comment: The notions, "We're all in this together," and "In a family treatment setting we are all responsible for what happens," while valid viewpoints in family process, can easily represent resistances. In this clinical vignette an attempt is made to individualize the experiences and participation in the therapy based on the individualized methods of payment, thus, to some degree, thwarting the resistant but traditional modes of interacting in the family.

Case #5: Avoidance of Coverage as Countertransference

In the treatment setting, reimbursement and insurance issues may play a role in the countertransference as well as in the transference. A supervisor was working with a beginning therapist who was treating a man who had been paying $50 an hour out-of-pocket. At one point the patient acquired Blue Shield and was now paying through Blue Shield only the profile amount, which, at that particular point in time, represented approximately $15 less of actual income to the physician. The therapist put on the table the fact that, if there was a payment through the insurance policy, a net dead loss of income to the doctor resulted. The patient considered this and agreed to pay the higher rate out-of-pocket and not to use his insurance policy as a matter of choice. There ensued an interruption of some period of time while the patient was on vacation; upon returning the patient began to talk about the large number of exploitative relationships he was in, where people were taking advantage of him here, there, or elsewhere. Catching on to some possible relevance to the therapy situation, the doctor called attention to this element. In fact, the patient had allowed several months to go by without bringing up his experience of this arrangement, namely, that he felt enormously upset and angry about the increase.

Comment: Under supervisory assistance, the therapist realized in retrospect that he should have accepted the decreased amount on a number of bases. Even though "balance billing" is illegal and fraudulent, he (the therapist) should have accepted a treatment arrangement in the long haul (while coverage lasted) at the profile fee. On introspection he was able to realize, however, that he was unable to tolerate that arrangement on narcissistic grounds. Thus, the physician's entitlement (an element of countertransference functioning as a resistance) and the patient's independent masochism all seemed in this example to interact to frustrate the legitimate use of insurance for reimbursement purposes.

Case #6: The Big Tip

A 23-year-old waitress was being seen for multiple unsatisfactory relationships with men and for shoplifting, for which she had been placed on probation with therapy as a condition for her not going to jail. She came from deprived economic circumstances and had a very cynical view of the world including money and men. When it came time for payment, she brought in two hundred $1 bills in a brown paper bag and presented it to the therapist. She had earned these dollars as tips, and she described the payment as "a big tip." In the process she simultaneously devalued the therapy and showed what a "big shot" or "big tipper" she was by being able to pay with this mountain of money; thus payment was not an adult purchase of a consultation, but a generous gratuitous "gift" for comparable menial service. She also implied that the therapist might collude with this cash payment and not report it to the Internal Revenue Service, and she challenged the therapist to count it out in front of her to assure its accuracy. At one stroke she thus invited the therapist into collusion and invited him to accuse her of possible duplicity—two serious alliance threats! A review of the significance of the payment method with her allowed for further exploration of her longstanding characterological problem.

Case #7: The Check Bouncer

A 42-year-old business executive was being seen for alcohol problems and physical violence toward his wife. He became superficially involved in therapy as he focused on his personal behavior and his third turbulent marriage. He denied any other problems in his life. When time came for payment, he presented the therapist with a check which was returned two weeks later for insufficient funds. Angrily, he denounced his bank and brought the therapist cash. The next month the exact same thing happened. He presented the check, assuring the therapist that he was sure it was OK, but the check was returned once more. Again, he blamed the bank, refusing to acknowledge or even discuss other possible explanations (including his devaluing the therapist and the therapy) or to admit that he was having business difficulties. When this happened for the third time, he persisted in insisting that this was the bank's problem and not his. He also felt that he was getting nowhere in therapy and terminated abruptly with "a gift" to the therapist of the referral of "his best friend," whom he described as "exactly like" himself in relation to lifestyle and drinking problems. His friend, indeed, seemed superficially a carbon copy of this patient, and it was with some trepidation that the therapist accepted his first check. However, this man continued in therapy for two years, cutting back dramatically on his alcohol consumption and remarrying with great satisfaction. He never bounced a check. Parenthetically, it should be noted that he mentioned that his friend who had referred him had filed for personal bankruptcy several months after terminating therapy.

Comment: It appears that the bounced check expressed both ambivalence about payment and denial of the severity of the financial straits; the referral for "vicarious treatment" is especially interesting.

Ethical and Countertransference Issues for the Psychiatrist

Case #8: Fraudulent Entitlement and Collusion

Grace was a 48-year-old woman with four children being seen four times weekly for psychotherapy for a moderately severe unipolar depression, which was exacerbated by her hostile-dependent relationship with her somewhat successful husband, who was a stockbroker. After one year of treatment, the patient had shown slight improvement but was feeling pressure to decrease appointments because of a decrease in her husband's business. When she appealed to her psychiatrist for help, he tolerated and participated in a plan for him to bill the insurance company as if he were treating each member of her family, thus increasing the coverage five-fold.

Case #9: Billing for a Child Psychiatric Evaluation Not Rendered Directly

Michael was a seven-year-old boy who suffered a 10 percent burn injury and had preexisting encopresis which worsened after the burn. He was evaluated in a private group practice with his parents by a fully trained clinical social worker but never saw the child psychiatrist for whom the social worker worked. Michael improved considerably with play therapy and parent guidance work combined with appropriate pediatric attention to the differential diagnosis of the causes of encopresis. No organic etiology was found. Following the completion of therapy, billing was made directly to Michael's parents by the child psychiatrist, not stating that services were rendered by another professional. The parents were angered to be charged at the psychiatrist's usual fee and refused to pay, causing the psychiatrist to undergo a process of painful soul-searching.

Case #10: The Symbiotic Dyad

Roger was a healthy 21-year-old college student who presented to Dr. A for assistance in resolving his conflict about whether to pursue a career in academe or in business. After five sessions it had become clear that Roger's neurotic attachment to his father, of which he was well aware, and from whom he was attempting to separate, was the source of his conflict. When he recognized this, he easily made his decision to pursue his business interests. When he thanked Dr. A for his assistance and sought to end the therapy, Dr. A pointed out that Roger had not completely worked through his neurotic conflicts with his father although the presenting complaint had been resolved. He also pointed out to Roger that he might as well remain in therapy as long as his insurance benefits were available. Roger, intensely grateful to Dr. A for his assistance with his decision-making and sad at the thought of ending their relationship, agreed to the new extended "treatment plan."

Comment: Situations such as the foregoing are not too unusual. Whether or not this constitutes abuse is not always clear. The therapist is often seduced into a misalliance with the patient's character pathology and must be alert to potential ethical compromises therefrom. The insurance carrier may be viewed as a common enemy or victim of patient and therapist entitlement, often in a manner that recapitulates pathologic relationships. At the least, in the last example the psychotherapy appeared to be extended because of available coverage beyond the necessary short-term period required to resolve the presenting problem. At the worst, such situations can represent greed in the name of patient advocacy.

Case #11: The Passive Dependent Therapist

Dora was an intermittently suicidal, borderline, but intelligent, attractive young woman who sought help for her loneliness and depression from Dr. Q, a senior, experienced, but somewhat tired psychiatrist. He was independently wealthy and, in his usual fashion, paid little attention to the fee arrangements, simply billing Dora the usual $45 per hour at the end of the month. After two years of work with her, he felt increasingly drained of energy following sessions with her, and eventually concluded that, for his efforts, he might consider increasing her fee, though this was not his customary practice once a therapy had gone on for so long. Although most other psychiatrists with less experience charged $65 per hour, he—with great difficulty—eventually sent her a bill for $50 per hour. He was bewildered and angry when the third party paid him at the same $45 per hour as they always had. When he asked his patient to find out why this was, she reported that his usual and customary fee, according to them, was $45 and that they would not revise the usual and customary profiles for another year. Following this experience, Dr. Q decided that in the future he would no longer agree to bill third parties since they interfered with the therapeutic process.

Comment: Here the therapist inappropriately blames the insurance arrangements for difficulties that stem from his ignorance and inexperience of the system and from his passivity.

Case #12: The Unremitting Chronic Schizophrenic

Hazel was a 56-year-old divorced mother of three grown children who had had six hospitalizations for schizophrenia in 14 years. Several were lengthy, and she was growing less responsive to phenothiazines and other antipsychotic drugs as well as pessimistic that any psychotherapist could help her to improve her level of functioning. She was admitted because of increasing psychosis and recurrence of suicide risk, which Dr. R did not feel could be managed with her as an outpatient. She was admitted to Private Psychiatric Hospital B and placed on a unit with other chronic patients, several of whom had extensive inpatient coverage. She entered into psychotherapy four times weekly with Dr. R and a sequential trial of the latest antipsychotic agents, which had little effect. She remained confused, hallucinating and occasionally mildly combative when paranoid delusions predominated. After 60 days, her insurance benefits were exhausted, and it was decided to transfer her to a state hospital for further care.

Comment: This patient is the type which seems to benefit little from the present psychiatric care system. The private hospital, peer review, and third-party systems are all organized in ways which militate against optimal care. The implications for ethics in psychiatry were recently reviewed and debated (10). Hazel perhaps should not have been admitted to a hospital of this type with such limited coverage. Utilization or peer review criteria might judge her to be "custodial" or having "received maximal benefit of care," which may not be at all true. The third party, with its rather arbitrary benefit package, may, in fact, directly contribute to the discontinuity of care and, therefore, the relapses seen in such cases.

When Should We Insist on Cash or Turn to the Collection Agency?

Case #13: The Sociopath's Victim

John was referred to Dr. S for treatment by a court because he had threatened the life of a former employer who refused to rehire him. A condition of parole was that the patient enter treatment. John participated in several interviews, all covered by a small insurance company, and he consistently disavowed and rationalized the hostility which was at the source of his murder threat to his former boss. He seemed, nevertheless, in no danger of violent threats to anyone in the near future, so Dr. S permitted him to terminate the therapy, with payment having been made for 70 percent of the fees. Subsequent billings were refused by the insurance company since the basic benefit had been used up, and John mailed in a check for $2 after receiving repeated monthly billings.

Comment: Dr. S was obviously the victim of John's unworked-through hostility in this case. Such situations are not rare in treatment of severe character disorders as outpatients, and psychiatrists can only protect themselves up to a point. Some psychiatrists insist on payments in cash with such patients because of the risks involved and the undependability of third-party reimbursement. Some utilization review criteria would eliminate a patient such as this from coverage, but that would obviously only deprive patients with severe character disorders and potentially dangerous to society of psychiatric treatment, It should be added that such patients are notoriously difficult to treat, and restrictive coverage discourages any effort.

Case #14: Narcissistic Injury—Fee Payment Withheld

Homer was a 61-year-old man who had suffered a heart attack six years before and subsequently developed a perversion; he intensely wished to have breasts constructed via plastic surgery. He was referred by the surgeon for psychiatric evaluation, which ultimately revealed cerebral atrophy. The psychiatrist did not advise breast augmentation for this man, and Homer retaliated by making only partial payment of the balance not covered by his insurance policy.

Comment: The risk of such reactions is common where psychiatrists are used as consultants or sought for second, and often unwelcome, opinions. Had the psychiatrist realized that Homer's policy would not cover the full evaluation, she would have insisted on cash payment.

Case #15: Parental Neglect of the Child Psychiatrist

Timmy was the product of the marriage of his entrepreneurial father to his schizophrenic mother, and he was referred for child psychiatric evaluation by the school psychologist because of his poor attention span in school and disruptiveness in the classroom. Timmy entered into weekly psychotherapy with Dr. T for a period which extended over two years. Over that period much of the therapy consisted of limit-setting, which neither of his parents had done or been able to do when he was younger. Timmy grew to trust Dr. T and to become more motivated in school. The parents in their therapy developed some capacity for listening to their son and responding to him with warmth or firmness as the situation required. When the therapy ended, a sizable outstanding balance remained to be paid by insurance. When that was not forthcoming, the parents expressed disappointment with the therapy and refused to pay. The psychiatrist, after many months, began civil litigation and was eventually paid in full.

Comment: Cases such as this reveal the practical and psychotherapeutic naivete of the psychiatrist. It is likely that the parents of this child did not fully complete the termination process with Dr. T and kept him alive for themselves by failing to pay and devaluing his help. They repeated with the psychiatrist the neglect and failure to set limits (this time on themselves) which they had earlier done with Timmy. Such problems are more, not less, common with complex reimbursement and peer review systems.

Summary

The different types of therapeutic problems in these situations are as variable as the character types of the psychiatrists, the policies of the hospitals and third parties, and the character types of the patients. The masochist and sadist, sociopath and substance abuser, murderer and pervert, borderline and schizophrenic will manifest styles of handling money as individualized as their fingerprints. It is small wonder that "doubly taxed" therapists do not welcome the presence of yet other parties to complicate the situation.

The case examples, all cases of individuals with characterological problems, are the other side of the reimbursement dilemma: the important clinical and ethical meaning of the economic transaction. The third-party payer and the fiscal contract are caught in a web of meaning that is central to the therapeutic enterprise. Only through alert clinical attention to the meaning as well as details of the payment transaction can ethical standards be maintained and the therapeutic process successfully furthered.

RECOMMENDATIONS TOWARD A HOPEFUL FUTURE

It is clear that the practicing psychiatrist must be very mindful of the dilemmas inherent in third-party payments for treatment of patients with characterological problems, as well as the interaction of money as a therapeutic issue in the initiation and follow-through of the economic contract. Aside from being aware of these issues, there are other recommendations which could assure some third-party financing even for these most problematic of psychiatric diagnoses.

What is required in the short run is closer attention to peer review as a key mechanism in assuring the fiscal accountability of the third-party system. The American Psychiatric Association currently has contracts with the CHAMPUS program and 18 commercial insurance carriers, and, to date, this program has an excellent track record of reviewing care and, in some instances, containing costs. When a third-party claims reviewer questions expensive long-term treatment for questionable diagnoses, a much more preferable solution is to refer that case to local peer review for advice rather than questioning the insurance benefit itself.

In the long run it is important to develop a research strategy which prospectively studies our treatments of characterological problems in terms of cost-effective outcomes. Prognostic outcome criteria could be developed from these studies which would aid peer reviewers in making the decision on long-term or intensive treatment of the individuals with certain kinds of characterological problems. The impact of psychotherapy and psychoanalysis on productivity, job stability, absenteeism, and other measures of economic return are important to build into any assessment. Other outcome measures of economic concern include health offsets, such as number of hospital days and certain life satisfaction measures which yield benefits, for example, in the social and emotional health of children. One such study was done some 30 years ago at the Central Institute of Psychogenic Illness of the Berlin General Insurance Office. A prospective study was designed with evaluation criteria for 1,000 patients entering intensive psychotherapy in the early 1950s. Descriptions of symptoms and duration of illnesses included a large number of people with characterological problems. These patients were evaluated before and at the end of treatment (average number of sessions equals 100) and were followed up after five years. Data on the use of general health services and on the patients' work capacities, as well as their self-evaluations of their treatments, were the key outcome indicators. For the 850 patients followed up after five years, the hospitalization rates were significantly lower than the comparison group; absenteeism was lower; productivity was higher. As a result, in the early 1960s, national health insurance in West Germany began to include a 250-visit lifetime psychotherapy benefit, which was closely allied to a peer review system (11).

We would recommend that such a study be designed and carried through in the United States. Although this country does not have national health insurance, it is an idea which will probably return to the public policy arena, and, at that time, if we have the cost-effective data, it might be possible to overcome the problems inherent in psychiatric treatment for individuals with characterological disorders. Surely the scope of the problem is considerable, and an investment on the part of society in ameliorating the personal and social pain is worthwhile. These efforts should begin now.

REFERENCES

1. SHARFSTEIN, S.S.: Third-party payers: To pay or not to pay. *Am. J. Psychiat.*, 135: 10, October 1978.

2. GUTHEIL, T.G. (Ed.): Money as a clinical issue in psychiatry. *Psychiat. Annals*, 7: 50-111, 1977.
3. SHARFSTEIN, S.S., and TAUBE, C.A.: Reductions in insurance for mental disorders: Adverse selection, moral hazard, consumer demand. *Am. J. Psychiat.*, 139: 1425-1430, 1982.
4. STODDARD, F.J., ALTMAN, H.G., SHELDON, M., SENGER, H., and VAN BUSKIRK, D.: Psychiatric benefits and insurance regulation in Massachusetts: A national model??? *Am. J. Psychiat.*, 140: 327-331, 1983.
5. Hewitt Associates "Spec Book." Chicago, 1980-1981.
6. *Diagnostic and Statistical Manual of Mental Disorders*, Third Edition. Washington, D.C.: American Psychiatric Association, 1980.
7. McGUIRE, T.G.: *Financing Psychotherapy: Costs, Effects, and Public Policy*. Cambridge, MA: Ballinger Press, 1981.
8. NEWHOUSE, J.P., ET AL.: Some interim results from a controlled trial of cost sharing in health insurance. *New Engl. J. Med.*, 305: 1501-1507, 1981.
9. SHARFSTEIN, S.S., TOWERY, O.B., and MILOWE, I.D.: Accuracy of diagnostic information submitted to an insurance company. *Am. J. Psychiat.*, 137: 70-73, 1980.
10. BURSTEN, B., and STODDARD, F.J.: Opinion and comment: "Medical responsibility" in institutional settings. *Am. J. Psychiat.*, 137: 1071-1078, 1980.
11. DUEHRSSEN, A.: Die berteilung des behandlungserfolges in der psychotherapie. *Z. Psycho-som. Med.*, 3 (3): 201-210, 1957; and Katamnestische ergebnisse bei 1004 patienten nach analytischer psychotherapie. *Z. Psycho-som. Med.*, 8: 94-113, 1962.

Subject Index

217

Neuropsychopharmacology, 98-99
Neuroses, 9
    character, 10-18
    in continuum of ego defenses, 13
    selfobject relations disorders and, 37
    violence and, 59
Neurotic character disorders, 110
    insight psychotherapy for, 119-20
Normality, 17-19
    in continuum of ego defenses, 12
    narcissism in, 39-55
Norms, 39, 71

Object permanence, 149-50
Object relations
    alcoholism and, 88, 89, 95, 106-9
    in borderline patients, 144-45
    idealization in, 53-54
    narcissism and, 47-48
    See also Selfobject transferences
Obsessional personality, 111
Obsessive-compulsive personality, 11, 17
Oedipal complexes, 37
    in borderline patients, 153
    narcissism and, 50-52
    in short-term anxiety-provoking psycho-
        therapy, 123, 125, 131, 132, 134-36
Old Testament, 84-85
Orality, 14-15
    alcoholism and, 85
Organic mental disorders, 59
Organic personality syndrome, 59-60
Outpatient treatment, insurance coverage for,
    198-200
Overburdening, 32
Overstimulation, 32

Paranoid defenses, 34
Paranoid ideation, 74
Paranoid personality
    alcoholism and, 110-11
    borderline personality disorder and, 153
    violence and, 63-64
Partial fragmentation, 31, 32
Pathology. *See* Character pathology; Psycho-
    pathology
Patuxent (prison), 186, 190
Payments, 196-97
    as clinical issue, 204-13
    in coercive therapies, 187
    from third parties, 197-203
Peer group pressures, 13, 187
Peer review, 202, 211, 214
Personality, character and, 159, 162

Personality disorders, 11
    alcoholic, 84-92, 95, 105-6
    borderline and narcissistic, diagnosis of,
        140-46
    criminal, treatment of, 186-92
    diagnosis of, 153-54
    involving selfobject relations, 33-35
    See also Character disorders
Personality theory, 105
Personality typologies, 95
Pharmacodynamic psychology, 90
Pharmacologic-cognitive paradigm, 99-100
Pharmacologic theory, 91-92
Pharmacothymia, 85
Physicians, 159-73
Prediction of behavior, 182-84
Premorbid personality
    alcoholism and, 96
    violence and, 59
Proctologists, 16
Psychiatry
    alcoholism not major interest to, 101, 102
    legal interfaces with, 175-93
    payment for, 196-214
Psychoanalysis
    alcoholism and, 85-90, 101
    approach to crime in, 62
    character typology in, 34-35
    "character" used in, 161
    insurance coverage for, 199-200
    interpretations in, 26
    self neglected by, 27
    for selfobject relations disorders, 36, 37
    self psychology in, 25
    for transference neuroses, 120
Psychoanalytic ego psychology, 89-90
Psychoanalytic structural theory, 88-89
Psychodynamic theory, 120
Psychologists, 203
Psychoneuroses, 37
Psychopathology, 9-10
    body build and, 7-8
    within normality, 18
    of selfobject relations disorders, 30-33
    violence and, 61, 63-68
Psychopaths, 186-87, 190, 191
    sexual, 189
Psychoses, 9
    in adolescents diagnosed as having conduct
        disorders, 79, 81
    in continuum of ego defenses, 12
    merger of self and other in, 144
    selfobject relations disorders as, 30, 37
    violence and, 59, 66

Name Index

Abel, G.G., 189
Abraham, K., 85
Adler, Gerald, 140-55
Anglin, M.D., 102-3
Aristotle, 161

Bacon, M.K., 92
Balint, M., 88, 146
Barry, H., III, 95
Bazelon, David, 181
Bean, M.H., 90
Bettleheim, Bruno, 42-43
Bleuler, E., 8
Boswell, James, 171
Bowlby, J., 62
Brandeis, Louis D., 188
Brendtro, L.K., 187
Buie, D.H., 148
Burnham, D.G., 144
Butler, Samuel, 161

Carney, F.L., 186
Chein, I., 87
Cleckley, H.M., 63
Clemenceau, Georges, 159
Colarusso, C.A., 54-55
Cooper, Arnold M., 39-55
Costello, R.M., 95, 102
Crawshaw, , 163
Crichton, Michael, 171

Dante, 171

Ellis, Havelock, 42
Erikson, Erik, 40, 47
Eysenck, H.J., 61

Fairbairn, W.R.D., 110, 144, 146
Fenichel, O., 85
Fraiberg, S., 149, 150

Frazier, Shervert H., 59-68
Freud, Anna, 40-41
Freud, Sigmund, 24, 27, 40, 42-44, 47, 85, 101, 161

Glasser, W., 187
Glueck, E., 61
Glueck, S., 61
Goring, Charles, 60
Greeley, A.M., 92
Grinker, R.R., Sr., 17
Grunberger, B., 14
Guntrip, H., 146
Gutheil, Thomas G., 196-214
Guze, S.B., 61

Hall, C.S., 105
Hallack, Seymour L., 175, 184-86
Hare, R.D., 61
Hartmann, H., 42
Henderson, D.K., 61
Heraclitus, 161
Hewitt, L., 70
Hill, Lewis B., 11
Horney, K., 47-49
Hooten, E.A., 60

Isenberg, Phillip L., 59-68

Jacobson, E., 45, 144
James, William S., 59-68
Jellinek, E.M., 103-4
Jenkins, R.L., 70-71
Jung, C.G., 8

Kammeier, M.L., 96
Karpman, B., 61
Kernberg, Otto, 17, 43, 45, 47, 88, 144-46, 148
Khantzian, E.J., 89
Knight, Robert, 88

223